MISSION BENGAL

Praise for *Lalgarh and the Legend of Kishanji*

'*Lalgarh and the Legend of Kishanji: Tales from India's Maoist Movement* by Snigdhendu Bhattacharya explores the enigmatic and doomed personality of the Maoist leader, and the "Lalgarh" movement that he spearheaded – one of the most violent and bloody periods in the state's recent political history. The author, having covered the Maoist movement in the state, weaves in personal experience with hard facts and takes the reader deep into the heart of the violence and the ruthless politics surrounding the movement. It is this anecdotal aspect that makes the book fascinating to read not just for students and academics but also for the general public.'

– *Frontline*

'Even keen watchers of West Bengal's politics … will find much to learn from the book. And for anyone studying the phenomenon of Maoism in India – what former prime minister Manmohan Singh called the "biggest internal security challenge facing our country" – this book is a must-read.'

– Scroll.in

'Snigdhendu Bhattacharya's book on Kishanji does a thorough job of detailing how the Maoist leader's clarion calls were perennially undercut by episodes of grisly violence.'

– *The Hindu BusinessLine*

'*Lalgarh and the Legend of Kishanji* is an essential read for every politically involved and socially-motivated citizen of this nation.'

– The Wire

MISSION BENGAL

A SAFFRON EXPERIMENT

SNIGDHENDU BHATTACHARYA

HarperCollins *Publishers* India

First published in hardback in India by
HarperCollins *Publishers* in 2020

HarperCollins Publishers India, Cyber City, Building 10-A, Gurugram,
Haryana-122002, India
www.harpercollins.co.in

2 4 6 8 10 9 7 5 3 1

P-ISBN: 978-93-5357-949-4
E-ISBN: 978-93-5357-950-0

Typeset in 11/14.2 Centaur MT Std at
Manipal Technologies Limited, Manipal

Printed and bound at
MicroPrints India, New Delhi

MIX
Paper
FSC FSC® C218906

This product is made of FSC®-certified and other controlled material.

HarperCollins Publishers, Macken House, 39/40 Mayor Street
Upper, Dublin 1, D01 C9W8, Ireland

To Sreemanti Sengupta,
a poet, literary editor and my partner in life and crime,
without whose sacrifices this book would not have seen the light of day

Contents

Introduction

THE RASHTRIYA SWAYAMSEVAK SANGH'S national plan for expansion in 2009, after Mohan Bhagwat took charge as the sarsanghchalak, or the chief of the Sangh, coincided with the beginning of the decline of the Left in West Bengal. The Left Front government had, during its regime of three decades, tried its best to keep the Sangh at bay. But from 2009, with the maverick Trinamool Congress supremo Mamata Banerjee rising as an imminent threat to the regime, the Left was in no position to keep a tab on the Sangh's activities. Mamata Banerjee had started resorting to overt appeasement of the Muslims since 2008, but the Sangh Parivar was keener on seeing the fall of the Left than on training its guns on her.

In 2013, a sheer political vacuum in West Bengal – with the Left and the Congress appearing to be on a path of steady decline – coincided with the emergence of a pro-Bharatiya Janata Party (BJP) wave around Narendra Modi that touched almost all parts of the country. It was also the year when the RSS launched its online recruitment drive, 'Join RSS'.

West Bengal turned into a political laboratory thereafter, with the saffron camp contrasting the atrocities against Hindus in Bangladesh with the 'appeasement' of Muslims in West Bengal, accusing the Mamata Banerjee government of importing Islamic fundamentalism from Bangladesh, and vowing that the BJP would prevent West Bengal's transformation into

'West Bangladesh'. And Mamata Banerjee, once described as *'Maa Durga'* at an RSS event in New Delhi in 2003, had become 'Jihadi Didi' for the saffron warriors.

For the record, Hindutva, which the RSS describes as 'Hindu cultural nationalism', had its roots in the undivided Bengal of the nineteenth century, in the post-Renaissance period. The coinage of 'Bharat Mata', the first possible use of the word 'Hindutva' in print, the 'Bande Mataram' slogan, the iconic image of Bharat Mata, and even the notion that Hindus were in danger of extermination – all originated in Bengal and later spread to other parts of the country. Bengal, simultaneously, was also one of the key centres of Muslim separatism in India.

Ironically, despite the Sangh's first political wing, the Bharatiya Jana Sangh (BJS), being founded by a stalwart Bengali politician – Syama Prasad Mookerjee –BJS's ideological and organizational successor, the BJP, remained a fringe player in West Bengal until Modi arrived on the scene in 2014.

For Mamata Banerjee, the battle was not against the BJP alone; she was fighting the entire Sangh Parivar, as the RSS in Bengal had declared that the Mamata Banerjee government had become a threat to national security and that opposition to its rule was no longer a task to be left exclusively to political parties. About three dozen outfits belonging to the Sangh Parivar were active in Bengal, and nearly half of them recorded exponential expansion of activities between 2010 and 2018. The saffron camp's push for Hindutva, with 'Jai Shree Ram' as the central slogan, also triggered a revival of dormant Bengali regionalist sentiment, and 'Joy Bangla', a slogan used during the Bangladesh Liberation War, had a rebirth in West Bengal, post-2017. The role of the Left, its leaders and workers, added a further twist to the changing socio-political dynamic.

And then there was the mother of all controversies – the one over citizenship, involving the National Register of Citizens, the Citizenship Amendment Act and National Population Register – the trio of 'CAA-NRC-NPR', in short. It is widely believed in West Bengal that this Pandora's box on the question of citizenship was opened with the sole agenda of polarizing the state. Modi started to talk about driving out Bangladeshi

Muslim infiltrators from the time of his 2014 Lok Sabha election campaign itself, and this later grew into a national issue. Even in 2019, the BJP had mentioned the NRC in their national publication on the CAA only in the Bengali edition while at the national level they maintained that the CAA was entirely unrelated to the NRC.

The Sangh Parivar's battle was not easy though, as Mamata Banerjee's social welfare and industrial policies, focused on micro and small-scale industries, had created a large base of beneficiaries. If the BJP dealt the TMC a rude blow in the 2019 Lok Sabha elections by increasing its tally from two in 2014 to eighteen – with the TMC's numbers coming down from thirty-four in 2014 to twenty-two in 2019 – the assembly bye-elections held six months later signalled that the BJP might not even be halfway through its Mission 2021. The entry of political strategist Prashant Kishor as the Trinamool's advisor in June 2019 added a further twist to the narrative, with Kishor coming up with ingenious ideas to help the TMC regain lost ground.

As West Bengal stands poised for a high-voltage duel between Narendra Modi and Mamata Banerjee in the run-up to the 2021 assembly elections, this book attempts to put the battle for Bengal in its historical perspective, closely examining the workings of various RSS-affiliated organizations, the policies of Mamata Banerjee and the strategies of Prashant Kishor's team, and chronicles the myriad political experiments and changing socio-political equations of this period.

ONE

Rise of the Sangh

The Warning

RASH MATH, BARUIPUR, 8 June 2014: 'Listen carefully, Sajahan Sheikh, Arabul Islam, Kaiser Ahmed, or whoever you are, we know how to retaliate. You would be shortened by six inches from the top or buried six feet beneath the earth should you try to continue with your terrorizing tactics', said the stout, mustachioed, middle-aged man speaking from the dais. He had salt-and-pepper hair and wore khadi kurta-pyjama. The dais was decked in saffron. This was twelve days after Narendra Modi was sworn in as the prime minister.

The audience, about 3,000 to 4,000 strong, cheered him with a thunderous '*Bharat Mata Ki – Jai!*'

Sajahan Sheikh was a leader of the Trinamool Congress (TMC)[1] in the Sandeshkhali area of Basirhat sub-division in North 24 Parganas district, the two others named by the speaker being TMC leaders from the neighbouring district of South 24 Parganas. Both districts had sizeable Muslim populations; South 24 Parganas was 35.57 per cent Muslim, and North 24 Parganas 25.82 per cent.

A handful of journalists, including this author, were present at the event that day. Everyone was somewhat surprised with what the man had just publicly said. That he had a special liking for this 'six inches or six feet' phrase would be evident a couple of years later, when he would start repeating it in his public speeches.[2] Here, his tirade continued: 'You have adopted the same Marxist approach of terrorizing the opponent. Do inquire from your Marxist friends in Kerala. Ask for the scorecard. If we are down by one, they [Marxists] are down by two.'

The gathering erupted in applause. '*Bharat Mata Ki Jaaaai!*'

The event was organized by the Rashtriya Swayamsevak Sangh (RSS), the parent organization of the Bharatiya Janata Party (BJP), to protest the atrocities against RSS organizers perpetrated by Mamata Banerjee's TMC. This was the RSS's first 'protest rally' in Bengal in thirteen years. The last was in 2001, a public meeting to protest the killing of four swayamsevaks at Sonakhali in South 24 Parganas district, allegedly by a local Revolutionary Socialist Party (RSP) leader, who was a Muslim. At that time, the newborn TMC, which was emerging as the principal opponent of the Left Front, leaving the Congress behind, was part of the BJP-led National Democratic Alliance (NDA) government at the Centre with Atal Bihari Vajpayee as the prime minister. Now, in 2014, Mamata Banerjee was the Modi-led BJP's sworn opponent.

In the 2014 Lok Sabha election, the TMC had bulldozed its rivals in Bengal, winning thirty-four of the state's forty-two seats. The party won all five Lok Sabha seats in North 24 Parganas district and all four in South 24 Parganas. However, the elections also marked the pinnacle of BJP's electoral success in Bengal – its vote share jumping to 16.8 per cent from 6.1 per cent in the 2009 Lok Sabha election, and from 4.06 per cent in the 2011 assembly election. Besides, it managed to win a Lok Sabha seat entirely on its own for the first time[3] in the state.

This meeting at Baruipur Rash Math was held when memories of the high-voltage verbal duel between Modi and Mamata were still fresh. The man behind the microphone speaking Bengali with a slightly Hindi accent was Dilip Ghosh, a name completely unfamiliar in Bengal politics and not very familiar among West Bengal's Sangh Parivar either. He was introduced as the organizing secretary of the Hindu Jagaran Manch, an organization hardly heard of before in the state.

The leadership of the RSS's south Bengal chapter was on the dais. They included south Bengal pranta sanghachalak (president/chairperson of the state unit) Atul Kumar Biswas and prachar pramukh (head of publicity/spokesperson) Jisnu Basu. Baruipur town sanghachalak Indrajit Sarkar and South 24 Parganas district karyavaha (secretary) Swapan Saha were also present. Three senior leaders of the state unit of the BJP were there too: former president Tathagata Roy (who would soon be made the governor of Tripura), and vice-presidents Subhas Sarkar and Swarup Prasad Ghosh. They claimed they were attending the meeting in their capacity as swayamsevaks (volunteers).

One speaker after another warned the TMC of bloody retaliation if the party continued harassing RSS volunteers involved in social work. Tathagata Roy, who was also a national executive member of the BJP, said, 'I want to make my message clear. Do not dare touch us. We are not Gandhians. We won't be silent spectators when we come under attack… Syama Prasad Mookerjee had said we needed to protest, resist and even retaliate if necessary.'

As many as four leaders from the Hindu Jagaran Manch (HJM) were on the dais. Apart from Dilip Ghosh, there were Swarup Dutta, general secretary of HJM, and Sudip Ghosh and Mriganka Roy, two state-level organizers. Dutta threw an open challenge to the TMC. 'RSS would lead the battle against the Trinamool's *goondaraj* from the front. If anyone comes under attack from the Trinamool goons, simply inform RSS or HJM. We'll take up the matter.'

Atul Kumar Biswas, the south Bengal sanghachalak, called for a '*dharmayuddha*'. He referred to former Marxist chief minister Buddhadeb Bhattacharjee's 2002 remark[4] that a number of madrasas had turned into breeding grounds for terrorists, and lambasted Mamata Banerjee for her promise to establish 10,000 new madrasas.

'We have all seen how Buddha-babu's own party forced him to deny the truth to please the Muslim vote-bank. It shows to what extent they can go. They compromised national security. And this present government too is taking the bread out of the Hindus' mouth to give undue advantage to the

Muslims. We must participate in this dharmayuddha. Even if we die, we'll find a place in heaven,' Biswas said.

However, the man who drew everybody's attention was Dilip Ghosh with his fiery speech. In all RSS-affiliated organizations, the position of organizational secretary[5] is reserved for an RSS pracharak, a term that loosely translates as 'preacher' or 'campaigner', and refers to the bachelor-whole-timers who have left home and family life for the Sangh. Ghosh, being HJM's organizing secretary, was a pracharak.

After he got down from the dais, this author went up to him for a formal introduction and was greeted with a hearty smile. 'Did I say a little too much?' he asked. His body language indicated he knew the answer, but he wanted to know the author's reaction.

'Well, I was not expecting such strong words.'

'We have to speak the language TMC's goons understand', Ghosh said. He looked relaxed.

Inside an RSS Camp

Tantiberia, Howrah, 14 May 2014: The Lok Sabha elections were over. The results were awaited.

Leaders of the south Bengal RSS already looked buoyed at the inauguration of a state-level, twenty-day residential camp, as the number of attendees at this annual event had witnessed a spike. Besides, over the past one year, the Sangh had recorded a stunning growth in the number of shakhas – its basic units that gather daily for an hour or so for physical and intellectual exercises.

The venue of this first-year officer training camp, or OTC in Sangh parlance, was Sarada Shishu Mandir, a school run by Vivekananda Bidya Bikash Parishad (VBBP) and affiliated to the West Bengal Board of Secondary Education. VBBP is the south Bengal chapter of the RSS's education wing Vidya Bharati. About 300 participants, aged eighteen to forty, had come down from all south Bengal districts, paying for their own uniforms, transport and food. They were selected from among the participants of the week-long initial training camps, or ITC, held in the districts.

Two more similar camps started on the same day in the state, one a first-year OTC at Raiganj in North Dinajpur district of north Bengal, with ninety-one attendees, and the other a second-year OTC for the eastern region, with about 230 participants, also at Raiganj. The RSS had two state units in West Bengal – one for south Bengal and another for north Bengal. However, with north Bengal accounting for only one fifth of the state's population and geography, it was the south Bengal unit that mattered most.

Back at the camp at Tantiberia, instructions for the drill in the evening were all in Sanskrit. The few hundred participants clad in 'ganavesh' or uniform – white half-sleeved shirt, khaki shorts, black cap and black shoes – and carrying a 'danda' (stick) followed them comfortably. They swung to 'attention' mode the moment the instructor shouted '*dakshah*'. They turned back as the instructor ordered '*ardhavrittah!*' To the cry of '*aramah*', they stood at ease; with '*prochaloh*' they marched forward.

The top leadership of the south Bengal RSS was also present – Vadla Bhagaiyah, the akhil Bharatiya bauddhik pramukh (all-India intellectual chief), who was based in Kolkata; Tilak Ranjan Bera, the karyavaha or secretary of the south Bengal chapter; Ramapada Pal, south Bengal's prant pracharak (loosely, chief preacher; in effect the key person of a prant or state unit); Pal's deputy Bidyut Mukherjee, the saha-prant pracharak; and Jisnu Basu, prachar pramukh or head of publicity/spokesperson at the south Bengal unit. Of them, Bera was also a member of the working committee of the Vivekananda Bidya Bikash Parishad, which ran the school – one of the large, spacious ones in the neighbourhood, a two-storeyed building with thirty-four rooms, a large hall, two playgrounds, forty-five latrines and filtered drinking water facilities. The camp was being held during the summer holidays.

The inaugural session started on the dot at 7 p.m. in the hall, which was large enough to accommodate about 500. The dais had pictures of Bharat Mata, RSS-founder Keshav Baliram Hedgewar and the second sarsanghchalak of the organization, Madhav Sadashiv Golwalkar.

The session started with a song that called for the awakening of the Hindus. A swayamsevak sang it without musical accompaniments. Its lyrics are as follows:

'Jagorey Hindu Bajao Bijoy Turjyo,
Supto Singho Thekona Alos Shoyane…
Panchojonye kapuk saptasindhu
Jonogonomono mahajagoroni ganey
Hindur kobhu hridoy kapeni kapeni hridoy bhoy-e
Mar somman tai to roksha torey
Jujhechhi amra jhilam er teerey
Haldighat er ron-e
Kargil a tar diyechhi proman debo aro proyojon-a
Aji o oshoni bharot akash manob akash jurey
Shotru shapod nokhor shanito kore
Songhoboddho Hindu miliya bijoy barta aney
Poro ronosaj cholo cholo aj shotru songharone
Songho montre jagroto desh jagorito ashwas-e
Kompibe joto shotrur hiya tras-e
Juddho hobei dormo juddho dhormo ronangone
Joy o hobei parther moto parthasarathi son-e'

('Wake up Hindus, blow the trumpet of victory
O lion, rise from thy slumber
Let the Panchajanya and the song for the awakening of the masses
Make the seven seas tremble.
The heart of the Hindus never shivered in fear
We fought on the banks of Jhelum and in the battle of Haldighat
to protect the honour of our mother
We gave a proof in Kargil too and will do it again
Thunder has covered the skies of India and of the human race today
Enemies and wild beasts are sharpening their claws
United Hindus will bring the news of victory
Put on the battledress, let's eliminate the enemy

The sangha's mantra has awakened the country
The enemy's heart will tremble in fear
The war will take place – the war for dharma on the battlefield of dharma
And victory will be ours, like that of Partha's with Parthasarathi beside him.')

The atmosphere was charged. The discipline one witnessed was awe-inspiring. The attendees included college students and schoolteachers, unemployed youth, government employees and workers of private firms. Everybody sat upright and followed the proceedings with rapt attention.

The RSS leaders sounded upbeat while addressing the trainees. Vadla Bhagaiyah spoke of the 'winds of change'. 'Our movement has picked up pace in Bengal ... it will now increase in speed. It is time for a change in the state', he said. 'The winds of change are sweeping across the villages of West Bengal. We have to save the Hindus from being dishonoured. They need protection. The Hindus want to be organized. More people are waiting to join us. We have to learn from this camp how to organize the Hindus. Each of us needs to do it in the villages we live in.'

The daily schedule at the camp was tight. Between waking up at 4 a.m. and going to bed at sharp 10.15 p.m., there were two physical drill sessions and three to four classes and discussion sessions. Participants had to wash their own clothes and utensils. Simple vegetarian food was served four times a day. No one was allowed to keep their mobile phones with them, and no one allowed to be lazy.

The RSS, founded in Maharashtra in 1925, had only a marginal presence in West Bengal for a long time, even though the two most important figures of the organization had special connections with the state. Hedgewar studied in Kolkata and had links with the city even after returning to Maharashtra. Golwalkar, who took charge of the RSS after Hedgewar's death in 1940 and shaped the organization over the next three decades, first came to Bengal in 1936 after leaving the RSS, with plans of pursuing a spiritual life. He had joined the Belur Math's first branch at Sargachhi Ashram in Murshidabad district to learn yoga from Swami

Akhandananda, one of the direct disciples of Ramakrishna Paramahamsa.[6] However, after his guru's death in February 1937, Golwalkar returned to Nagpur and rejoined the RSS. He came back to Bengal in 1939, this time to initiate RSS activities in the state. He spoke to the headmaster of a school at Maniktala in Kolkata, and the first shakha was started with the students of this school at Telkol Maath in the Garhpar area of north Kolkata.

Golwalkar went back to Maharashtra by early 1940 after Hedgewar's health deteriorated, but by then the Sangh had started opening new shakhas. By 1944, the RSS had opened shakhas at Berhampore, Nabadwip, Burdwan, Suri, Uttarpara, Midnapore and Malda towns, besides in the Maimansingh and Nababgunj areas in present-day Bangladesh (where the organization was disbanded after Partition).[7]

The RSS's growth in West Bengal witnessed a spike during the 1965 Indo-Pakistan war and later again in 1991, riding the wave of the Ram Mandir movement. Pradip Dey, a pracharak who was serving as RSS south Bengal's office secretary and lived at its state headquarters of Keshav Bhavan, told this author in 2014 that the organization got around 100 pracharaks in Bengal in 1991 alone. In 1992, an enthused RSS leadership organized a three-day camp in Kalyani, Nadia district, and 17,000 swayamsevaks from different parts of Bengal attended it. It was their biggest show of strength in the state. During that time, the number of shakhas increased to 1,500.

The high tide in favour of the RSS continued till 2000. By 2001, the Left had made it one of their primary tasks to push the RSS back, especially following the bloody turf war between the Left and the TMC–BJP alliance at the tri-junction of West Midnapore, Bankura and Hooghly districts in 1998–2000. By 2003, the number of shakhas had declined to about 1,000. By the time the Left regime fell in 2011, the number of shakhas was down to 800.

However, an expansion drive by the RSS central leadership across the country[8] in 2009 coincided with the creation of a 'favourable' situation for them in Bengal. First, the fall of the Left Front regime looked imminent after the 2009 Lok Sabha elections. In any case, the Left had been put on the back foot. It was in no position to divert its attention from the TMC and could barely challenge the RSS. Second, the TMC did not care about the RSS, the least as a challenger. And third, the TMC took to overt Muslim appeasement.

There was another development that prompted the RSS to give special focus to West Bengal. And that was demographic change.

A 10,000-word article written in 2009 by Mohit Ray, a Sangh-associated BJP ideologue, throws some light on the saffron camp's concerns. In the article, titled 'Idea of West Bengal: Eroded from the Very Emergence', which appeared in *Dialogue,* an English-language publication of Astha Bharati, an organization affiliated to the RSS, Ray wrote:

> Demographic danger is already a reality. Recent changes of electoral constituencies in West Bengal show the impact. While the Hindu-dominated areas have lost constituencies, seats have shot up in the Muslim-dominated areas. Kolkata, which earlier had 21 Legislative Assembly seats, now has only 11. Again, Hindu-dominated Purulia and West Medinipur districts lost two constituencies each, one each in Bankura, Burdwan, Birbhum and Hooghly. Muslim-dominated areas, e.g., in Murshidabad, the number of seats increased by three and for both North Dinajpur and Nadia the increase was by two seats each. Malda and South Dinajpur gained one each. Now see the demographic change at the 0-6-year level. The amazing 2001 census results show that while the Muslim population in state is 25.25%, their children (0-6 years) constitute 33.17%.

The RSS's expansion programme in West Bengal primarily focused on social work among the downtrodden and the backward classes through a web of associated organizations that makes the Sangh Parivar. After the fall of the Left Front government in 2011, they decided to push for opening new shakhas and all-round expansion of their activities. A three-day residential camp accommodating about 10,000 swayamsevaks was planned. Named Vivekananda Yuva Shivir, it was held at Gayeshpur Goshala Maidan, Kalyani, during 11–13 January 2013 to mark the 150th birth anniversary of Swami Vivekananda. It was after a gap of twenty-one years that such a large camp was being organized in Bengal.

The swayamsevaks were segregated into twelve groups – mostly along the lines of the districts they came from – and each group had its own routine and space for its various sessions. The participants were accommodated in camps where they shared mattresses and blankets, had frugal meals and a tight schedule of bouddhik (intellectual) and sharirik (physical) sessions. From time to time, all groups would gather at a central location for physical drills and to hear addresses by the top RSS leaders. Suresh 'Bhaiya-ji' Joshi addressed the inaugural session. Mohan Bhagwat and former Indian Space Research Organisation chairman, G. Madhavan Nair, addressed the concluding session.

The push yielded fruit. According to Jisnu Basu, the number of shakhas shot up from about 820 in March 2013 to 1,010 by March 2014. Besides shakhas, there were 520 weekly gatherings called milan and 2,536 monthly gatherings called mandali in West Bengal.

So, what impact did the much-talked-about 'poriborton' (change) in Bengal – the toppling of the Left Front regime by Mamata Banerjee in 2011 – have on the RSS's expansion plans, this author asked RSS leaders present at the Tantiberia camp. Tilak Ranjan Bera, Ph.D., a chemistry teacher at a school in Kharagpur, admitted that the fall of the Left Front regime had helped them take up an expansion initiative. Both Bera and Bhagaiah blamed the Left for subjecting grassroots-level RSS organizers to terror. Communists had suppressed those who held opposing ideas during their rule, Bhagaiah said, adding that 'a little bit of freedom' had come to Bengal 'in the spheres of thought and expression'.

Jisnu Basu, Ph.D., worked at the Saha Institute of Nuclear Physics. He acknowledged that the Left regime had created 'an ideological barrier' to the growth of the Sangh. 'Left leaders of the early days profited from the image of those who sacrificed their lives for the sake of the people. A number of people were direct beneficiaries of the land reforms. These leaders held influence on the people. But Left leaders of later days lost that image and people were disillusioned. In their lookout for an organization with a solid ideological base, they found the RSS.'

And what has been the role of the TMC behind their growth?

Bera had a prompt reply: 'TMC's overt Muslim appeasement is prompting Hindus to look for an alternative.'

Changing Political Landscape

The post-Independence Congress rule in West Bengal for about two decades remained eventful, marked by the rapid increase in influence of a militant Left movement among workers, refugees, teachers, students and farmers, even though reputed freedom fighters Prafulla Chandra Ghosh, Bidhan Chandra Roy and Prafulla Chandra Sen led successive governments that were based on a solid foundation of a two-thirds majority in the state assembly. In 1967, Bengal sunk into total chaos following a split in the Congress, marking the birth of Bangla Congress,[9] and a split in the Communist Party of India (Marxist), popularly known as the CPM, too, marking the launch of the Naxalite (Maoist) movement[10] that aimed at armed overthrow of the Indian state.

During these times of armed revolt, three successive, unstable non-Congress coalition governments, with four chief ministers, and three terms of President's Rule did nothing to help matters. Siddhartha Shankar Ray, once a Union minister and a close collaborator of Indira Gandhi, who looked after West Bengal on behalf of the Centre during the third tenure of President's Rule in the state, led the Congress in West Bengal in the 1972 assembly election, which is quite widely regarded as one of the dirtiest elections in India, allegedly marred by widespread rigging.[11] The ensuing Congress rule, headed by Ray, a London-educated barrister who would later be dubbed as 'Bengal's last aristocrat politician', earned a very bad reputation for political and administrative highhandedness and undemocratic attitude. In fact, the Left had boycotted the state assembly for the entire duration of this Congress government until 1977. In several following elections they pegged their campaigns against 'Siddhartha Ray-er kalo jamana' ('the dark regime of S.S. Ray').

In contrast, the CPM-led Left Front regime was rather humdrum. Since coming to power in 1977, there had been no major political movement – the Congress had been overwhelmingly rejected by the people – that could threaten their stay in power or create major law and order problems. Jyoti Basu, a London-educated barrister-turned-trade unionist, created a national record of holding on to the chief minister's chair for twenty-three years straight.[12] The land reforms, the refugee movement, the teachers' and students' movements, the cooperative movement and the Left Front government's acceptance of their demands had created a huge beneficiary base for the Left.

There had, of course, been major controversies: the Marichjhapi massacre of 1979[13] and the Bijon Setu Massacre of 1982.[14] But even in the immediate aftermath of Indira Gandhi's assassination in 1984, only two political entities in India withstood the wave of sympathy in favour of Congress: the newborn Telugu Desam Party that had formed the Andhra government barely a year ago bagged thirty of the state's forty-two Lok Sabha seats, and the Left Front in Bengal won twenty-six of the forty-two Lok Sabha seats.

It was in the same year that Mamata Banerjee, a self-made politician with no lineage or backing, entered the Lok Sabha at the age of twenty-nine, defeating the Marxist heavyweight Somnath Chatterjee.

Mamata Banerjee has been called a maverick, theatrical, unpredictable, eccentric, firebrand, a born fighter, a born rebel and 'Bengal tigress', among many other names, and has been the biggest political phenomenon in Bengal since the Left came to power. She had made her mark even before she entered the Lok Sabha. She entered politics joining the Congress's student wing, Chhatra Parishad, in 1972. Within three years, she hogged the headlines after blocking the convoy of Indira Gandhi's prime opponent, socialist leader Jayaprakash Narayan, who was scheduled to attend an event at an auditorium at Calcutta University on 18 April 1975.[15] She famously mounted Narayan's Ambassador car and, as several media reports put it, 'danced on the car's bonnet'. By the time she defeated Somnath Chatterjee from the red citadel of Jadavpur, she had already made a name for herself.

She lost the 1989 election but an attack on her at Kolkata's prominent thoroughfare of Hazra Crossing – she was hit on the head with a stick – brought her back into the limelight. According to a news report, 'When Marxist goons assaulted Mamata Banerjee in August 1990 they made her a

Bengali Joan of Arc.'[16] She returned to the Lok Sabha in 1991, this time also bagging a ministerial berth in the Narasimha Rao government as minister for sports and youth affairs. She became the state Youth Congress president in the same year. However, her mercurial rise in the Congress also benefited the Left to some extent, as while projecting herself as an uncompromising warrior against the CPM she also declared war against Congress's existing state leadership, presided over by Somen Mitra. She contested against Somen Mitra for the post of Congress state president in 1992 and narrowly lost.

This defeat possibly made her resolve stronger. In November of the same year, she addressed a massive meeting at Kolkata's Brigade Parade Ground, from where she announced her resignation from the Union ministry to devote herself entirely to the cause of freeing Bengal from Marxist rule. In July 1993, a rally led by her under the Youth Congress banner, demanding inclusion of photographs in voter ID cards and, curiously, seeking to capture the state secretariat of Writers' Building, had resulted in the death of thirteen Youth Congress activists in police firing in the heart of Kolkata. But this posed no threat to the Left government as a majority of Bengal's senior Congress leaders, including Union Minister A.B.A. Ghani Khan Chowdhury and Somen Mitra, thought Mamata had been reckless. They did not stand by her in building a major movement against the Left government around this firing.

According to a report in *India Today*'s 31 October 1993 issue, Mamata Banerjee had already become 'synonymous with the "real" opposition in the state.' The same report said, 'For the CPM, of course, there is nothing more satisfying than to see its rival's house ablaze and it is sitting back and enjoying the fireworks.'

Mamata Banerjee was relentless, though. In November 1993, she picked up the issue of the disappearance of a jute mill worker, Bhikhari Paswan, in Hooghly district – he was allegedly abducted by the police – and launched a hunger strike seeking a CBI investigation after the district administration disallowed her from entering the area. A CBI probe was finally ordered. A news report put it like this, 'Whenever inertia has gripped West Bengal politics, the firebrand Trinamool Congress chief has sought to liven things up by getting into skirmishes with the state's Marxist Government.'[17]

She indeed turned into the 'real Opposition' after declaring war against the Somen Mitra-led state unit, accusing it of being 'CPM's B-team in Bengal',[18] and breaking away and launching her own party, the Trinamool Congress, on 1 January 1998. She tied up with the BJP, which had so far had only a fringe existence in Bengal. Her argument was simple: since the Congress was more preoccupied with fighting the BJP at the national level it would always keep the CPM in good humour, and the BJP was the only force that would stand by her in her bid to uproot the Left government. In the two Lok Sabha elections in 1998, Trinamool bagged seven seats, against only one by the Congress in the state. In 1999, the TMC won eight, against three by the Congress. The BJP won one seat in 1998 and two in 1999. A new political equation had started unfolding in Bengal.

In 1999, Banerjee bagged the ministerial berth for railways in Atal Bihari Vajpayee's cabinet, but was perhaps more occupied with West Bengal, where the assembly elections were due in 2001. She resigned twice in 2000 – once in September, to protest the steep hike in petroleum prices, withdrawing her resignation after Vajpayee's assurance of having a relook at the decision; and the second time in December, owning responsibility for a railway accident in Punjab that claimed forty-six lives. Vajpayee rejected this resignation too. In March 2001, she again resigned and pulled the TMC out of the NDA, this time demanding Defence Minister Geroge Fernandes's resignation and an impartial probe into the *Tehelka* tapes. She resigned despite Fernandes's resignation. Her resignation was finally accepted.

By that time, the arts and culture-oriented Buddhadeb Bhattacharjee, a leader with a spotless image, had replaced Jyoti Basu in West Bengal. Banerjee smelt an opportunity with this change of guard and tied up with the Congress in Bengal for the 2001 assembly elections. She lost. The Left Front bagged 199 of the state 294 seats, their poorest performance since 1977, but still well above the required number of 147. The TMC won only sixty seats. By 2002, she was trying to get closer to NDA again. In May 2002, the TMC supported the Vajpayee government in the Lok Sabha while voting on the motion brought by opposition parties to censure the Modi-led Gujarat government for the riots.[19] She formally went back to the NDA fold in 2003 but witnessed her party's worst electoral performance in 2004: she was the only TMC MP in the new Lok Sabha. The Trinamool contested the 2006 West Bengal assembly elections in collaboration with the BJP, and faced yet another disastrous result.

With the turn of the new century, the Left looked invincible. They put up one of their better performances in the 2004 Lok Sabha elections, winning thirty-five of the state's forty-two Lok Sabha seats. The 2006 assembly elections saw them bag 235 of the state's 294 seats.

As soon as it formed the government for the seventh consecutive time in the state, the Left launched an extensive land acquisition drive to facilitate the setting up of mega industrial projects: the Tatas' Nano plant on 1,000 acres in Singur, the Salem group's chemical hub in Nandigram on 5,000 acres, and the Jindal steel plant in Salboni. And that was the beginning of the regime's end.

The farmers' agitation triggered by the land acquisition drive gave the electorally devastated Mamata Banerjee an opportunity to revive her party. She pounced on the issue, her policies taking a Left bent as she tried to win over the Left intelligentsia that was already crying foul over the CPM's policy of applying force to acquire land for these projects. By 2007, she had dumped the BJP and aligned herself with the small Left parties, fringe Left groups, rights organizations and the Left-leaning intelligentsia. She praised 'genuine Leftist ideology', hijacked the Left's slogan of 'land to the tillers' and invoked the Left cultural stalwarts of yesteryears. Portraying herself as a champion of the poor and the powerless, she stalled the land acquisition drive.

She dealt the Left a blow in the 2008 panchayat elections, and yet again in the 2009 Lok Sabha elections, this time in alliance with the Congress. And finally, in 2011, she toppled the Buddhadeb Bhattacharjee government. She promised to deal with the newly revived Maoist movement through dialogue rather than by force, and promised to release all political prisoners. She received the backing of a majority of Bengal's Left-leaning and liberal cultural personalities. She had the support of a large number of MLAs – significantly more than what constituted an absolute majority.[20] There was no perceivable threat to her government for many years. In September 2012, the TMC quit the UPA II government and, subsequently, the Congress quit the West Bengal government.

As the Left went down a path of steady decline, which became evident from the results of the 2013 panchayat elections and college union elections, and with the Congress camp looking hopeless anyway, Modi saw an opportunity and seized it. He picked on Mamata Banerjee's 'folly' of 'Muslim appeasement' and the scandalous cases of corruption in the state. Political commentators on TV channels and newspapers had been talking about the need for a credible and strong Opposition in the state. While none of the commentators could foresee any party fitting that role, Modi addressed eight election rallies in Bengal, a number unmatched by any other prime ministerial candidate, creating the momentum for opening a new road to politics in Bengal.

An analysis of the voting patterns in the forty-two Lok Sabha constituencies of the state in 2014 reveals that the TMC led in 216 of the state's 294 assembly segments, while the Left led in twenty-nine segments and the Congress in twenty-eight. The BJP led in twenty-one. But both the Left and the Congress were on the path to decline.

It was BJP's time to take on the TMC.

Dial 'D' for Delhi

Clashes between the supporters of the TMC and BJP broke out on the very day Modi was sworn in as prime minister of India on 26 May 2014. At Haldarbheri village in North 24 Parganas district's Sandeshkhali, a part of the Sunderbans, altercations broke out over BJP supporters celebrating Modi's swearing-in by bursting firecrackers in front of the residence of a local TMC worker. The next day it developed into a full-blown clash. Twenty-one BJP supporters, four TMC workers and a policeman were injured as crude bombs and bullets flew. Following the clash, several BJP supporters were admitted to the SSKM hospital in Kolkata.

On 31 May, a BJP delegation which included Mukhtar Abbas Naqvi, Meenakshi Lekhi, Siddharth Nath Singh, the two West Bengal MPs Surinder Singh Ahluwalia (Darjeeling) and Babul Supriyo (Asansol), and state unit leaders Rahul Sinha and Samik Bhattacharya, entered the area in the afternoon with a convoy of about four dozen vehicles. It had rained heavily since morning. The BJP leaders negotiated the slippery, muddy roads to meet the relatives of the injured. Several hundred people had gathered to narrate the incident to them. They showed the delegation empty cartridges – proof of bullets having been fired – that the villagers had collected from the spot of the clash. A police camp had been set up in the village, but the residents looked terrified. They feared attacks once the camp was withdrawn.

From Sandeshkhali, the delegation went to the SSKM hospital to meet the injured, and from there to the state secretariat where they met Chief Secretary Sanjoy Mitra. Mamata Banerjee was not present.

This was a turning point. There had been numerous political clashes between the supporters of the TMC, the Left and the Congress over the past three years. The central leadership of the Left and the Congress hardly ever visited the affected areas. Here were the BJP leaders now, promising that their national leadership will stand by victims of political atrocities. 'If Kolkata (state leadership) cannot give you support, Delhi (national leadership) will', Naqvi told the villagers in Sandeshkhali.[21]

Speaking to journalists, the party's state unit president Rahul Sinha explained the changing political equations with the following remarks: 'This visit of central leaders is not a one-off incident; let me tell you clearly, we will emerge as her [Mamata's] main opponent soon. We will lead protests and we will protect the protesters.'

They kept their word. Rahim Sheikh, a BJP supporter, died at Kanur village, within Ilambazar police station limits in Birbhum district, on 7 June. Five days later, the BJP announced a five-member central delegation that would visit the village. The team comprising Siddharth Nath Singh, Rahul Sinha, Kirti Azad, MP and Abdul Rashid Ansari (national president of BJP's minority morcha) was led by Balbir Punj, national vice-president. They reached Birbhum on 15 June. Bengal unit leaders Tathagata Roy and Samik Bhattacharya accompanied them.

Hundreds from several neighbouring villages gathered at Kanur to speak to the delegation, according to a report published in leading Bengali daily *Anandabazar Patrika* the next day. The report said that local BJP supporters who had been staying away from home to evade possible arrests came back to meet the BJP delegation. The entire village was simmering in rage against the TMC, according to a report published in Bengali daily *Ei Samay* on 16 June.

Punj and others spoke to dozens of BJP supporters – mostly Muslims – and later addressed a public gathering in front of the party's office in Ilambazar town. 'I assure you, no one needs to fear the TMC. The party ruling the country is with you. Central ministers are with you,' Punj said.[22]

While Punj was busy reassuring them, a district-level conference of Bharatiya Kisan Sangh (BKS), the farmers' wing of the RSS, was stalled after the venue was vandalized, allegedly by TMC workers, in the presence of BKS state unit's organizational secretary Anil Chandra Roy. It happened at Chatra village, within Bhadur gram panchayat area in Goghat of Hooghly district. Goghat still had a Left MLA, Forward Bloc's Biswanath Karak, but thanks to the change of power in the state, the TMC made a clean sweep in the 2013 rural elections there.

Mission 2016

The BJP's state executive met in Kolkata over 7–8 June 2014 to evaluate the post-poll scenario and derive strategies from it. The party's national general secretary (organization) Ramlal was present, along with the party's Bengal in-charge, Siddharth Nath Singh. After two days of brainstorming, the BJP announced its 'Mission 2016 – Trinamool-Mukt Bengal'. Addressing a press meet at the state committee office at 6, Muralidhar Sen Lane in North Kolkata, Rahul Sinha and Siddharth Nath Singh said the party was prepared to lead the unseating of the Mamata Banerjee regime and usher in 'true poriborton (change)', referring to Mamata Banerjee's 2011 slogan of Poriborton.

It sounded a tall claim, given the BJP's electoral track record in the state since its foundation in 1980. Most of the party's candidates lost their deposits in the several Lok Sabha elections that followed – they lost their deposits in all the nine seats they contested in 1984, in all the nineteen contested in 1989, in thirty-six of the forty-two contested in 1991, all the forty-two seats in 1996, and thirty-nine of forty-two in 2009. Assembly election performances were not better. Even in the 2014 Lok

Sabha elections, when they put up their best electoral show in the state, BJP candidates in twenty-one of the forty-two seats in the state lost their deposits. They fared better only when they fought in alliance with the TMC. As of June 2014, the BJP did not have a single MLA, did not run a single civic body and or control a single panchayat samiti in the state. The party was entirely banking on the 'Modi wave' coinciding with a vacuum in the Opposition space in West Bengal.

During the state executive meeting, Ramlal asked party leaders to focus on building the organization, without which, he said, popular support would never translate into votes. For this they needed to take the organization to the booth level. But the party had no presence in over half the state's 78,000 polling booths. The state leaders were also asked to strengthen their IT cell, for which adequate guidance would be coming from Delhi, and form a Right to Information (RTI) cell.

For a statewide agitation, the controversy around the Teachers' Eligibility Test (TET) was chosen. The exams were marred by charges of corruption, manipulation and nepotism at various levels. BJP leaders in the districts were asked to focus on getting in touch with TET aspirants from their areas. Earlier, when the Left and the Congress tried to organize protests on the TET issue, the police often resorted to baton charge and even arrest of TET aspirants to demoralize the agitators. The BJP, if it had to win the TET aspirants' confidence, had to assist them in legal matters and, when necessary, provide financial help to family members of those landing in jail or becoming victims of violence. Therefore, strengthening its legal cell became another priority for the BJP.

There was another plan – a subtler and more important one – on which the BJP and RSS would work together: to revive the name of Syama Prasad Mookerjee, whom the BJP considered one of its founders, portraying him as the 'creator of West Bengal'. In June 2014, an RSS-backed organization, Poschimbonger Jonyo, was floated by Mohit Ray, an environmentalist and earlier a Left-leaning human rights activist who had turned into an intellectual face of Bengal's saffron camp. The plan was to highlight Mookerjee's role in securing 'a homeland for the Bengali Hindus'. The new organization decided to celebrate 'Poschimbongo Dibos' (West Bengal Day) on 20 June, commemorating the historic day in 1947 when the undivided Bengal assembly voted favouring division of Bengal on religious lines.

'Poschimbongo Dibos' was an indoor event, held at the auditorium of the Theosophical Society in Kolkata. Three days later, on 23 June, Mookerjee's death anniversary, the BJP took out a rally in Kolkata, observing Mookerjee's 'atmobolidaan dibos' (self-sacrifice day). State unit president Rahul Sinha, Bengal in-charge Siddharth Nath Singh, Tathagata Roy, and the two MPs S.S. Ahluwalia and Babul Supriyo, walked the three-kilometre stretch from College Square to Esplanade in central Kolkata. Besides, the RSS's Bengali newsweekly *Swastika* brought out two cover stories on Mookerjee. Its 23 June issue was titled *'Poschimbondo Sarkar-er Kachhei Obanchhito Poschimbonger Sroshta Syama Prasad Mookerjee.'* ('Bengal's government doesn't care for Bengal's creator'), and its 7 July issue chronicled in brief the journey of the RSS's political wing – from the Jana Sangh to the BJP.

'It is with discussions around Mookerjee that we plan to revive the idea of West Bengal as a homeland for Bengali Hindus', Amalendu Chattopadhyay, an RSS pracharak who had been serving as West Bengal BJP general secretary (organization) for more than a decade, explained to this author during a conversation at the West Bengal BJP headquarters in June 2014.

Sensing a kill

Ahead of the May 2014 Lok Sabha elections, the BJP asked Samik Bhattacharya to fight a losing battle. He was chosen as the party's candidate for the Basirhat Lok Sabha seat, where Muslims constituted more than 65 per cent of the population. The BJP, understandably, stood a very thin chance, if at all they had any, of winning. Bhattacharya pegged his electoral campaign on being a 'minority candidate'. 'The Hindus are a minority here and I am the only Hindu candidate among the major political parties. I am here to represent the Hindus', he said repeatedly. He stood a distant third in the Lok Sabha elections after the TMC and the Left, even though BJP's vote share in the constituency rose from below 7 per cent in 2009 Lok Sabha elections to over 19 per cent. Of the seven assembly segments in Basirhat Lok Sabha, the TMC led over the Left in five, the Left over the

TMC in one, and the BJP over the TMC in one. That one segment where the BJP took the lead was Basirhat Dakshin.

The Left's eight-time MLA from Basirhat Dakshin assembly constituency, Naranyan Mukhopadhyay, died in March 2014 in the run-up to the Lok Sabha elections. This required a bye-election to the assembly seat. After the Election Commission announced 13 September 2014 as the date of the by-poll (along with elections for the Chowringhee seat in Kolkata vacated by a disgruntled TMC MLA), the BJP leadership promptly nominated Bhattacharya to try his luck one more time.

The Basirhat Dakshin assembly constituency was an ideal choice for any party looking to polarize votes on religious lines – 54 per cent of its voters were Hindu, Muslims comprising the rest. The assembly segment consisted of the municipal towns of Basirhat and Taki, where Hindus were in overwhelming majority, and the Basirhat I community development block, where Muslims constituted the majority.

This time, for the September 2014 assembly bye-election, Bhattacharya started from an advantageous situation. In the Lok Sabha elections, he had bagged 38.39 per cent of votes in Basirhat Dakshin assembly segment, while the TMC got 23.23 per cent and the Left only 21.22 per cent. To add to his advantages, he was the only candidate in the fray who had the experience of contesting an election here just a few months ago. The turf was known and the people knew him. Also, a number of grassroots-level Left workers and organizers had joined the BJP since the Lok Sabha election. The TMC, on the other hand, took over Basirhat municipality from the Congress by poaching four of its councillors.

For the BJP, the opportunity was too big and crucial to be taken casually. It would help the party maintain the Lok Sabha election's momentum. Mamata Banerjee did not take it lightly either. She named former India football captain Dipendu Biswas as the party's candidate. Biswas was a local. Mukul Roy, the virtual 'number two' in the TMC, camped there to oversee the functioning of the party's election machinery.

The assembly bye-election battle was closer and the polarization sharper. Bhattacharya won, marking the BJP's first assembly seat victory in Bengal fighting on its own. He managed to retain almost the same share of votes in the bye-poll compared to the May 2014 Lok Sabha elections. He got

71,002 of 189,691 votes polled, or 37.4 per cent in September 2014. However, he won by a narrow margin of only 1,586 votes because the TMC had increased its share by eating into the Left and Congress vote-banks. It now drew 36.59 per cent (69,416) of the votes polled. The Left and the Congress were pushed to the fringes, with 13.09 per cent and 11.57 per cent vote-share, respectively.

The other bye-election that took place at the same time was in Chowringhee, in the heart of Kolkata. The local TMC MLA was Shikha Mitra, wife of Somen Mitra, the former state Congress president against whom Mamata Banerjee had rebelled and quit Congress to form the TMC in 1997. Somen Mitra, funnily, later joined the TMC, accepting Mamata Banerjee's leadership. Somen Mitra became a TMC MP in 2009 and Shikha Mitra a TMC MLA in 2011. However, Mitra fell out with Banerjee around 2013, went back to Congress and contested the 2014 Lok Sabha elections on a Congress ticket against the TMC incumbent. Mitra came fourth and lost his deposit. Shikha Mitra then resigned from the assembly, necessitating a by-poll. The voting pattern reaffirmed the trends observed in Basirhat Dakshin.

New political equations were beginning to unfold.

Seeking 'Jihadi-Mukto Bangla'

The BJP's 'Mission 2016', which was aimed at making the party the main Opposition in West Bengal, had three aspects to it – a war on the ideological front, the highlighting of administrative failure, and organization building. On the ideological front, the party was to contrast the persecution of minority Hindus in Islamic Bangladesh with the appeasement of minority Muslims in Hindu-majority West Bengal. On 2 October 2014, a blast on the first floor of a two-storeyed house at Khagragarh, a non-descript Muslim neighbourhood in Burdwan town, about 130 km north of Kolkata, blew the lid off a mushrooming network of the banned terror outfit, Jamaat-ul-Mujahideen Bangladesh, or JMB, in West Bengal. The BJP had got its issue.

The blast happened in the afternoon of the auspicious maha-ashtami, the third day of the five-day festival of Durga puja, the state's largest annual festival. It killed two persons on the spot and left one grievously injured. Police later found the house full of explosives. The state police, who did the initial investigations, suggested involvement of local criminals. But the National Investigation Agency (NIA) proactively threw itself into the investigations and very soon unearthed a cross-border terror network.

Complicating matters for the TMC, the house where the terror suspects were living as tenants belonged to a local TMC leader, Nurul Hassan Chowdhury, who had not sought any document from the prospective tenants before renting out the house to them. The tenants – two families – used the first floor as their residence and the ground floor as a tailoring unit. The ground floor had even been used as an election office of the TMC during the Lok Sabha elections in April-May before being rented out in June. It was possible that the terror suspects chose this house to avoid police vigilance by virtue of its being owned by a TMC leader and its having served as an office of the ruling party.

The BJP leaders held press conference after press conference, took out rallies and carried out campaigns with posters and leaflets. 'It has become apparent that the Trinamool is trying to cover up its links with terror outfits. Otherwise, why is it so opposed to the NIA stepping in? By belittling an issue concerning the nation's security, the Mamata Banerjee government is causing embarrassment to the entire nation,'[23] BJP's West Bengal in-charge Siddharth Nath Singh alleged at a press meet at the party's state headquarters. Various organizations belonging to the saffron camp put up posters at railway stations and bus terminuses and around government offices in prominent towns, seeking 'Jihadi-mukto Bangla' (A Bengal free from Jihad).

The RSS newsweekly *Swastika* had back-to-back issues with 'cover stories' on this subject. The 20 October issue had a cover title that said, '*Shashok Doler Sathe Jongi Jogsajos?*' (Has the ruling party terror connections?). It carried an advertisement for its 27 October issue that read, 'Bengal turning into the second Kashmir, courtesy the TMC.' One of the articles branded the TMC as 'Jamaat-ul-Trinamool'. The 27 October edition, titled '*Onuprobesh er Kufol*' (the ill effect of infiltration), linked terror in the state with infiltration (of Muslims) from Bangladesh.

Several of the arrested persons' links with various madrasas became another point of embarrassment for the Mamata Banerjee government, as it was proudly proclaiming success in promoting madrasa education. Increasing the TMC's embarrassment, Reuters on 28 October reported that the NIA had unearthed a plot by JMB's West Bengal network to kill Bangladesh prime minister Sheikh Hasina and the key Opposition leader, former prime minister Khaleda Zia. Reuters quoted three anonymous officers of the NIA in its report.

The news was all over the Bengali media in no time and prominently featured in the media in Bangladesh too. Several Dhaka-based newspapers reported that Dhaka was worried about the news of these terrorists getting shelter in West Bengal. Nothing could have been more embarrassing for Mamata Banerjee, as Hasina, while speaking to journalists at her residence in Dhaka on 30 October, cautioned anyone against providing shelter to fundamentalists and terrorists. 'Anyone sheltering or harbouring terrorists must realize how dangerous it could prove to be'[24], she said, and expressed hopes that India would punish those sheltering terrorists.

Later on the same day, in an exclusive interview to *Anandabazar Patrika*, the Bengali daily with the largest circulation in West Bengal, Hasina said, 'It saddens me every time I hear that terrorists are taking shelter in West Bengal to hatch conspiracies against our government, our country and our people … the people of West Bengal will never tolerate this. They will eliminate terror from their soil.'

Mamata Banerjee was coming under pressure. In a matter of a few days, following interrogation of the arrested persons and sharing of intelligence between the anti-terror agencies of India and Bangladesh, investigating agencies realized that the five most-wanted accused in the Khagragarh blast – Sunny, Kausar, Hatkata Nasirullah, Talha Sheikh and Farooq – were none other than Salahuddin Salehin, Bomaru Mizan, Sohel Mahfuz, Shyamal Sheikh and Jamai Farooq, respectively, all of them wanted by the Bangladesh police. There was relentless discussion on the Khagragarh blast in the mainstream and social media.

Mamata Banerjee responded with conspiracy theories. She started blaming the BJP for using central agencies to spread a misinformation campaign against her. Besides, her administration began to target the RSS.

On 21 November, the top leaders of the RSS in south Bengal, Atul Kumar Biswas, Bidyut Mukherjee, Jisnu Basu and Srimanta Chanda (saha prant karyavaha or assistant secretary), met Governor Keshari Nath Tripathy and complained that the police had interrupted two shakhas – at Baruipur and Gosaba, both in South 24 Parganas district. In the letter written to Tripathi, Biswas alleged, 'Subrata Kanshabanik, inspector in charge, Baruipur police station, South 24 Parganas has instructed the swayamsevaks to perform RSS shakhas only inside closed rooms.'[25]

'Trinamool would do anything to please Jihadi elements that now form the backbone of the party. We will, of course, not abide by such unlawful orders (by the police) and will take legal course if necessary,' Jisnu Basu told journalists after meeting the governor.

Was the RSS getting a little more politically oriented in Bengal than in other states, this author asked Jisnu Basu a few days later. 'Could be', he said after thinking for a moment, and then explained: 'No other chief minister has sacrificed the country's national security as much as she [Mamata] has. Her police were about to suppress the Jamaat links with the Khagragarh blast. It is only because of NIA's proactive role that a danger to the country of such great magnitude could be identified and dealt with. Saving the state from this government is no longer a task limited to the sphere of politics.'

There were whispers within the state BJP that a change in leadership was in the offing and that more RSS leaders could be deputed to the state unit. Early in 2014, the RSS deputed its pracharak and former prachar pramukh of south Bengal, Subrato Chattopadhyay, to the BJP as joint-general secretary (organization). He was to assist another pracharak, Amalendu Chattopadhyay, who had been serving as Bengal BJP's general secretary (organization) for more than a decade. The buzz got louder after November 2014, when the RSS deputed its pracharak Dilip Ghosh, who had been serving as the organizing secretary of Hindu Jagaran Manch, to West Bengal BJP. Ghosh, of whom we have already spoken, was designated as one of the general secretaries of BJP's state unit.

TWO

Bengal, Islam, Hindutva

Bengal

THE BENGAL DELTA, THE world's largest, and also one of the most densely populated regions of the Indian subcontinent[1], is the land of a civilization more than 3,000 years old.[2] This land of the Bengali-speaking people is a huge tract of deltaic plain – at present politically divided into West Bengal and Bangladesh. *Nodimatrik Bongodesh* – child of Mother River – has been sujalam, sufalam, and shashya-shyamalam (full of water and fertile tracts of land green with crops), as described by the Bengali novelist Bankim Chandra Chattopadhyay. There has been no dearth of rain in this hot and humid land, and rice and fish are available in abundance. Its distinct geographical features also led to the development of a distinct identity over hundreds of years – one united by language and a common cultural heritage.

According to Niharranjan Ray's *Bangaleer Itihas* and Sukumar Sen's *Bangala Sahityer Itihas,* Bengal was dominated by non-Aryan races prior to the rule of the Gupta dynasty in north India. 'Since Bengal was inhabited by the non-Aryan races, it was prohibited for north-Indian Aryans to travel or settle here. After a visit here, they would not be accepted back in society without undergoing purification,' Sen wrote[3]. Indo-Aryan migration to the lower Gangetic plains is estimated to have taken place from the fifth century onwards. Ray wrote[4] that the Brahmanical system had found no acceptance in Bengal before the establishment of the Gupta dynasty's rule (approximately AD 319–543).

Bengal's geographical location has frequently been called its 'fortune'. In *History of Bengal*,[5] an 1813 book often described as the first work on the subject in English, British orientalist Charles Stewart wrote that the province of Bengal was one of the most valuable acquisitions 'ever made by any nation'. Stewart wrote, 'On the north and east it is defended by impenetrable mountains; and on the south by a line of inhospitable and dangerous seacoast, containing but one harbour capable of admitting vessels of any size; and even that one guarded by innumerable shoals. Its western frontier, although exposed to invasion, is, in many places, so strongly defended by nature, that fewer troops are requisite to protect it than any other country of similar extent on the continent of Asia.'

He added, 'Its numerous navigable rivers, in the possession of a maritime nation, are also so many sources of defence, that should the English ever be driven from all the other parts of India, they may find in Bengal an asylum where no enemy will venture to follow them.'

Except during the period of the Maurya and Gupta dynasties, Bengal was governed by independent kingdoms ruling different parts during different times – Pundra and Gaud in the north; Banga, Samatata and Harikela in the east; and Sumha, Tamralipti and Rarh in the west – for most of the first millennium and before.

Buddhism was the first major organized religion to influence the people of this region and even received state patronage, especially during the Pal (Pala) dynasty from the middle of the eighth to the end of the eleventh century. Orthodox Hinduism and the Brahmanical caste system triumphed over Buddhism in the twelfth century, especially in southwestern Bengal during the Sen (Sena) dynasty, whose founders hailed from the Deccan. The rulers described themselves as Brahmin-Khsatriyas – Brahmins who rule as Kshatriyas.

The Sen dynasty not only ensured strict implementation of the caste system but also introduced Kulinism, a practice of hypergamy that finally led to upper-caste male polygamy, with people having dozens of wives. Hinduism spread to central and northern Bengal with the increasing influence of the Sen dynasty, but after a little more than a century's rule, at the beginning of the thirteenth century, a Turk army led by Ikhtiyar al-Din Muhammad Bin Bakhtiyar Khalji defeated Laxman Sen of the dynasty and marked the beginning of Islamic rule in the region. The year was AD 1203 or 1204.

In *Social History of the Muslims in Bengal (down to AD 1538)*,[6] Abdul Karim wrote that the entry of Islam 'completely changed the socio-religious pattern of Bengal.' In the words of Sukumar Sen, 'The Turki invasion at the very beginning of the thirteenth century acted as a stunning blow to Bengal, which, under the rule of the Pala, Candra, Varman, Sena and other kings had achieved a singular cultural distinction.'[7]

Muslims ruled Bengal for the next five centuries, until the British defeated Bengal's last independent nawab, Siraj-ud-Daula, in the Battle of Plassey in 1757.

Islam in Bengal

The publication of the report of the first census in India in 1872 created a demographic puzzle after it revealed Islam's exponential growth in Bengal, especially in the eastern part, in complete isolation from the Muslim areas of western and northern India. The census report showed Hindus made only 50.68 per cent of Bengal's population (18,100,438 Hindus and 17,609,135 Muslims). In a striking difference from the Muslims of north and western India, Muslims in Bengal lived in the rural areas and not around the old capitals or urban settlements. By 1881, Islam had emerged as Bengal's largest religion, Muslims making up 49.69 per cent of the population, thanks to its steady growth in the eastern part of the region.

The question that rang aloud was, how did Bengal, one of the last provinces to be conquered by the Muslims, turn into a Muslim-majority area?

The 1872 census report[8] referred to 'wholesale conversion' of low-caste Hindus to Islam in eastern Bengal. Several Muslim scholars, including Abu

A. Ghuznavi in 1872 and Khondkar Fuzli Rubbee in 1895 contested this analysis and claimed that the Muslims in Bengal were essentially high-born immigrants.[9] The immigration theory was finally discarded by most, as even though immigration of Arabs, Turks and Afghans as imperial employees and fortune-seekers did take place from 1204 onwards, there was no evidence of immigration of such a magnitude that the immigrants would outnumber the original inhabitants. The 1901 census report reiterated the 1872 observation that conversions were taking place.

'The Namasudras aggregate about 18,61,000 and the Pods nearly half a million: but large numbers have been converted into Muhammadanism and now call themselves Sheik. There are ten and a half millions of Muhammadans in the Dacca and Chittagong divisions, and it has been shown that a great majority of them are the descendants of the converts from the ranks of these two castes,' reported the census of 1901.

Three separate serological studies (analysis of blood groups) between 1938 and 1960 supported the theory of conversion. The first was conducted by Eileen W. Erlanson Macfarlane in 1938, and the second by B.K. Chatterjee and A.K. Mitra, published in 1941. The third study, conducted by Dhirandra Nath Majumdar and C. Radhakrishna Rao, published[10] in 1960, stressed on the 'dissociation of the Bengali Muslims from those outside India, and even from the Shias and Sunnis of Uttar Pradesh.'

Later, in independent Bangladesh, Dhaka-based historian A.F. Salahuddin Ahmed wrote, 'The Muslims of Bengal form a distinct community and in their social and cultural life they are closer to the non-Muslim population of this region than to the Muslims living elsewhere in the subcontinent.'[11]

Scholars have later attributed the speedy growth of Islam only in the eastern part of Bengal to Islam's entry to east Bengal before Hinduism could spread its roots there. Richard Eaton wrote: 'Evidence indicates that Bengal's north-western and western sub-regions were far more deeply influenced by Indo-Aryan and Hindu civilization than was the eastern delta ... In 1204, when Muhammad Bakhtiyar's Turkish cavalry captured the western Sena city of Nudiya, most Hindu pilgrimage sites were built along the Bhagirathi-

Hooghly in the western part and there was virtually no pilgrimage along what is now known as Padma.'[12]

According to Md Shah Noorur Rahman, 'The people of eastern Bengal did not fully conform to Hinduism; rather they were followers of a corrupt and perverted form of Buddhism before the Muslim conquest. So, it failed to resist the onslaught of Islam.'[13]

Conversions have been attributed to two reasons essentially – fear of persecution and lure of material gains during the reigns of the Delhi Sultanate, the independent Bengal Sultanate and the Mughal era; and voluntarily, during and after the Muslim rule. Scholars have pointed out that Islam continued to grow here even after the British defeated the Muslim rulers, when the Hindus did not even need to express their subordination or gratitude to the Muslims. Voluntary conversions have been attributed to caste divides in the Hindu society in the backdrop of Islam's, especially Sufism's, appeal of a society free of divisions and untouchability.

Ramesh Chandra Majumdar's *History of Medieval Bengal* presents a picture that complements this view. 'Even for the slightest deviation from the rules of touch and purity the Hindus were cast out of society, with no chance of re-entry.... This, together with forcible conversion, and voluntary acceptance of Islam by temptation of material gain or benefit, rarely by conviction, resulted in the steady flow of the Hindus to the fold of Islam, which constitutes the most important change in the Hindu society during the middle ages.'[14]

This demographic change would ultimately lead to the battle for political dominance between the Hindus and the Muslims in the state, resulting in the Partition along religious lines in 1947. The east – which became East Pakistan – had the Muslim-majority districts, except for the Hindu-majority Khulna and the Buddhist-majority Chittagong Hill Tract. The west – which remained in India – got the Hindu-majority districts, and the Muslim-majority Murshidabad.

Islam, however, continued to grow in both parts of divided Bengal. Muslims accounted for 19.85 per cent of West Bengal's population at the time of Partition. As the Muslim population kept growing, Malda became West Bengal's second Muslim-majority district in 2001 and Uttar Dinajpur its third in 2011. The Muslim population in the state had grown to 27.02 per cent by 2011. In the eastern part, initially East Pakistan and later Bangladesh, the Muslim population went up from 76.9 per cent in 1951 to 89.6 per cent in 2011, with the Hindu population dwindling from 22.05 per cent in 1947 to 8.5 per cent in 2011.

This would have a significant impact on the politics of West Bengal from 2013 onwards, and we will come to that.

Birthplace of Hindutva

Nineteenth-century Bengal, the time and theatre of the Indian Renaissance from where many aspects of modern India originated, was also the birthplace of the idea of Hindutva, which the RSS describes as Hindu cultural nationalism. The very word Hindutva, the concept of Bharat Mata and the Bande Mataram slogan were all products of Bengal that spread across the country. The origin of the notion that Hindus are in danger – the principal reason that led to the creation of right-wing Hindutva organizations – can also be traced back to Bengal.

Hindu revivalism emerged in Bengal in the second half of the nineteenth century as a reaction to the influence of Western education and culture on the Hindu society during the first half of that century. The Hindu College, today's Presidency University, was founded in 1820, and eight years later, the appointment of a nineteen-year-old as a lecturer in English turned out to be a game changer. That young man, Henry Luis Vivian Derozio, rose like a radical star in a very short time, creating his own group of freethinking followers. In only three more years that he lived – during which he was also sacked for his 'ill-influence' on the pupils – Derozio ignited dozens of minds, who constituted what became known as the Young Bengal movement. They radically questioned the shastra (the scriptures), widely believed superstitions and practices of Hindu society and played a pivotal role in turning Calcutta into a cradle of liberal thinking. Some of them eventually denounced Hinduism and embraced Christianity or Brahmoism.

Brahmoism was a monotheistic socio-religious reformist movement born out of the Hindu society's exposure to Western education. This movement sowed the seeds of the Bengal (or Indian) Renaissance. The movement denounced idolatry, faith in scriptures and avatars, and discrimination based on caste, creed and religion; it questioned superstitions and advocated women's education. Its journey started with the foundation of the Brahmo Sabha in 1828 by 'Rajah' Rammohun Roy, the social, religious and educational reformer often regarded as the 'father of Indian Renaissance' and the 'father of modern India', and Debendranath Tagore, father of Nobel laureate Rabindranath Tagore. The Brahmo movement drew some of Bengal's brightest sons and daughters[15] – most of the educated women of Bengal in the nineteenth century were either Christian or Brahmo – and raised a storm in the Hindu society with its social reform programmes, even though it remained an elite movement with little influence on the masses, who were somewhat scandalized by some of the radical proposals of the Brahmo movement.

The visualization and depiction of India as a 'mother' started gaining popularity during the late 1860s. The first published reference to the coinage 'Bharat Mata' has been traced to a satirical Bengali book, *Unabingsho Puran*[16] (the nineteenth purana), published in 1866 under the pseudonym of Krishnadwaipayana Vedavyasa. Bhudeb Mukhopadhyay, a scholar and writer, is generally regarded as its anonymous author. He was part of Bengal's Hindu revivalism. Discussing Mukhopadhyay and his times, linguist Suniti Kumar Chatterjee wrote[17] that the atmosphere in the colleges and high schools during 1840–1870 'was not healthy for the Bengali mind and culture' and that an 'inferiority complex' gripped the Bengali psyche – by Bengali, he meant Bengali Hindus – after exposure to Western education, knowledge and culture.

In 1867, Debendranath Tagore, along with poet-playwright-editor Nabagopal Mitra and essayist Rajnarayan Basu, took the leadership in organizing the Hindu Mela, which was alternatively called '*jatiyo mela*' (national fair). The fair was inaugurated with a patriotic song composed by Rabindranath's elder brother Dwijendranath –a polymath –addressing Bharat, the mother. '*Malina Mukhochandra, Maa Bharat Tomari*' (You look pale, mother India). In 1873, a play titled *Bharat Mata* was staged in Kolkata. Its author was Kiran Chandra Bandyopadhyay. Rajnarayan Basu's *Hindu*

Dharmer Shreshthota (The Superiority of the Hindu Dharma) was published in 1879. Towards the end of the 1870s, Bankim Chandra Chattopadhyay penned the hymn 'Bande Mataram'. The hymn became part of his landmark and controversial literary work *Ananda Math*, published in 1882. It was a landmark for its literary value and social influence, and controversial for its anti-Muslim sentiment. Also, in 1882, in an article titled '*Bangalar itihas sanmandhe koekti kotha*' (a few words about the history of Bengal) that appeared in *Bangadarshan*, which Bankim Chandra himself edited, Bankim refused to accept the history of Islamic rulers as the history of Bengal.

> In our consideration, not a single English book contains the true history of Bengal. These books contain merely a hotchpotch of the birth, death and family feud of the Muslims who used to relax lying down on their beds wearing useless titles such as the Badshah of Bangalah or Subah-dar of Bangalah. This is not the history of Bengal; this is not even an iota of the history of Bengal. This has no connection whatsoever with Bengal's history. The Bengali who accepts all this as the history of Bengal is not a Bengali. The one who accepts without questioning the versions of the Muslims, who are blind with self-pride are liars and Hindu-haters, is not a Bengali.[18]

He also called upon Bengalis, in the same article, to search for and chronicle Bengal's authentic history. By Bengalis, he meant Bengali-speaking Hindus.

Chadra Nath Basu's book *Hindutva* was published in 1892 by Gurudas Chatterjee. The first recorded use of the word Hindutva, at least in print, is believed to have been made in this book. In the *Calcutta Review*'s July 1894 issue (Vol. 99), the 'vernacular literature' section carried a two-and-a-half-page review of *Hindutva*. The review describes the book as 'evidently a work of Hindu revival'.

Though Hindu revivalism started as a counter narrative to Western education and culture, it gradually developed into Hindu nationalism seeking to confront the ruling British power. The primary sentiment was that Hindus are not inferior; they will not remain dominated.

In *The Swadeshi Movement in Bengal (1903-1908)*, historian Sumit Sarkar wrote:

> For a short while during its Derozian phase, the movement [the Renaissance] seemed to be heading for a really radical break with Hindu sectarian traditions and the achievement of a truly secular culture.... But as the century progressed, the awakening national pride of the Bengali *bhadrolok* sought sustenance more and more in images of ancient Hindu glory and medieval Hindu resistance to Muslim rule.... Patriotism tended to be identified with Hindu revivalism, 'Hindu' and 'national' came to be used as synonymous terms.[19]

Ananda Math had emerged as an exemplar of the idea of Hindu nationalism. And in its aim of ousting the British, it did not consider taking the Muslims along. The first edition of the book merely excluded the Muslims in the Hindus' fight against the British. In the second edition, though, the enemy changed from *gora* (white), British and *sena* (army) to '*Nere*' and '*Jobon*' – two derogatory terms by which the Hindus referred to the Muslims in Bengal.

According to Ahmed Sofa,[20] a legendary public intellectual in Bangladesh, none influenced Bengal's society and politics as much as Bankim did, and the influence of *Ananda Math* in Bengal's socio-political life is comparable only to that of Jean Jacques Rousseau's *Social Contract* in France. In *Shotoborsher Ferari Bankim Chandra Chattopadhyay*, while acknowledging Bankim's literary genius, Sofa stressed that it was his thoughts on nation building that earned Bankim a distinct place. He was 'more than merely a powerful writer,' Sofa wrote, 'He was the first to dream of establishing a Hindu Rashtra', and added, 'If a single person is to be blamed for the Partition of Bengal, it is Bankim Chandra.'

By the end of the century, secret revolutionary societies started taking shape in Maharashtra and Bengal. In Bengal, Anushilan Samiti – a name inspired by Bankim Chandra's 1888 essay 'Anushilan' – was formed in 1902. The Jugantar Dal emerged as one of its wings in 1906. Members of these groups were mostly bhadrolok – wealthy, upper-caste and educated Hindu Bengalis – but there were members from the lower castes too. These groups drew inspiration from the Bhagavad Gita, the writings of Bankim Chandra, the call of Swami Vivekananda and his Irish disciple Sister Nivedita, and the autobiography of Mazzini, the latter particularly because it contained a chapter on guerrilla warfare.

Muslims were not part of these groups. It appeared from the accounts of Bhupendranath Dutta[21] and Hem Chandra Kanungo[22] that Muslims were not welcome either. An integral part of their programme was taking oath on the Gita, while 'Bande Mataram' was their war cry. The members included some of Bengal's most revered revolutionaries – from Bagha Jatin and Kshudiram Bose to Master-da Surya Sen – who literally terrorized the British administration.

Hindu revivalism took a different shape at the beginning of the twentieth century, with the numerical increase of the Muslims, and the Muslim elites' efforts to secure rights and benefits for the community.[23]

Through June 1909, a string of letters, titled '*Hindu: A Dying Race*', written by Lt Col. U.N. Mukerji, an Indian Medical Service officer, appeared in *Bengalee*, a Kolkata-based English-language newspaper owned and edited by veteran Congress leader Surendranath Banerjea. Historians identified these letters, later compiled into a pamphlet and also published as a book,[24] as the founding basis of the notion that Hindus were in danger and they needed to wake up and act.

'There are various ways people have dwindled and finally disappeared from their own country,' Mukerji wrote, 'and we are in a fair way of sharing their fate.' He then explained how the Maoris of New Zealand and the natives of the US and Hispaniola disappeared following foreign invasions: 'We are also a decaying race. Every census reveals the same fact. We are getting proportionately fewer and fewer.... Year after year they [the Hindus] are being pushed back, the land once occupied by them is being taken up by Mohammedans, and their relative proportion to the population of the country is getting smaller and smaller.'

'They look forward to a united Mohammedan world – we are waiting for our extinction,' he wrote, and added, 'The Mohammedans have a future and they believe in it – we Hindus have no conception of it. Time is with them – time is against us. At the end of the year *they count their gains, we calculate our losses.*'

The series of letters and the pamphlet stirred such a debate that Mukerji was invited to deliver a speech at the Bengal Provincial Congress Committee's 1911 session at Faridpur in east Bengal. Earlier that year, the census had revealed that Bengal accounted for 36 per cent (24 million) of the total number of Muslims in India.

His writing also influenced people living beyond the borders of Bengal. Punjab-based Swami Shraddhananada, who later became a prominent leader of the Akhil Bharat Hindu Mahasabha and was shot dead by a Muslim in 1926, wrote in his book *Hindu Sangathan: Saviour of the Dying Race* that he was deeply impressed by Mukherji when he met him in Kolkata in 1912. Shraddhananda had also spoken about the influence of Mukherji's book on him in a speech he gave at Patna in 1925.[25] Shraddhananda and his book, a 1924 publication, had a lasting impact on right-wing Hindu organizers in northern and western India during the formative days of the ideology of Hindutva, as did V.D. Savarkar's 1923 book, *Essentials of Hindutva,* which later became popular simply as *Hindutva.* '*They count their gains, we calculate our losses,*' became an oft-repeated phrase by the Hindu rightwing in the following days. In 1976, the Vishwa Hindu Parishad published a book under this title.

The Communal Divide

Tracing the roots of Muslim separatism in Bengal in the latter half of the nineteenth century, Nitish Sengupta cited the impact of the Permanent Settlement of 1793 that turned zamindari into a monopoly of the wealthy Hindus in Bengal, while the hurt pride of the Muslims for the loss of their reign to the British pushed the community into a cocoon[26] and resulted in a decline of the Muslim aristocracy. Sengupta wrote, 'Nowhere else in the subcontinent were Muslims as worse off as in Bengal, as, paradoxically, few other communities derived as much benefit from the British rule as the

Bengali Hindus.'[27] He went on to quote William Hunter from the latter's book[28] *Indian Mussalmans*, published in 1871: 'A hundred and seventy years ago, it was almost impossible for a well-born Muslim in Bengal to become poor. At present, it is almost impossible for him to continue rich.'

Apart from the Permanent Settlement, there was another impact. Two Muslim reformist movements took place in Bengal in the first half of the nineteenth century. According to historian Amalendu De,[29] 'Though there were some differences between the Faraizis and the Wahabis,[30] these two movements were directed mainly with the object of purifying Islam in Bengal by removing un-Islamic practices from it.' This, in effect, further differentiated the Muslims from the Hindus, as before these movements Hindus and Muslims in the state had many common practices. A British administrative report of 1911[31] says the Hindus and Muslims of the cultivating classes 'until lately attended the religious festivals of either sect with great impartiality.' The author wrote 'until lately', because later in the article he talked about the increasing influence of Wahabi radicalism among the Muslims. 'Even now, it is not uncommon for them to apply mutually to the deities or saints of the other religion when they imagine that application to their own will prove ineffectual,' the report said.

The fault line between the Hindu-dominated west and the Muslim-dominated east emerged rather clearly during the movement against the first Partition of Bengal, which was proposed in 1903 and – despite Kolkata and its surroundings turning into a hotbed of anti-British struggle – enforced in 1905. Protests continued in the western part seeking reunification of the Bengali-speaking territories, but the Muslim-dominated eastern part, which initially offered a lukewarm response to the west's call, later largely welcomed the bifurcation.

According to Sumit Sarkar, the bhadrolok who were blissfully disconnected from the Muslims and had a lack of regard for them as their social counterparts[32] made overtures to the Muslims in the post-Partition days, trying to make common cause against partition. While the educated and elite among Muslims were favouring partition because the government of East Bengal made it a norm to prefer Muslims over Hindus for job recruitments, the East Bengal peasantry, consisting mostly of Muslims, saw the partition as an opportunity to free themselves from the clutches of their West Bengal-based Hindu landlords. Even patriotic Muslims were isolated or distanced by the Hindu revivalist bent of the Swadeshi movement. 'Hindu-Muslim relations posed the greatest challenge before the Swadeshi movement, and ultimately proved its greatest failure,' Sarkar wrote.

The communal relations started souring over the question of sharing political space after the suspension of the non-cooperation movement and the collapse of the Khilafat movement in 1922. Communal riots were increasing in number and magnitude. The year 1926 alone witnessed at least eleven riots, including in Kolkata, Dhaka, Pabna and Kharagpur, as also in small towns such as Patuakhali (Barishal). Hindu–Muslim relations turned worse after 1929, when the Communal Award first came into discussion. It proposed proportional representation of various communities in the legislatures. Muslims alone would elect Muslims, Hindus would elect Hindus, and Europeans would elect Europeans.

This, if implemented, would surely diminish the influence of the Hindus in Bengal.

In the existing structure of the Bengal Council, Hindus had forty-six seats, against thirty-nine for Muslims. Now, of the 250-seat proposed Bengal Assembly, Muslims were allotted 119, or 47.6 per cent, even though they were 54 per cent of Bengal's population in 1931. Hindus got eighty-two seats, or 32.8 per cent of the total, while their population stood at 44 per cent. Of these eighty-two, ten were for the backward classes and two for women. Europeans, who formed less than 1 per cent of Bengal's population, were given eleven seats.

Bengal's newly appointed governor, the Second Marquess of Zetland Lawrence Dundas,[33] had objections to the proposed seat-sharing formula. In *Bengal Divided: Hindu Communalism and Partition 1932-1947*,[34] Joya Chatterjee wrote that 'Lord Zetland' had a four-point objection. She quoted Zetland from one of his official notes, which is now part of the Zetland Collection of papers:

'(I) It is putting an advanced people in a position of subordination to a backward people;

(2) It will enormously increase communal bitterness;

(3) It will create a sense of injustice which will not easily be forgiven or forgotten;

(4) It will give rise to increasing agitation and will inevitably give an immense stimulus to subversive movements.'

His objection yielded no result, and Delhi and London decided to go ahead with the plan. Hindus continued to organize themselves for a prolonged protest. The rift between the communities continued to widen.

Suranjan Das, in one of his works[35] on the subject of communal conflict in Bengal, pointed out that 'The question of "music before the mosques," which had hardly bothered inhabitants in most areas for hundreds of years, was raised as a central point of communal dissension in large parts of Bengal by the 1930s.'

With the growing influence of the Muslim League[36] and with the Hindu Mahasabha's entry into politics in 1937, Subhas Chandra Bose, the tallest political figure of Bengal of that time, carried out a sustained ideological propaganda against communal politics. In an editorial titled 'Congress and Communal Organizations', which appeared in the 4 May 1940 issue of the weekly *Forward Bloc* that he edited, Bose referred to the Mahasabha and the League as 'communal organizations' and remarked that 'these communal organizations have become more communal than before'.

Eight days later, while addressing a public gathering at Durga Maidan in Jhargram on 12 May, he lashed out at the Mahasabha. A report in *Anandabazar Patrika's* 14 May 1940 issue quoted 'Netaji' as saying: 'Hindu Mahasabha has sent out trident-carrying monks begging for votes. Hindus bow whenever they see the trident and the saffron clothes. Hindu Mahasabha has emerged in the political scene, using religion to pollute it. Remove these traitors from the national life. No one should listen to them.... No lie is greater than saying that Hindus and Muslims had different interests. Floods, famines and epidemics spare none.'[37] However, with Bose leaving India for good in 1941, there was no one left of his stature to prevent the complete communalization of politics in Bengal.

Jana Sangh to BJP – The Bengal Story

Syama Prasad Mookerjee, Calcutta University's youngest vice-chancellor, had been loosely associated with the Congress since 1929 and served as a member of the Bengal Legislative Assembly from the Calcutta University constituency.[38] He joined the Hindu Mahasabha in 1939, two years after Savarkar oriented the organization politically. Mookerjee was initially appointed its national working president, but soon, owing to Savarkar's failing health, he took charge as president. His clout grew in Bengal politics, especially after Subhas Chandra Bose left India for good in 1941. At the time of India's Independence, Mookerjee was among Bengal's influential politicians. Despite being the leader of the Hindu Mahasabha, he entered the Constituent Assembly in 1946 as a Congress-nominated member. When the first cabinet of independent India was formed in 1947, Mookerjee was appointed minister of industries and supplies.

His most important role during 1946–47 lay in mobilizing public opinion in favour of creating a separate province with Bengal's Hindu-majority districts – a homeland for the Bengali Hindus – by partitioning Bengal.

Mookerjee's acquaintance with the workings of the RSS goes back to April 1940, when he had attended a shakha at Telkol Maath (grounds) on Raja Dinendra Street (in the Garhpar area in north Kolkata) in the presence of Balasaheb Deoras. The swayasamsevaks gave Mookerjee a guard of honour. In May 1940, he called on an ailing Hedgewar at Nagpur while returning from Mumbai. The RSS and the Hindu Mahasabha became close during 1946-48, especially after Mookerjee formed the Hindustan National Guard, a volunteer force aimed at combating Muslims.

Mookerjee resigned from the Hindu Mahasabha in December 1948 and the Jawaharlal Nehru cabinet in April 1950. He evidently failed to fit in at any of the existing political formations. That was when RSS organizers Balraj Madhok, Vasantrao Oke and Eknath Ranade contacted him. The need for a political wing was felt by a good number of pracharaks and swayamsevaks after the Congress in 1949 closed its doors to RSS members. Mookerjee later had discussions with M.S. Golwalkar, the second sarasanghachalak who was then at the helm of affairs of the RSS, in Kolkata and in New Delhi. Golwalkar did not want his organization to get involved in politics but agreed to lend some of his best men to work with Mookerjee for building a new political organization. The Bharatiya Jana Sangh was launched in New Delhi on 21 October 1951 as the political platform for swayamsevaks.

The newly launched party failed to create much of an impression in India's first parliamentary elections held soon after, during 1951–52. Contesting ninety-two of the 347 Lok Sabha seats, BJS won only three, two of them from West Bengal – Mookerjee from South Calcutta and Durga Charan Banerjee from Medinipur. Umashankar Trivedi won the third seat, Chittor in Rajasthan. Overall, the BJS ranked second in thirty-three seats – fourteen in Uttar Pradesh, four in Madhya Pradesh, three in Punjab, two in Bengal, three in Madhya Bharat, three in Delhi and one each in Rajasthan, Himachal, Ajmer and Vindhya Pradesh. The assembly elections held during 1951–1952 presented no brighter future for the party. Contesting 725 of the total 2,718 seats across India, they won only thirty-five. Except for West Bengal, where they won nine seats, all other seats came from the 'Hindi heartland' – areas represented by today's Rajasthan (eleven), Madhya Pradesh (six), Delhi (five), Uttar Pradesh (two) and Haryana (two).

In Bengal, their electoral success was limited to the south-western corner – now covered by the districts of West Midnapore, East Midnapore and Jhargram – from where eight of the nine winning seats came. The BJS would have required putting up a tough fight in West Bengal to surpass the Left as the Congress's main rival, but Mookerjee's untimely death – at a jail in Kashmir in 1953 – nipped its prospects in the bud. In the 1957 state assembly elections, the Jana Sangh and the Hindu Mahasabha fought in alliance but failed to win even a single seat. The BJS candidates' deposits were forfeited in thirty-one of the thirty-three seats the party had contested.

In 1962, when the party had established itself as a strong force in Uttar Pradesh and Madhya Pradesh, winning forty-nine of 430 seats and forty-one of 288 assembly seats, respectively – and had also spread its influence in Rajasthan, Punjab, Haryana and Bihar – West Bengal recorded one of their worst performances. All the twenty-five candidates lost their deposits. The Jana Sangh had a presence only on signboards in the state of its founder.

On the other hand, the Communist Party of India's vote share in West Bengal rose from 10.76 per cent in 1952 to 17.81 per cent in 1957 and to 24.96 per cent in 1962.

The Jana Sangh leaders in the state, Debaprasad Ghosh, Haripada Bharati and Vishnu Kant Shashtri, were reputed educationists and intellectuals. Ghosh, a linguist of good repute, served as the Jana Sangh's Bengal unit president and later as national president, during 1956–59, 1962–63 and 1964. Bharati was a renowned professor of philosophy. Shastri was a professor of Hindi and loved to write.

For organizing the BJS in West Bengal, the RSS sent two pracharaks to the state in 1951 – Ramprasad Das and Prabhakar Faijpurkar. Ramprasad Das continued as organizing secretary of BJS's Bengal chapter till 1964, when he was entrusted with leading the newborn Vishwa Hindu Parishad in the state. Shibaprasad Das, another pracharak, stepped into his shoes and continued as the BJS organizing secretary until it merged into the Janata Party. Ramdas Kalaskar, an RSS pracharak who was working in the Jana Sangh's Maharashtra unit, was sent to the Bengal unit during the late 1960s.

Electoral success, however, remained elusive. The first assembly election success after 1952 came in 1967, when G.N. Mondal got elected from the Scheduled Caste-dominated Gosaba seat in the Sunderbans region of South 24 Parganas district, securing 38.7 per cent of the vote. Another member got entry to the assembly in 1971, when the BJS won from Jalangi in Murshidabad district. Both seats were along the Bangladesh border. Haripada Bharati and Vishnu Kant Shastri made it to the Bengal assembly in 1977, but the Jana Sangh had by that time merged into the Janata Party and they had contested as Janata Party members.

When the BJP was formed in 1980, Bharati became the first state unit president. Pracharak Bidyut Dutta was sent to the BJP as general secretary (organization). Dutta was also the founder of BJP's youth wing, Bharatiya Janata Yuva Morcha, in Bengal.[39]

The next big name in the Bengal BJP after Bharati and Shastri was Tapan Sikdar, who later served as a junior minister in the Vajpayee government, winning the 1998 and 1999 Lok Sabha elections from Dumdum, largely by virtue of the BJP's alliance with the TMC. During the 1990s, Sikdar was synonymous with the BJP in Bengal. He had joined the Jana Sangh in 1969–70, after a three-year-association with the RSS's student wing, the Akhil Bharatiya Vidyarthi Parishad (ABVP) in Malda College, and rose up the ranks to become a protégé of Haripada Bharati.

Tathagata Roy, the other big name of the Bengal BJP, was an active swayamsevak since the late 1980s and underwent RSS's third-year OTC training in Nagpur. A civil engineer who had served as the general manager of RITES and as head of Jadavpur University's civil engineering department, Roy was, however, more of an ideologue than an organizer. Industrialist Purshottam Das Chitlangia was an RSS man, having served as the national president of Friends of Tribal Society, or Vanvandhu Parishad, from 1991 to 2003. For most of this period, he was also a vice-president of the BJP's West Bengal unit.

The BJP had to wait for nineteen years since the party's formation to get its first MLA elected in West Bengal. In 1999, BJP's Badal Bhattacharya won a bye-election from Ashoknagar, a constituency bordering Bangladesh in North 24 Parganas. That seat came with the TMC's support, though. It would be another fifteen years before the second BJP member entered the assembly.

While the BJP's vote share during these years did not increase much – mostly hovering around the 6 per cent mark – its membership kept increasing. The number of primary members had increased from 43,418 in 1980 to 2,62,822 in 2007. The number of active members rose from 532 to 11,563.[40]

Syama Prasad Mookerjee, meanwhile, had been relegated to history in Bengal politics. The Left's abhorrence for Mookerjee's brand of politics was no secret. In 2000, Deputy Chief Minister Buddhadeb Bhattacharjee refused to share the dais with Prime Minister Atal Bihari Vajpayee in Kolkata at an event kicking off Mookerjee's birth centenary celebrations. Bhattacharjee told the media on 5 July, on the eve of the event, 'I cannot go because our party is opposed to Dr Mookerjee's political thinking.'[41]

In 2017, when the BJP and RSS were busy reviving the memory of Mookerjee, Jisnu Basu, secretary of the south Bengal RSS, alleged in an article – shared a lot on Facebook and WhatsApp – that the Left and the

Congress had together hatched a conspiracy to drive people's attention away from the causes espoused by Mookerjee. He wrote that the Congress was unnerved to see the crowd of thousands that had gathered at the airport to receive Mookerjee's body at the dead of the night and was scared that the people would seek justice for this 'murder, heinous crime'. It was at this juncture that the CPI came to the rescue of the Congress by diverting the people's attention, Basu alleged.

He wrote:

> Syama Prasad passed away on 23 June (1953). The plan started exactly seven days later. Calcutta Tram Company was a British commercial venture. Such Leftist parties as the CPI, SUCI and RSP burnt down one tram after another, protesting a hike in the ticket price by one paisa. The Congress government arrested Jyoti Basu, Subodh Bandyopadhyay and Satyapriya Bandyopadhyay and gave them royal treatment in jail. The Left, protesting this (the arrests), called for a general strike in West Bengal on 8 July. Not a fortnight had passed since the death of Syama Prasad.[42]

Six decades later, the saffron camp was to compete with the Left again – a declining Left this time – to emerge as the principal challenger to Trinamool Congress. Time stood in their favour.

THREE

From Laddu to Fish Fry

Laddu Goes Sour

IN 2014, NARENDRA MODI started his campaign in Bengal trying to keep Mamata Banerjee in good humour. At his meeting at Kolkata's Brigade Parade ground on 5 February, his first in the state, Modi offered a new proposition – 'Let Didi work for you (people) here and let Modi work for you in Delhi. You will have laddu in both hands.'[1]

This was one month before the dates for the 2014 Lok Sabha elections were announced. Modi had already been nominated as the BJP's prime ministerial candidate. The crowd was not thick – at least when compared with the shows the Left and the Trinamool usually put up at this venue – but the atmosphere was charged. It was barely three years after a new government had taken charge of Bengal following the end of a thirty-four-year regime. The BJP's state unit leaders were expecting Modi to take on Mamata Banerjee to help the state unit reap the benefits of the anti-incumbency climate in Bengal, at a time when the Left and the Congress were struggling to combat the TMC.

Modi, at the beginning of his speech, asked the audience if West Bengal got to taste true poriborton – the 'change' that Mamata Banerjee had promised. The gathering answered in the negative – largely as a result of the Mamata bashing by the state's BJP leaders that had preceded Modi's address. The party's state unit president Rahul Sinha had insisted in his speech that there was no possibility of the BJP joining hands with the TMC.

'We were with her for ten years. We won't commit the same mistake,' Sinha said in his high-pitched speech targeting the Mamata Banerjee regime.

However, the speeches delivered by the national leaders were in stark contrast to those made by the party's state leaders. National president Rajnath Singh went soft on the TMC supremo and even supported her demand for a moratorium on the interest the state needed to pay the Centre, arguing that it was the misrule by the Left regime that had emptied the Bengal exchequer.

Modi too was evidently in no mood to irk Mamata Banerjee. All his salvos were directed towards the Left and the Congress. He told the crowd:

> Bengal is not facing the assembly elections. There is a government at the helm. They have promised change. You are waiting. Will you do one thing? Will you? I have always felt that Bengal has led the way in charting out a new course, a new direction for the country. It has happened for ages. Are you ready for an experiment in the coming elections? Ensure a win for the BJP in these Lok Sabha polls. Why? Let me explain. You have the Trinamool government here. They have promised to work. Ask them about their achievements, about their promises. And after voting for the BJP you come and ask me, Modi-ji what have you done?[2]

He even referred to President Pranab Mukherjee, the first Bengali to occupy the Rashtrapati Bhawan, and told the gathering that it would be 'tripple laddu' for the people of Bengal, with Mamata in Bengal, Modi in Delhi and Pranab Mukherjee as the president.

'Let us have a friendly competition,' Modi said, 'Let Mamata-ji's government work for the betterment of the people of West Bengal, and in 2014, when the BJP government comes to power in Delhi, let them too work for you. If we have this friendly competition, who will benefit?'

Modi argued that the state government alone would not be able to accelerate development in the state without 'a sympathetic government' in Delhi. He also tried to trigger anti-Congress sentiments by indicating that the Congress leadership had denied Pranab Mukherjee a chance to be India's first Bengali prime minister despite him being an able contender for the post:

> Today, I shall tell you about Congress politics. When Smt Indira Gandhi was assassinated, Rajiv Gandhi was in Kolkata. He went back. The senior-most minister in the cabinet was Pranab Mukherjee. It would have been right if he had been made the prime minister of the country. They didn't do it. The family even refused to include Pranab-da in the council of ministers. Do not forget these things. In 2004 again, Pranab-da was the senior-most leader. If madam Sonia-ji was so reluctant (to be the prime minister), he (Mukherjee) should have been made the PM. But Manmohan Singh was chosen and Pranab-da was again overlooked. We must understand the modus operandi of the Congress.[3]

In the evening, CPM state secretary Biman Bose addressed a press conference at the party's state committee office on Alimuddin Street. He said that Modi had refrained from criticizing the TMC to keep the door open for a post-poll alliance. 'He did not utter a single word on the burning issue of safety and security of women in the state,' Bose said.[4] Following several brutal incidents of rape, gang-rape and murder in the state, the Left had been targeting the state government for 'absolute absence of women's security on roads,' an allegation that state BJP leaders raised as well. Citing Modi and Rajnath Singh's silence against TMC's misrule, Congress's Manas Bhuniya too asked for the TMC to clarify its stand on the BJP.

Mamata Banerjee was not pleased. Muslims comprised a major chunk of Trinamool Congress's vote bank. She could not have allowed the Left and the Congress to create confusion among the Muslims. It had taken a great deal of effort on her part to win the confidence of the Muslims in the state. The TMC's secretary general, Partha Chatterjee, responded that very evening, 'We do not need a certificate from anyone.'

Mamata responded about two weeks later. In an interview to the *Economic Times* that appeared on 23 February, she ruled out joining hands with the BJP under any circumstance. 'We are fighting the Congress, the CPM and the BJP, and that perhaps answers your question,' Banerjee said. She batted for a federal government to be formed by various regional parties, the paper reported: '… the federal government which she is angling for will most definitely not include the Congress and the BJP.'

Throughout March, she repeatedly branded[5] the BJP as 'dangabaaj' (rioters) and referred to Modi as 'dangar mukh' (the face of the riots)[6].

By the time Modi returned to Bengal in April, he had made up his mind. At his rally at Matigara in north Bengal on 10 April 2014, he said the Mamata Banerjee government had betrayed the faith of the people and New Delhi needed a 'bada masterji' to put the government on the right path. He did not hide his displeasure at being Mamata Banerjee's prime target. 'I thought she would be more interested in criticizing the Congress and CPM. Now I find that she criticizes me hundred times a day.'[7]

Hitting where it would hurt Mamata most, Modi sought from people an opportunity to punish the culprits of the Saradha chit fund scam.

The Saradha group's ponzi scam[8] that was busted in 2013 got branded as Bengal's biggest scam in many years, and the TMC's name got linked to it because a number of the party's leaders had close associations with the group. Kunal Ghosh, group CEO in charge of Saradha's media activities, was also a Rajya Sabha MP of the Trinamool Congress and had been seen with chief minister. He oversaw operations that included a Bengali daily, an English daily and two TV news channels that ran pro-TMC propaganda. The Left and the Congress had been alleging Mamata Banerjee's direct involvement in the scam, a charge that the TMC had always rubbished. If anyone in the party had done anything wrong, it had been done in their personal capacity, was the official stand of the party.

This was a good opportunity for Modi to corner the TMC.

The battle lines were drawn. The gloves were off.

Thereafter, with every rally of Modi's and Mamata's the tempo of their verbal duel only rose. The war of words further intensified after Modi, at his

Serampore rally in Hooghly district at the end of April, raised for the first time the issue that would dominate West Bengal's political conversations, not only over the remaining days of the electoral campaign but also in the days to come.

He dropped the 'Bangladeshi bomb'.

Refugee vs infiltrator

Serampore, Hooghly, 27 April 2014: The atmosphere was electric and the crowds energized. Traffic choked in the small, centuries-old town – a former Danish colony where the first printing press in Bengal was set up in 1800 – as hundreds of BJP supporters from various neighbouring areas came down to listen to their leader-in-the-making.

A stronghold of the Congress, and later of the Trinamool Congress, Serampore had never seen such craze over a BJP rally, local residents told this author. The streets, which had been taken over by hundreds of youths clad in saffron bandanas shouting, '*Jai Shree Ram*' and '*Har Har Modi*' with unending enthusiasm, were festooned with saffron flags.

The party's candidate was Bappi Lahiri, the music composer of Bollywood fame, whose most important announcement to the voters was that if he was elected he would hold concerts at Serampore for free. But the applause that Lahiri's promise elicited was eclipsed soon by the roar of a thousand voices cheering 'Moooodiii ... Moooodi ...'

When Modi said, 'You (Mamata) have done greater damage in thirty-five months than what the Left did in thirty-four years,' a wave of 'Modi Modi' interrupted his speech for half a minute. The same happened when he dared Mamata Banerjee to reveal the identity of the buyers of her paintings that allegedly fetched astronomical prices, or when he said, 'You (Mamata) find the people from Bihar, Odisha as alien but your face glows when the Bangladeshis come. [It is] as if your relatives from some seven generations have arrived!'

Modi then paused, and delivered a threat: 'Brothers and sisters, note it down, the Bangladeshis will have to pack their bags after May 16.'[9]

Applause. 'Jai Shree Ram! Bharat Mata Ki Jai!'

As the news of this threat spread, panic and confusion took over in different pockets of the state – Hindu-dominated and Muslim-dominated areas alike. There are innumerable people of east Bengal origin who had settled in the western part after Partition. Estimates hover well above the one crore mark, whereas the state's population stood at nine crore in 2011. The migrants include Hindus and Muslims. During Partition, the population exchange in the two parts of Punjab took place rapidly, but in Bengal, a one-way migration continued for the next six decades.

Hindus migrated to West Bengal in phases, and in the thousands. There were periods of surge – during the 1950s and 1960s, during the Bangladesh Liberation War in the early 1970s, in the early 1990s, when Hindus in Bangladesh faced the repercussions of the demolition of the Babri Masjid and then, in the beginning of the new millennium, after Khaleda Zia became the prime minister of Bangladesh, with the backing of Muslim fundamentalist forces.

Hindu migrants were the target constituency of the RSS and Bharatiya Jana Sangh in the immediate post-Partition period. Bastuhara Sahayata Samiti was founded in 1950 to create a strong base among these persecuted Hindus who came fleeing from the east, selling their property and belongings to the Muslims for a pittance or often simply leaving everything behind. The RSS had built its base in northern and western India banking on these Hindu migrants from west Punjab. In Bengal, however, the Left movement had gained strength in both parts by the late 1940s, especially during the days of the militant Tebhaga movement. Many of those who crossed over to the west had connections with the communist party in the east. The Communist Party of India-led United Central Refugee Council (UCRC)[10]captured the refugee movement, and thereafter, until the decline of the Left, beginning in 2008–09, these refugee-dominated pockets/colonies served as the Left's trusted vote bank.

Bangladeshi Muslims too were migrating to West Bengal. An article written by West Bengal's Marxist chief minister Jyoti Basu, which appeared in the CPM's Bengali mouthpiece, the daily *Ganashakti* on 11 October 1992, said that before the Bangladesh Liberation War, it was mainly the Hindus who came to West Bengal. 'But from 1979, even Muslims started coming into India from Bangladesh. Between 1977 and April 1992, a total number of 235,529 Bangladeshi migrants had been identified and were sent back by the BSF. Of them, 68,472 were Hindus and 164,132 were Muslims ... this is the right time to stop cross-border migration.'

The figures quoted by Basu give an idea of the extent of Muslim migration that was happening. The Left, which always propagated the adoption of humane refugee policies, helped both Hindu and Muslim migrants to settle in the state. The migrants were given ration cards and, subsequently, their names were included in the voters' list in the state.

In a 2009 article titled 'Idea of West Bengal: Eroded from the Very Emergence', the BJP's refugee cell leader, Mohit Ray, gave his version of how the Left captured the east Bengal refugees. 'The Left leadership could channelize the movement to their "anti-imperialistic" goal, suppressing the atrocities of Islamic rule in East Pakistan. So, the UCRC processions started to raise slogans totally irrelevant to the refugee problems, such as slogans against imperialism in Korea or slogans for peace not war and against Anglo-American imperialism. Not only that, one UCRC convention in 1952 adopted a list of resolutions which included: "vii) Exploitation of the country by foreign powers and discrimination against Russia and China in the field of international trade must be ended and viii) Equipment should be imported from Russia for the improvement of indigenous heavy industries."'[11]

In 2014, the saffron camp was focused on winning the refugees over. It was in the refugee colonies spread across the state that various Sangh-affiliated organizations escalated their activities since 2013. These organizations include the Hindu Jagran Manch and the Vishwa Hindu Parishad. Modi's Serampore speech had triggered panic in these areas.

A number of state-level TMC leaders condemned Modi's 'divisive plan', claiming that they were 'aimed at destabilizing Bengal's socio-cultural ethos'. Mamata responded five days later. At a rally at Nandigram in East Midnapore district, an angry Mamata thundered, 'Touch a single person and you will see.' She referred to Modi as a 'paper tiger' and warned him of the existence of 'a Royal Bengal tiger'.[12]

The next day, 4 May, Modi addressed rallies in Bankura and Asansol. This time, he came prepared to clear all confusion. He distinguished between 'refugees' and 'infiltrators':

> 'Two kinds of people came from Bangladesh. One is the refugees who have been forced out, and they were thrown out in the name of religion. Tell me, now, if someone carrying true Indian blood lands in trouble in any part of the world, shouldn't the person be coming to India, irrespective of the colour of their passport? If people of Indian origin who are living in Fiji for centuries are persecuted there, where else other than India will they come to? Should Bharat Mata refuse her children? And that is why, those who are driven out of Bangladesh – the ones who were the children of Bharat Mata – those who love Bharat Mata and celebrate Durgashtami and speak Bengali till date, are my brothers. Their security, honour and pride will be equal to that of any Indian. But the infiltrators who are pouring in due to vote-bank politics must go back. Those who are eating into the earnings of our youth will have to leave. Our priority is to provide income-generation opportunities for the country's young workforce. We cannot deprive our youth of their rights for mere vote-bank politics.[13]

The verbal battle intensified. On 9 May, Mamata said that Modi should be 'sent to jail with ropes tied around his waist'.[14]

Modi's stand was nothing new for West Bengal, though. From the early 1990s the BJP state unit had started demanding that Hindus, who had come from Bangladesh, be granted citizenship and Muslim infiltrators pushed back. Tapan Sikdar, BJP's state unit chief, wrote an article, titled 'How West Bengal Congress is providing fillip to Muslim infiltrators', which was published in BJP's fortnightly, *BJP Today*, on 1 October 1992.

In the 1998 Lok Sabha election, which the newborn TMC fought in alliance with the BJP, Sikdar had made the point of differential treatment for Hindu and Muslim migrants from Bangladesh as one of the main electoral issues. Sikdar won from Dumdum, marking BJP's first Lok Sabha seat from Bengal. In the Lok Sabha election that took place the next year, also fought by the BJP in alliance with the TMC, the party again made infiltration one of their key issues. This time they won Dumdum and Krishnanagar.

Even in 2007 – when Mamata Banerjee had started distancing from the BJP but had not yet announced disassociation with the NDA – in a report on infiltration in West Bengal in *Frontline*[15], Suhrid Sankar Chattopadhyay wrote that BJP's state unit president Tathagata Roy, 'in keeping with his party's line, seeks to distinguish between Hindu and Muslim immigrants: the former, for him, are asylum-seeking refugees whereas the latter are illegal immigrants'. Roy was quoted as saying, 'India does not have riches coming out of its ears that it can take the burden of supporting surplus Bangladeshi population, especially when Bangladesh receives a huge amount of aid from oil-rich Arab countries of West Asia.'

Times had changed now. Mamata Banerjee was desperate to erase from public memory her past association with the BJP. She would allow no distinction between migrants on the basis of religion.

Amid their escalating war of words, Modi and Mamata addressed three rallies each in West Bengal on 7 May, exchanging barbs. Modi raked up Mamata Banerjee's past. Retaliating to Mamata's 'royal Bengal tiger' remark, Modi said that Mamata had, indeed, acted like 'a lone tigress' (*'akeli sherni jaisi'*) on the floor of parliament when she had protested, seeking action against infiltrators. '*Didi parliament mein aag laga ke rakkhi thi*' (She had set parliament on fire!),' Modi said.[16]

Modi was referring to the incident in the Lok Sabha on 4 August 2005 that had received huge publicity at that time. Mamata Banerjee was the lone MP of her party in the Lok Sabha. West Bengal assembly elections were due next year and she was trying to build a movement alleging that there were false names in the voters' list. In Lok Sabha, her adjournment motion for discussion on her finding of 'Bangladeshi infiltrators' names in West Bengal's voters' list, was rejected by Speaker Somnath Chatterjee – who, incidentally, belonged to her arch-rival party, the CPM. Video footage of what happened showed Mamata, furious at this rejection, got down into the well, walked straight to the chair of the speaker, at that time occupied by Deputy Speaker Charanjit Singh Atwal, threw a bunch of papers on his table and walked out of parliament displaying anger and disgust. She was with the NDA at the time. She also shot off a resignation letter, which was not accepted on account of a technical error. She never entered the Lok Sabha for the rest of her tenure, in any case.

Referring to that day, Modi asked, 'How did Didi change so drastically? She is calling me a criminal when I, as a brother, am merely repeating what she earlier said.'

Banerjee, over the past few days, had been calling Modi many a name. At one rally, she asked, 'Is he a donkey?' and from another said she would have got Modi into jail if she had the authority. She frequently referred to him as 'danga babu' (Mr Riot).

'Modi has no right to say he will oust Bangladeshis from West Bengal. Who is he? He is nobody,' Banerjee said. 'I dare you to touch any of them (Bangladeshis),' she thundered.

'People of Bengal are being dubbed as refugees and shamed. Some people were being called infiltrators. If they try to divide Bengal, if they try to evict anyone, I will guard you. I will not let anyone touch you. He said I respect refugees. Who is a refugee? Does he understand what it means?'[17] she said, addressing a rally at the Muslim-dominated Budge Budge area in South 24 Parganas district.

The 'Bangladeshi' issue set the tone of West Bengal's 2014 Lok Sabha campaign.

Didi's U-turn

14 June 2008. Singur: Mamata Banerjee arrived at the venue agitated. It was about a month after the panchayat election results had been declared. The TMC had dealt a rude jolt to the Left by sweeping Singur and Nandigram, where the anti-land acquisition struggle had become the principal political issue in the state. Coming two years after the TMC's assembly election rout, Banerjee was buoyed.

On the dais, with the microphone in her hand, she was on fire. She made two significant announcements – one of which made headlines while the other remained in the footnotes. The first was that she would launch an indefinite sit-in demonstration in front of the Nano plant two months later if her demand for the return of 400 acres (out of 997.11 acres) of land to the farmers, who were unwilling to part with their land, was not met. She argued that by voting overwhelmingly for the TMC, the people of Singur had made it evident that they were against forcible acquisition of farmers' land.

This threatened demonstration, which would eventually go on for sixteen days at twenty-one camps along the eastern boundary of the Nano plant, blocking a five-kilometre stretch on Durgapur Expressway (national highway 19), would force Tata Motors to withdraw from Singur in October 2008.

The announcement that remained less reported was her statement on an incident that was generally being considered an accident. Two bikers had died on a highway within the limits of Singur's neighbouring Chanditala police station. A bus ran them over while they tried to overtake another bus. This was what journalists in Hooghly district, including this author, knew since the afternoon of that day from their sources in the police. No journalist was interested in the deaths. But Banerjee announced from the dais that on her way back to Kolkata she would stop at Chanditala to meet the families of the accident victims.

'Two of our Muslim brothers were killed this morning. They were our supporters. Attempts are being made to show it as an accident but it's a conspiracy of the CPM,' she alleged.[18]

Her use of the phrase 'Muslim brothers' was striking. This was not how she had been referring to incidents of alleged political murders previously.

Certainly, times were changing.

Barely two years ago, she fought the state assembly elections in alliance with the BJP. It was not long ago that she and the RSS mutually exchanged praises. On 15 September 2003, when she was a Union minister without a portfolio[19] in Atal Bihari Vajpayee's ministry, Banerjee paid a visit to an RSS function in New Delhi where she sought the RSS's help in ending 'red terror' in Bengal.

That event was the launch of a book, *Communist Terrorism,* compiled and edited by Tarun Vijay, then editor of the RSS mouthpiece *Panchajanya.* The book dealt with the alleged incidents of atrocities perpetrated by various brands of communists in India and Nepal. Smita Gupta, covering the event for the *Times of India,* wrote 'Though top RSS functionaries Mohan Bhagwat, Madan Das Devi and RSS elder H.V. Seshadri as well as Defence Minister George Fernandes were present, Mamata was clearly the star speaker.' BJP Rajya Sabha MP Balbir Punj had introduced her as '*pyari behen*' and '*shakshat Maa Durga*', and Banerjee returned all this sweetness extended to her by calling the RSS leaders 'true patriots'.

Kay Benedict reported in the *Telegraph* Mamata's talk to the gathering that day: 'I have never got to meet so many RSS leaders, though I have met some individually. You people are true patriots. I know you love the country, you care for even small, remote areas of the country.'[20]

She described the communists as 'fascists' and 'hypocrites' who practised 'double standards'. She told the RSS leadership: 'We are with you in your fight against the communists', and sought their help in turn. She claimed that since the Congress was ready to make common cause with the Left, the BJP and the TMC made for 'natural allies'. 'If you give us even one per cent help in Bengal, we'll be able to do wonders,' the *Times of India* quoted her as saying.[21]

Until the time of the 2006 assembly elections, the state's Muslim-dominated pockets remained strongholds of the Left and the Congress. However, this was changing since the publication of the Justice Rajinder Sachar Committee report in 2006 that revealed the backwardness of Muslims in West Bengal, compared even to those in Gujarat. In an article in *Frontline,* veteran journalist Suhrid Sankar Chattopadhyay had cited three incidents between 2006 and 2008 that led to the Muslims' disenchantment with the Left: the publication of the Sachar Committee report in 2006, the land-acquisition drive during 2006–07 in areas with significant Muslim population (Nandigram and Bhangar) and the mysterious death of Rizwanur Rahman. He was a thirty-year-old computer teacher who married the daughter of industrialist Ashok Todi and allegedly came under pressure from the police to get divorced.

These developments offered Mamata Banerjee a good opportunity to wean the Muslims away from the Left. The 2008 panchayat elections had clearly indicated the TMC's rise, virtually from the ashes. The party had now tasted its first success in gaining the Muslim vote in Nandigram and in the district of South 24 Parganas, riding the wave of anti-land-acquisition movements. By that time, Muslim religious and social leaders were crowding her daises whenever she spoke. She saw a realistic chance of dealing the three-decade-old Left regime a death blow. By mid-2008, with Lok Sabha elections due in less than a year, Mamata Banerjee oriented herself more towards winning the trust of the Muslims. She started appearing with the saree wrapped around her head in the style of a hijab.

In a 2009 article,[22] Abhijit Dasgupta, a professor of sociology at the University of Delhi, wrote, 'After six decades of Independence, Muslims in West Bengal are beginning to find themselves on the margins.' He also pointed out that West Bengal turned into an infertile ground for community-based politics since Independence, resulting in the political mainstreaming of the Muslims who preferred the Congress and the Left over Muslim parties, but the emergence of Hindu nationalist politics at the panchayat level resulted in 'more community-centric mobilizations of Muslims' that 'only alienated the minority community'.

By the 'emergence of Hindu nationalist politics', Dasgupta was mostly likely referring to the 1998 and 2003 panchayat elections that the BJP fought in alliance with the TMC.

In a 2011 research paper[23] by Kenneth Bo Nielsen, titled 'In Search of Development: Muslims and Electoral Politics in an Indian State', the author wrote that West Bengal Muslims were 'in many respects excluded from both the developmental and political processes', 'score significantly lower on a range of socio-economic indicators compared to other sections of the population,' and that the 'recent years have witnessed an increasing mobilization of Muslim organizations seeking to address and overcome this 'development deficit'.

Not surprisingly, the CPM started reminding the Muslims of Banerjee's past association with the BJP and how she and the RSS had heaped praise on each other. The more the CPM did this, the more desperate Banerjee became to appease the Muslims. Her approach became even more blatant after the party's Lok Sabha election surge - from a one-MP party in 2004 to bagging nineteen seats in 2009 – and her subsequent bagging of the railway portfolio in the UPA II government. In September 2009, the railway ministry published large advertisements in Bengali, English, Hindi and Urdu, announcing that Mamata Banerjee would inaugurate two projects on the occasion of Eid – a nursing training college in a Muslim neighbourhood in Kolkata and the doubling of a rail route. What caught everybody's eyes was Mamata Banerjee's photo in those advertisements – she had her saree wrapped around her head, in the style of a hijab.

The BJP and the RSS were yet to start attacking her on this issue – they were keener on seeing the fall of the Left regime first. However, a breakaway faction of the RSS, named Hindu Samhati,[24] had started referring to her as 'Mamata Bano'. Veteran RSS pracharak Tapan Ghosh had formed this group in 2008 after quitting the RSS, accusing the organization's Bengal chapter of 'lacking courage'.

Evidently, when Mamata Banerjee took to overt Muslim appeasement, the ground was already prepared for this new brand of politics in West Bengal. Thereafter, the Kolkata Municipal Corporation, which the TMC captured in 2010, organized at the Park Circus ground what was pegged as the biggest iftar in Kolkata that year. After coming to power in 2011, Banerjee announced stipends for imams and their helpers, the muezzins. And her government, in 2012, revealed its controversial, and later botched, plan for a hospital exclusively for the minority communities.

Fish Fry

Returning a courtesy to Chief Minister Mamata Banerjee earned a Left delegation a great deal of embarrassment one Monday evening. On 9 June 2014, a delegation comprising top leaders of the Communist Party of India (Marxist), the Communist Party of India, Revolutionary Socialist Party and Forward Bloc called on the chief minister to submit a complaint about the atrocities committed against Left workers by members of the ruling TMC. The Left leaders were surprised when they got the appointment in the first place. On several previous occasions the chief minister had declined to meet them. Instead, government officers used to receive those deputations.

More surprises awaited the Left leaders. On the thirteenth floor of Nabanna, the state secretariat building overlooking the river Hooghly, Mamata Banerjee was standing outside the door of her chamber, with her hands folded in the gesture of a namaskar and a smile on her face.

The scene was in complete contrast to what Nabanna had witnessed on 31 May, when a BJP central delegation came down, after visiting Sandeshkhali, to make a submission to her. She was aware of the team's visit but did not attend office that day. The BJP team had to leave after meeting the chief secretary.

Now, the Left leaders were served Darjeeling tea, fish fry, cakes and cream rolls as they took their chairs.

Inside the room were Banerjee, CPM's Biman Bose and Rabin Deb, CPI's Manjukumar Majumdar, RSP's Kshiti Goswami, Forward Bloc's Jayanta Roy and the state education-cum-parliamentary affairs minister, Partha Chatterjee. Mamata patiently listened to the allegations made by the Left Front chairman Biman Bose, who said that 48,500 Left workers and supporters had been driven out of their homes and that many were barred from harvesting their crops. She calmly responded to Bose's threat of hitting the streets if nothing changed, and promised action.

Then she came to her own business. It was her turn to complain: 'Workers of your parties are joining the BJP in numbers. You must do something about it. Please put your house in order!'

None in the Left delegation was expecting this. This was the least expected message from the chief of a party that had launched a poaching drive to leave the Opposition parties leaderless. Her insatiable hunger for Opposition-free functioning had put her party on the path of political poaching – a new phenomenon in Bengal politics. Despite winning 184 of the state 294 assembly seats, the TMC poached thirteen MLAs – nine from the Congress, two from the RSP and one each from the CPM and Forward Bloc – between June 2011 and June 2014. The poaching happened on a greater scale at the panchayat and municipal levels.

The TMC had not resorted to political violence for the first two years but the manhandling of Finance Minister Amit Mitra in New Delhi on 9 April 2013 by members of the CPM's student wing resulted in vandalism and the closure of several hundred CPM offices over the following months.

And now she was telling Biman Bose she believed that to protest against atrocities was a right, and a duty as well, of a political party. She was advising them on protecting their house from the BJP. The Left leaders were stumped. They failed to tell her to her face that it was because of the TMC's poaching drive, the political terror it unleashed, and harassment by the police that Left workers were going to the BJP in search of shelter. Biman Bose reportedly responded by saying that the Left are committed to fighting the RSS and would readily offer help in combating 'a communal force'.

Mamata Banerjee told them that she did not fear Modi and would take the RSS head on in the state.

Sensing that the meeting was going to end on a cordial note, Rabin Deb broached the issue of government-created complexities related to the land plot where the CPM had planned the Jyoti Basu Centre for Social Studies and Research. She assured the delegation they would be resolved.

The meeting continued for about seventy minutes and ended with Banerjee sharing her personal mobile number with the Left leaders and requesting them to get in touch with Partha Chatterjee or herself in case they received information about any conspiracy being hatched by the BJP–RSS. Chatterjee came down to the ground floor to see the delegation off.

Outside, dozens of television and print journalists were waiting for them. Biman Bose said the discussions were cordial and that Mamata Banerjee patiently listened to them and had assured them of action. He, however, also expressed his lack of trust in Mamata Banerjee's words.

Soon, nothing that happened at the meeting was a secret anymore, as the journalists extracted every detail from the individuals present at the meeting. 'She was so courteous that we could not refuse the refreshments offered,' one of the participants at the meeting told this author, requesting anonymity.

What followed was a political uproar.

Were the Left and the TMC coming closer to fight the saffron camp?

A section of Left workers and ground-level leaders was enraged. How could they have nibbled at fish fry served by the person responsible for the torment of hundreds of Left workers? Shouldn't they have refused her refreshments? Are these leaders at all worthy of trust to fight the TMC? These questions began to be asked aloud. It was construed that the Left had surrendered before Mamata Banerjee.

The BJP pounced on the development. From state unit president Rahul Sinha to state unit spokesperson Samik Bhattacharya, one BJP leader after another said the meeting formally marked the beginning of a new era in Bengal politics. 'This is her official acknowledgement that the BJP, and not the Left, is now her principal opponent. I appeal to Left workers to see the difference between the attitude of our leaders and those of the Left. If you want to fight the TMC, ours is the party you ought to be in', Rahul Sinha told the media at the party's state unit office the same evening.[25]

Over the months of June and July, a number of Left leaders quit their respective organizations and joined the BJP. They identified the BJP as the 'true anti-TMC force'. The defectors included Anirban Chowdhury and Ajay Agnihotri, the state secretary and state president of Forward Bloc's youth wing Yuva League, former FB MLA Bithika Mondal, senior FB leader from West Midnapore district Sukumar Bhuniya and women's wing leader Asma Khatun; and CPI's trade union leader Ashok Senapati and CPM's Antara Bhattacharya – the last two from West Midnapore district. Antara Bhattacharya had served as the zilla parishad sabhadhipati, or chairperson of the district council, the head of a district administration who enjoys minister-of-state status. All of them said the Left leadership was incapable of fighting the TMC and that joining the BJP was the only way to fight 'a fascist TMC government'.

'I tried my best to resist the TMC but got no support from the party (CPM). Workers pressured me to quit the party and join the BJP,' Antara Bhattacharya told this author.[26]

FOUR

Grassroots Grow Greener

Bhag, Mukul, Bhag!

VETERAN CONGRESS MLA ABDUL Mannan and former Kolkata Mayor, the CPM's Bikash Ranjan Bhattacharya, moved the Supreme Court in June 2013 to get the Rs 2,459 crore[1] Saradha chit fund scam probed by the Central Bureau of Investigation (CBI), overriding the Mamata Banerjee government's strong objection. Earlier, they had approached the Calcutta High Court, which turned down their appeal. The apex court order came on 9 May 2014, transferring to CBI the investigation of forty-four chit fund companies – including the Saradha Group – suspected of running Ponzi schemes in the states of West Bengal, Odisha, Assam, Jharkhand and Tripura.

Causing panic among the TMC leaders, who used to hobnob with the Saradha group helmsman, the Supreme Court in its order[2] asked the CBI to probe the 'larger conspiracy' angle and the role of persons holding influential positions. Besides, the Enforcement Directorate (ED) was running a parallel investigation. Everything was now in place to corner the TMC. Celebrations broke out in Bengal's Left and Congress camp on 9 May, but the situation was not in their favour, as in Delhi Modi had assumed charge barely two weeks after the order. The BJP now had a good opportunity to cultivate the land ploughed by the Left and Congress.

The political temperature over the chit fund scam had been rising since April 2013, when the Saradha boss, Sudipta Sen, fled Kolkata. The names of two TMC Rajya Sabha MPs – journalist-turned-politician Kunal Ghosh and media house owner Srinjay Bose, both of whom had been working closely with Sen – frequently featured in the allegations of opposition leaders. Ghosh was also named in an FIR lodged at Park Street police station by the employees of Channel 10, a Saradha group news channel that had been running for three years. The Trinamool supremo, however, was still standing by Ghosh and Bose. A visibly irate Mamata Banerjee told a party meeting on 3 May 2013: *'Kunal chor? Tumpai* (Srinjay Bose) *chor? Madan* (Mitra) *chor? Mukul* (Roy) *Chor? Ami Chor? Ar ora sob sadhu?'* (Is Kunal a thief? Is Tumpai? Is Madan? Is Mukul? Am I? And are they (opposition) all saints?)

This tirade would become famous, to be oft-quoted for months to come. Mamata Banerjee's defence of Kunal Ghosh did not last long. Ghosh fell out with the party, presumably after sensing that he was being made a scapegoat, and started indicting the TMC and its various leaders for their involvement in the Saradha scam. Ghosh was first suspended from the party and later, in November 2013, the Mamata Banerjee-instituted Special Investigation Team for probing the scam had him arrested.

Within hours of his arrest, a statement was posted on his Facebook account naming multiple TMC leaders, including Mamata Banerjee, insisting that these people would be able to 'help' the CBI in its investigations. Ghosh even wrote a ninety-one-page letter that he somehow managed to smuggle out of jail and send to the CBI office in New Delhi. Even before this, at a time when his arrest looked imminent, Ghosh had been pressing for a CBI probe. He was ready to drown – if that was what was to happen – taking along with him all the others who were involved in the controversial Saradha dealings.

The CBI took into custody six persons, including Sudipta Sen and Kunal Ghosh, who were arrested by the state police. After grilling them over and over in June and July, the investigating team started summoning other suspects, from August onwards. They started with the small fry. On

14 August, a CBI team raided Rajat Majumdar's residence and seized some documents. Majumdar, a retired IPS officer who had served as the director general of police (armed forces), was a vice-president of the TMC. He also served as the Saradha group's security advisor. He was asked to appear before the CBI on 23 August.

Simultaneously, the ED stepped up its activities. On 18 August, they grilled the state textiles minister, Shyamaprasad Mukherjee, who had sold his loss-making cement factory to the Saradha boss; and on 25 August they questioned Ahmed Hassan Imran, a TMC Rajya Sabha MP, who had sold his Bengali daily, *Kalom,* to Sudipta Sen.

Sensing imminent danger to her party, Mamata Banerjee took digs at the CBI at a public rally in Kolkata on 28 August 2014. 'The actual criminals are being shielded. Moreover, all kinds of lies are being spread for political mileage. I would request (CBI) to investigate properly ... we will cooperate,' she said.[3]

Come September and the noose tightened around the TMC. The CBI arrested Rajat Majumdar on the ninth. On the tenth, it was the turn of Srinjay Bose, another Rajya Sabha MP, to face CBI grilling. Bose, editor of the Bengali daily *Sambad Pratidin,* had struck a deal with the Saradha group to provide it with editorial assistance.

'Who's next?' became the talk of Bengal.

With every progress the CBI made, BJP leaders Siddharth Nath Singh and Rahul Sinha thumped their chests. What is interesting is that whenever the TMC accused the CBI and the ED of acting in a politically motivated way, the BJP leaders said the Central agencies were acting under instructions of the Supreme Court. However, they also contended that swift action was being taken because Modi gave the agencies a free hand in probing the case without caring about the influence the suspects in the case wielded.

By the end of the year, the two Central agencies sent the TMC into a tizzy. Srinjay Bose was arrested on 21 November and the state transport minister, Madan Mitra, was sent a notice to appear before them. Mitra initially sought time and then suddenly took ill after the arrest of Srijnay Bose. He publicly announced he was suffering from claustrophobia and needed treatment.

The TMC leaders looked nervous and BJP leaders jubilant. At the BJP's 30 November rally in Kolkata, addressed by the party's new national president Amit Shah, among others, Siddharth Nath Singh made a controversially famous remark: 'It's Bhag, Madan, Bhag, in 2014. It will be Bhag, Mukul, Bhag, in 2015. And in 2016 it will be Bhag, Mamata, Bhag!'[4]

In December, after his release from the state-run SSKM hospital, Madan Mitra went to the CBI office on the twelfth and was arrested the same day after five hours of grilling.

Mamata Banerjee defended her minister. She said Mitra had tendered his resignation before going to the CBI office but she had decided not to accept it. She also lambasted the Centre, calling it 'autocratic', among other adjectives.

However, the eerie correspondence of Mamata Banerjee's 3 May 2013 remarks with the chronology of arrests brought alive a verbal duel between the TMC and its political rivals. She had said, '*Kunal chor? Tumpai* (Srinjay Bose) *chor? Madan chor? Mukul chor? Ami chor? Ar ora sob sadhu?*'

Now, Ghosh, Bose and Mitra were in CBI custody. Three of the five she had named, in exactly the same sequence. Fourth on her list was Mukul Roy, the party's de facto 'number two', Mamata Banerjee's closest aide.

On 12 January 2015, the CBI summoned Mukul Roy.

The 'Chanakya'

Mukul Roy, frequently referred to as the 'Chanakya of Bengal politics' in the Bengali media, was in New Delhi on 12 January 2015 when a CBI sleuth from the Kolkata office rang Roy's phone number and asked him to appear before them. Roy told the officer that he was preoccupied with work in Delhi but would make himself available in a few days.

He must have been expecting this call. Two Rajya Sabha MPs and a minister had landed in jail, and the media was agog with speculation as to whether it was Mukul Roy's turn now to get CBI summons. From mid-December, Roy was reportedly focused on gathering thorough legal advice.

As news of the CBI's call to Mukul Roy broke, the TMC swung into a condemnation mode. It was exactly a month after Mitra's arrest. Partha

Chatterjee, party secretary-general and Subrata Bakshi, state unit president, along with Mukul Roy, made the TMC's second level leadership. Of them, Roy was known to be the closest to Mamata Banerjee. The TMC leaders in the districts knew that it was Roy's opinion that mattered most when it came to finalizing organizational posts. Leaders in Kolkata knew that in the most confidential matters it was often only Roy who had knowledge of the party chief's mind.

Reaching Mukul Roy meant being just one step away from Mamata Banerjee. He was the party's all-India general secretary, the chairman of the parliamentary board and the leader of the party in the Rajya Sabha. The following sentence from a report in *Anandabazar Patrika* somewhat aptly summed up the talk of the town of the time: '*Doler du-nombor byaktike deke pathiye ebar karjyoto Trinamool er penalty box a dhuke porlo CBI.*'[5] Roughly translated, it means: By summoning the number two in the party, the CBI has virtually entered the TMC's penalty box.

Partha Chatterjee addressed journalists in Kolkata in the evening of 12 July, alleging that the BJP was involved in 'naked politics' and was 'using the CBI politically', ahead of the Kolkata municipal elections 'in a planned manner'. He threw a challenge to the CBI: 'The TMC can't be destroyed by sending notice to one Mukul. Lakhs of Mukuls are ready to hit the streets to protest this vindictive politics of the BJP.'[6]

Mukul Roy himself had other things in mind. His response to journalists who telephoned him for his reaction, including this author, struck a different chord: he was ready to cooperate in the investigation.

The Nephew

The rift between Mamata Banerjee and Mukul Roy possibly had its origin in the latter's response to the press on a controversial deal between the railway catering service IRCTC and the Saradha group. The day was 2 September 2014.

'I was not the railway minister at that time,' he said, much to the shock and surprise of his colleagues in the party.

Roy was right. Roy had served as railway minister between 2012 and 2014. The deal was struck in 2010, when Mamata Banerjee was the railway minister. In February 2010, Mamata Banerjee in her railway budget announced sixteen new special trains for package tours of India on various routes. In January 2011, Saradha Tours and Travels signed a deal with IRCTC. By end August 2014, news was going around that the CBI had unearthed unusual relaxation of norms in IRCTC's agreement with Saradha.

Roy himself had downplayed the issue on 1 September 2014, when journalists sought his response. 'One company got a contract from another. What's the case here?' he asked, adding, 'I knew the CBI was probing those cheated by Saradha. It now appears the CBI is looking for those who cheated Saradha!'

His answer was perplexing. The Supreme Court had clearly asked the CBI to investigate the 'larger conspiracy' and the role of influential people. It was very unlikely that Mukul Roy would not know that the CBI was also to probe those who duped Saradha or connived with the group.

When he shrugged off the responsibility for the IRCTC deal by saying that it was not struck during his stint, speculation ran rife. Was Mukul Roy keener on saving his own skin than on protecting his leader?

The IRCTC issued a statement on 4 September 2014, clarifying that Saradha Tours and Travels had received no favours. 'M/s Saradha Tours & Travels Pvt Ltd was empanelled as direct sales agent of IRCTC/East Zone for marketing of tourism products on travel agent's commission basis like several other agents empanelled,' said the statement.[7]

While the IRCTC's statement reduced political pressure on the TMC in one matter at least, the turmoil triggered within the party by Mukul Roy's remarks kept growing. His answer was construed – not only by his own party colleagues but also by the leaders of the TMC's rival parties – as a way of diverting blame towards the party chief.

In another month and a half, Mamata Banerjee gave the first indication of clipping Mukul Roy's wings. On 17 October 2014, three of 'Mukul's men' were shunted out of crucial organizational posts. She removed

Sankudeb Panda from the post of president of the party's student wing. He was replaced by Ashok Rudra, Burdwan district unit president of the TMC's student wing, a man close to Partha Chatterjee. Another decision had a greater impact. The party's youth wing, Trinamool Youth Congress (TMYC), which had existed since the TMC's birth in 1998, and a parallel youth wing that was floated in 2011 exclusively to launch Mamata Banerjee's nephew Abhishek Banerjee, were merged. Mukul-confidante Saumitra Khan, who had been heading TMYC since June 2014, lost his post to the nephew. Saumitra was a Congress MLA who had switched over to the TMC ahead of the 2014 Lok Sabha elections, courtesy Mukul Roy, and had gone on to become a TMC MP in the Lok Sabha.

Yuva, the parallel youth wing of the TMC, had a 'soft launch' ahead of the 2011 assembly elections. The launch was like a teaser campaign. Nothing about Yuva was revealed, but hoardings and banners bearing the name in tricolor and calling for poriborton (change) were put up across the state, though principally in Kolkata and its neighbourhood. After Mamata Banerjee came to power in 2011, Yuva was launched as another youth wing of the TMC, headed by Abhishek Banerjee. It was difficult for Mamata Banerjee at that time to place Abhishek Banerjee in a prominent position in the youth wing. It was being headed by Suvendu Adhikari, the party's 'hero of Nandigram' and one of the most popular TMC leaders after Mamata Banerjee. She did not want to displease Adhikari at that time.

Now, while appointing Abhishek Banerjee as the national and state unit president of TMYC, Mamata Banerjee also dissolved the entire existing committee. This also meant Mukul Roy's son, who was a vice-president of TMYC, lost his post.

The message was crystal clear to anyone following state politics with any interest and Mukul Roy could not have missed it. Mamata Banerjee had chosen her heir.

Fall from Grace

Roy created further trouble for the party on 13 January 2015. He admitted before journalists in New Delhi that he had met Sudipta Sen twice, once in Kolkata on 5 April 2013, immediately before Sen's empire collapsed and he fled; and the second time in north Bengal the previous year.

Roy's acknowledgement of the north Bengal meeting with Sen had special political significance. Since his arrest by the Kolkata police, suspended TMC MP and the Saradha group's media wing chief Kunal Ghosh had repeatedly alleged that a meeting between Mamata Banerjee and Sudipta Sen took place at the tourist bungalow at Delo in the Kalimpong hills, past midnight on 1 March and that Mukul Roy was also present. It was at this meeting, Ghosh said, that Sudipta Sen placed his proposal of using his media ventures to promote Mamata Banerjee nationally as the best prime ministerial candidate.

The TMC had never admitted to any such meeting. For the record, Mamata Banerjee had said after the Saradha scam broke that she knew nothing about the Saradha group until she saw the presenters of Tara TV, owned by the Saradha group, breaking down in tears during live telecast as they announced the closure of the channel on 14 April 2013, which was Poila Boishakh, the first day of the Bengali calendar.

Now, Mukul Roy was partially supporting Kunal Ghosh's claim by admitting that he had a meeting with Sen in North Bengal. The TMC camp was tense. Would he next admit that Mamata Banerjee was also there? Would he tell this before the CBI sleuths during his questioning?

Over the next few days, TMC leaders closely monitored Roy's activities. He met Mamata Banerjee at Nabanna on 14 January and then sought time from the CBI, twice. The Mamata Banerjee government approached the Supreme Court seeking the apex court's monitoring of the CBI investigation but the government's attempts to get the case quickly heard failed. The hearing got delayed for various reasons. Roy did not utter a single word against CBI during this period. Roy then finalized 30 January as the day for appearance.

He reached the CBI office in the Central Government Office complex in Salt Lake before the scheduled time on that day. While entering the complex, he told journalists, 'I reiterate, I am not involved in any unethical activity and I will lend my full cooperation to the CBI in its investigation.'[8] He advised party workers who had gathered outside the CGO complex not to agitate.

He was interrogated for nearly five hours in three phases but, unlike other TMC leaders questioned, he did not look exhausted when he came out. 'I will come again if they ask me to. I have nothing to hide. I want the truth to emerge.'

He attended the party's core committee meeting at Mamata Banerjee's residence the day after. On his arrival before the meeting, journalists asked him about his differences with the party on the question of dealing with the CBI investigation. His answer made the split clearer: 'The party is speaking party's view, I am speaking mine. I will speak of my views in today's meeting, too.'

Mukul Roy differentiating between the party and himself was an unmistakable sign. Mamata Banerjee did not miss reading it. Between 14 and 28 February 2015, Mamata stripped Mukul Roy of all his portfolios.

Dilip Ghosh

In November 2014, the RSS sent Dilip Ghosh to the West Bengal unit of the BJP and was soon inducted as a general secretary. The state committee already comprised two pracharaks: Amalendu Chattopadhyay holding the mandatory position of general secretary (organization) since 2004 and Subrato Chattopadhyay, who was appointed as BJP's joint general secretary (organization) in early 2014. With Ghosh's entry into the state unit as the third pracharak, murmurs began in the state leadership as to whether he had not been sent to lead the organization in the near future. Rahul Sinha's second three-year term as state unit chief was to end in 2015.

Rahul Sinha, who rose through the ranks during the 1990s, was not an 'RSS man', even though he had a good rapport with the RSS south Bengal prant pracharak, Sunilpada Goswami, and the Sangh's national in-charge for the BJP, Suresh Soni.

Rahul Sinha, the state president since 2009, had not been having a good time since early 2015. Even though the February 2015 bye-election to Bongaon Lok Sabha and Krishnaganj Vidhan Sabha revealed the BJP's steadily rising vote share, the party was yet to decisively surpass the Left as the TMC's principal opponent. Early in January 2015, the

BJP thought it had got a shot in the arm when a sitting TMC minister, Manjul Krishna Thakur, switched over to it after the TMC refused his son a ticket for the Bongaon Lok Sabha seat. The TMC's Bongaon MP, Kapil Krishna Thakur, died in October 2014, and the TMC decided to nominate his widow, Mamata Thakur. Manjul Krishna, Kapil Krishna's younger brother, did not have a good rapport with Mamata Thakur. Manjul Krishna switched camps after the BJP promised to nominate his son, Subrata, from Bongaon constituency.

The Thakur family of Thakurnagar in Bongaon area of North 24 Parganas district is the supreme religious family of the Matua sect of Dalit refugees who had migrated from east Bengal over the past seven decades, mainly in the face of persecution at the hands of Muslims. Binapani Devi, widow of late parliamentarian and Union minister P.R. Thakur, was the religious chief of the Matuas. It was P.R. Thakur's grandfather who had founded the Matua sect in the 1870s. The Matuas were BJP's 'natural support-base', as BJP's Bongaon Lok Sabha candidate in 2014, K.D. Biswas, himself a Matua leader, had said. However, since the TMC had won over the Thakur family well ahead of the 2011 assembly elections – Manjul Krishna, Binapani Devi's younger son, won on a TMC ticket and became a junior minister in the refugee rehabilitation department in the Mamata Banerjee government – Bengal's ruling party wielded influence on the majority of the state's Matua population.

In the 2015 bye-election, voters of Bongaon rejected Manjul Krishna's aspirations. The BJP stood third, after the TMC and the CPM. The silver lining for the BJP from the bye-election was an increase in its vote share. In the Bongaon Lok Sabha poll, the TMC retained its 2014 share of 43 per cent of the polled votes. However, the Left share came down from 31.5 per cent in May 2014 to 26.3 per cent in February 2015. In contrast, BJP's vote share rose from 19.07 per cent to 24.17 per cent.

The Krishnaganj assembly seat revealed a greater swing in favour of the BJP. Not only did the BJP rank second but its vote share also rose from only 3.09 per cent in the 2011 assembly elections and 14.5 per cent in the 2014 Lok Sabha elections to 29.53 per cent in the by-poll. But the state civic polls held in April 2015 laid bare BJP's organizational deficiencies at the grassroots level. The party lacked faces popular in their own localities. Of the 2,094 seats where elections were held, the BJP won only eighty-one – or 3.86 per cent – of the seats. The CPM won 242 (11.55 per cent) seats, while the Congress won 187 (8.93 per cent). The TMC stood far ahead of them all, bagging 1,428 (or 68.19 per cent) of the total seats. Of the ninety-one civic bodies, the TMC failed to gain a majority in only twelve.

In the Kolkata Municipal Corporation, the BJP won only seven of the 144 seats, while the TMC alone won 114. The Left won ten seats and the Congress only five. BJP's best performances were in Kharagpur (seven of thirty-five seats) in West Midnapore, Old Malda (five of twenty seats) in Malda, Rampurhat (four of eighteen seats) in Birbhum and Beldanga (three of fourteen seats) in Murshidabad.

Forget challenging the TMC, the BJP had not even surpassed the Left or the Congress to secure the position of the TMC's principal opponent. Realizing the weaknesses of the state unit, the central leadership decided to review strategy and add more firepower to it.

Among Amit Shah's new organizational appointments made on 18 June 2015 was that of former Madhya Pradesh minister Kailash Vijayvargiya as one of the national general secretaries. On 6 July 2015, Vijayvargiya was appointed as 'observer' for the West Bengal unit. He was a leader of higher standing than the party's existing 'observer' in the state, Siddharth Nath Singh. National joint general secretary (organization) Shiv Prakash, a pracharak, had already got deeply involved in core organizational work in Bengal. Within the BJP circles, Vijayvargiya was referred to as 'observer' and Shiv Prakash as 'organizational in-charge'. On the night of 8 July 2015, Amit Shah, national general secretary (organization) Ramlal and Shiv Prakash visited Keshav Bhavan in Kolkata to discuss the West Bengal situation with RSS leaders Vadla Bhagaiah, Pradip Joshi and Bidyut Mukherjee. On 12 July, Vijayvargiya met Bhagaiyah, Mukherjee and Jisnu Basu at Keshav Bhavan.

In another few months, Dilip Ghosh was appointed as the party's state unit chief. The appointment was made on 11 December 2015.

The very next day, 12 December, Ghosh was felicitated at Keshav Bhavan by Atul Kumar Biswas and Keshob-ji – Keshav Rao Dikshit – the senior-most RSS pracharak in West Bengal, in the presence of Subrato Chattopadhyay, another pracharak, who had been deputed to the state BJP ahead of the 2014 Lok Sabha elections.

This author interviewed Dilip Ghosh over telephone a few days after his new appointment. On being asked what he thought was the key issue in the state, Ghosh said, reflecting a deep sense of conviction, 'Issues concerning the Hindus are the only permanent ones on the agenda. The rest are fleeting issues. Hindus in West Bengal are in danger and we need to stand by them. No other party will stand by the Hindus or speak for them.'

A new political language had arrived in Bengal.

Heartbreak

14 March 2016: West Bengal was glued to television, watching what they had never seen before in the state politics. Footage of a sting operation showed people who resembled almost all of Mamata Banerjee's lieutenants accepting cash from the representative of a fictitious company, or instructing them where to deposit the money.

This was barely three weeks before the seven-phase assembly elections were to start. The leaders who had allegedly been exposed included Mukul Roy, ministers Subrata Mukherjee, Sovan Chatterjee, Firhad Hakim and Suvendu Adhikari, MPs Kakoli Ghosh Dastidar, Sougata Roy, Sultan Ahmed, MLA Iqbal Ahmed and jailed MLA Madan Mitra, among others. Narada News, the portal that conducted the sting, claimed that Subrata Bakshi flatly refused to meet them and they could not reach Abhishek Banerjee despite trying.

The footage became every TV channel's prime-time item, largely thanks to the BJP, which swiftly projected it on large screens in their state office at a press conference called minutes within release of the tapes by Naradanews.com.

The Opposition was rejuvenated. The TMC was already struggling with the Saradha scam and the CBI investigation into it. Now, its top leaders were seen purportedly accepting cash and discussing rates. Kolkata mayor and minister Sovan Chatterjee was seen accepting something wrapped in a towel.

Minister Suvendu Adhikari accepted something wrapped in paper. The man who looked and sounded like Firhad Hakim said Rs 5 lakh meant peanuts – 'meant for kids', he said. The one who resembled Sougata Roy MP was heard saying that Rs 5 lakh meant 'a lot of money'. Mukul Roy was heard asking for the money to be deposited with SMH Mirza, an Indian Police Service (IPS) officer. Mirza was separately seen accepting cash.[9]

There could not have been anything more embarrassing for a party going to seek a second term in the government. Mamata Banerjee had pegged the election campaign on the state government's development programme. The Narada tapes changed the discussions entirely. Some TMC leaders called the tapes fabricated and malicious. Banerjee called the sting a BJP-sponsored conspiracy. She could not possibly have said anything else. Whom would she penalize? Whom would she drop from her candidate list?

The BJP's target was to secure for itself the position of the TMC's principal opponent. Its prospects looked bleak once the Left and the Congress arrived at a seat-sharing formula. This coming together of the CPM and the Congress for an electoral tie-up was in itself a historic event, as it had happened for the first time. It was clear to the leadership of both parties that they stood no chance against the TMC if they fought separately. There was no formal alliance or common minimum programme. The CPM central committee would not allow that. They were Congress's archrival in Kerala, as also fighting the Congress in some other states. They did support the Congress-led UPA I government, but did so staying outside. They would help the Congress stay in power in a bid to stop the BJP but would not take part in the Congress's anti-people policies.

So, in West Bengal, the two parties simply did not field candidates against each other. Nevertheless, in a bid to send the message loud and clear that neither party had any hesitation about joining hands to take on the TMC, Rahul Gandhi and Buddhadeb Bhattacharjee shared a dais in Kolkata. Modi and Shah too invested a lot of time and effort. Modi addressed ten rallies during the campaign, lambasting the TMC for corruption and for failure in income generation – the same issues that the Left and the Congress highlighted.

Time, though, was on Mamata Banerjee's side. She had managed to create a large beneficiary base during her five years in power. Farmers were assured that their land would not be disturbed. Health infrastructure had improved. The existing infrastructure had been expanded and new infrastructure had been created, with treatment at government hospitals made free. The government had introduced fair-price medicine shops offering up to 70 per cent discount on MRP.

Knowing that attracting big industries would be difficult because of its land policies (the government would not acquire land for any private industry) and its declared opposition to special economic zones (SEZs), Mamata Banerjee had focused on the micro and small industries – handicrafts and textile, cottage industries, animal husbandry, food processing, tourism. West Bengal had the highest number of MSMEs in India – 52,69,814 establishments and 11.62 per cent of the national share, according to the Union ministry's report for 2016-17. To boost sales of MSME products, the government had organized a series of rural and urban fairs and festivals across the state that went on through half the year, linking economic and cultural activities, essentially the folk artisans and artists, with the market.

While the Left and Congress continued to mockingly call the Mamata Banerjee government 'myala-mochchhober-sarkar' – a government of fairs and festivals – these events indeed created a huge beneficiary base. According to Amitava Bhattacharya, a social entrepreneur and the helmsman at Banglanatak Dot Com, a private company working with folk artisans, 'The government's aggressive promotion of festivities and linking them with local produce, be it folk art, handicrafts or textiles, gave a boost to village industries.'

Besides, the public distribution system had improved, and in this case certification for Mamata Banerjee's government came from none other than Jean Dreze – the Belgium-born Indian economist and social scientist who served in the UPA government's National Advisory Council – though sometime after the assembly elections. Referring to a survey on PDS in different states, Dreze wrote in the *Indian Express*, 'The survey findings do suggest that the PDS in West Bengal has greatly improved in the recent past,' and added, 'Greater transparency, simpler entitlements and other PDS reforms seem to have led to a sharp decline in leakages.'[10] He wrote:

> Perhaps the most significant development in West Bengal is that food security has become a lively political issue. As elections approached, the state government threw its weight behind the NFSA and initiated bold PDS reforms. Judging from the survey, the results are similar to those achieved in other states (such as Chhattisgarh and Odisha) where political leaders have taken serious interest in food security. However, it remains to be seen whether West Bengal's renewed interest in food security proves durable or short-lived.

And then there were Mamata's social welfare schemes – a monthly stipend for folk artistes, old-age pension for handicraft artisans, handloom workers, and workers in the unorganized sector. And, above all, there was Kanyashree. Launched in 2013 with the aim of retaining girls in school and delaying their age of marriage, Kanyashree offered unmarried female students between thirteen and eighteen years of age, whose family income was under Rs 1,20,000 annually in urban areas, scholarships of Rs 750 a year. Besides, a one-time stipend of Rs 25,000 was provided to girls who continued to study after turning eighteen. This scheme created a huge impact. Besides, the government was also distributing cycles to all girl students in classes eight to twelve. During a tour of the Lalgarh area in Jhargram district in the run-up to the assembly elections, a middle-aged bidi worker's remarks on his supposed misfortune was an eye-opener for this author. He said, 'I have two children, and both are sons. Just think of my misfortune. Not a single daughter! I will get no assistance from the government.'[11]

Mamata emerged second-time lucky, first with Saradha – which failed to impact the panchayat elections in 2013 – and now with Narada – which had no visible impact on the assembly election results. She returned to Nabanna with more power in her hands. Her party's tally increased to 211 – as high as 72 per cent of the total strength of the house. The MLAs who were shown allegedly accepting cash all won, except for Madan Mitra, who had contested from jail.

The Left-Congress combination failed miserably. In the 294-seat assembly, their tally stood at seventy-six, with the Congress managing to win forty-four, and the Left reduced to thirty-two. Leader of the Opposition, Surjya Kanta Mishra, himself lost. Congress was the second largest party now, for the first time since the birth of the TMC in 1998.

The BJP fell behind – way behind. It won only three seats and its vote share, which had been 16.8 per cent in the 2014 Lok Sabha elections, was 10.16 per cent now. They even failed to retain Basirhat Dakshin, which Samik Bhattacharya had won in the September 2014 bye-election.

FIVE

The Widening Fault Lines

Us and Them

MAMATA BANERJEE DID NOT get much breathing space despite her resounding victory, as the communal fault line between the Hindus and the Muslims in the state kept widening. The first riot in her second term happened on 28 May, a day after she was sworn in. One contentious matter in the public sphere that was heating up was around skull caps and helmets. From around 2013–14, when Kolkata Police decided to strictly implement traffic rules and fine as many violators as they could, Hindus of various affiliations started pointing out that the rule books did not apply in the city's Muslim-dominated areas – Park Circus, Rajabazar, Mallick Bazar, Kidderpore, Mominpore, Ekbalpore and others.

People were talking about this everywhere – in their offices, on their commutes in trains, buses and auto-rickshaws, in the adda sessions at tea stalls or in clubs where they gathered to play cards or carom; and, of course, on social media. Photos showing bikes with three riders wearing skull caps going past policemen flooded Facebook and WhatsApp.

A few examples from social media discussions should throw some light on the nature of the conversations. On 14 November 2015,

Bimochan Bhattacharya, who called himself 'a declared Leftist' and had more than 2000 followers on Facebook, criticized the 'secular' voices for not condemning and not even accepting the reality of Islamic terror and fundamentalism. In his Facebook post[1] he alleged that Muslim youths in and around his neighbourhood of Belgachhia in north Kolkata were brazenly violating traffic rules but the police were imposing fines on riders without helmets only when the offenders were Hindus. He claimed to have asked a traffic sergeant about this discrimination and the sergeant reportedly said the police were scared of inviting trouble by booking Muslims. 'I asked a cop at Duttapukur crossing. The reply was that he would be attacked with daggers by a group of ten in case he slapped one case. When living in Rome, it's better not to quarrel with the Pope.' Bhattacharya's post was shared 142 times. The subject continued to be a talking point and the voices of the saffron camp were getting louder.

On 16 July 2016, Sabyasachi Bhattacharjee, a Hindutva propagandist, wrote on Facebook: 'Slap me with as many cases you want, I will not wear a helmet. I would wear it the day the administration shall be able to make the Muslims of Razabazar, Metiabruz, Garden Reach and Park Circus wear helmets. If Muslims get off scot-free by wearing skull caps, I too should be spared for wearing a tilak on my forehead ... and I shall beat up then and there whoever would dare prevent me.' This was shared 196 times.

By that time, even Trinamool Congress supporters were talking about it. On 18 July 2016, Prabir Biswas, a TMC supporter and blogger followed by more than 10,000 people, wrote a rather long post, titled *Prosongo Helmet* (On Helmets). Here is a paragraph from his post: 'A lot is being spoken about wearing a helmet and enforcing it.... Bike and scooter riders will have to wear full-mask helmets and that too with ISI mark. A great proposal. However, in some areas of Kolkata, particularly Kidderpore, Metiabruz, Park Circus and Rajabazar, anyone wearing a skull cap can care a hoot about the traffic rules. The police look the other way even when there are three riders on a bike. Even moving into a no-entry zone is not considered a violation then. The police must stop practising double standards.'

There was no counter to this perception. At least, there was no visible effort at one by the ruling Trinamool Congress or the police. The counter-narrative started coming from a newly emerging outfit, a Bengali rights group, Bangla Pokkho, and some radical Left activists, towards the end of 2017. Bangla Pokkho argued that the police go soft on traffic-rule violators in areas dominated by Hindi- and Urdu-speaking 'rowdies', meaning the Hindus and Muslims who have come from Bihar and Uttar Pradesh. 'All areas infamous for traffic rule violations are dominated by Hindi and Urdu-speaking people. If in Kolkata's Razabazar you need skull caps, in the Barrackpore industrial belt you merely need to be chewing gutkha and spit everywhere to avert police action,' Bangla Pokkho's Garga Chatterjee said in street corner meetings, as also in a telephonic interview with this author. Radical Left activists pointed out that groups of bike-borne Hindu pilgrims heading to Tarakeswar and Gangasagar never faced police harassment either.

But these were minority voices, and the perception about the police's communal approach kept growing.

The Bangladesh Impact

On 20 November 2016, when Professor Abul Barkat, one of Bangladesh's leading political economists, made a bombshell announcement in Dhaka about the country's demographics, the tremors were greater around Kolkata. Addressing a ceremony at the Senate Bhaban of Dhaka University to launch his new book, *Political Economy of Reforming Agriculture: Land Water Bodies in Bangladesh,* he said no Hindus would be left in Bangladesh after thirty years if their exodus continued at the present rate.[2]

Professor Barkat had been working on Hindu migration out of Bangladesh into India since the late 1990s. In 2016, after analyzing the rate at which the share of Hindus in the population was diminishing in the country over the past few decades, Barkat drew the conclusion that 'from 1964 to 2013, around 11.3 million Hindus left Bangladesh due to religious persecution and discrimination'. He was quoted as saying, 'It means on an average 632 Hindus left the country each day and 230,612 annually.'

Bengalis on both sides of the border have shared a common history and culture but have had different destinies. Leaving behind the bitterness of the Partition on religious lines in 1947, it was the linguistic sentiment that united the people from the two parts of Bengal during the Liberation

War of Bangladesh in 1971. The crowd at the Indira Gandhi–Mujibur Rahman joint rally in Kolkata's Brigade Parade Ground on 6 February 1972, celebrating the victory of the Liberation War, is still considered to be among the largest gathering of the masses at this venue, known for its many historic rallies. The replacement of the Islamic nation in erstwhile East Pakistan with the secular country of Bangladesh created hopes of greater proximity between the two parts of Bengal, but they headed for different destinies in just about five years.

In 1977, the military dictator Ziaur Rahman's government removed secularism from the Bangladesh constitution[3] and inserted the clause of 'absolute trust and faith in Almighty Allah'. Meanwhile, in West Bengal, the Left Front, a staunchly secular and atheist force, was in power for a rather long term of three decades and a half. Religion remained far off the political mainstream in the west, while it took political centre stage in the east.

In 1988, the military dictator Hussain Mohammad Ershad announced Islam as the state religion of Bangladesh. In contrast, West Bengal witnessed secularization of Hindu religious festivals – for example, Durga puja became popular as Sharodotsab or the autumn festival – and when the demolition of the Babri Masjid in 1992 triggered riots in some major Indian cities, and had its repercussions on Hindus in Bangladesh, Kolkata stood as India's capital of communal harmony.

During the period 2013–16, the secular-liberal-atheist camp in Bangladesh had been at loggerheads with Islamic fundamentalists. The writings of atheist bloggers, blasting not only Islamist fanaticism and fundamentalism but often Islam itself, started making their way to West Bengal's social media sphere more frequently than ever before. Surprisingly though, these write-ups did not fetch great endorsement from the 'secular-liberal-atheists' of West Bengal. Articles by Bangladeshi atheist and liberal bloggers were being circulated in West Bengal by the warriors of Hindutva to highlight 'problems in the very basis of Islam'. West Bengal's Hindu right wing used in their propaganda the writings of Bangladesh's secular faces criticizing the atrocities perpetrated on the Hindus there.

The BJP was trying to contrast the atrocities against Hindus in Bangladesh with Mamata Banerjee's overt appeasement of Muslims in West Bengal. She was trying to turn West Bengal into 'West Bangladesh', the saffron camp contended. The BJP got ammunition for propaganda when sixteen Muslim organizations took out a massive rally in Kolkata on 30 March 2013 to protest the Bangladesh International Crimes Tribunal's award of death sentence to Delwar Hossain Sayeedi, a top ideologue of Jamaat-e-Islami Bangladesh, who was convicted for engineering mass killings in connivance with he Pakistan army in 1971. Some of the speakers in the Kolkata rally boasted about how they drove exiled Bangladeshi author Taslima Nasreen out of Kolkata (in 2007) and prevented Salman Rushdie from coming to the city (2012). Many of the speakers described Sayeedi as a great scholar.

While the Left and the TMC refrained from commenting on this rally, the first voice of concern over the event came from the saffron camp. Rediff.com published on 4 April 2013 an article by Anirban Ganguly, a Jadavpur University Alumnus and New Delhi resident who would have his own role in Bengal politics a few years later. Titled 'A rally for war criminals: Why are TMC, Left silent?',[4] the article said, 'It was for the first time that such a mobilization took place in Kolkata and it simply reinforced an emerging mindset which has begun trying to consolidate a pan-Bengal Islamic identity.'

Another response came in the form of an opinion piece, 'West Bengal, a zone of silence in India',[5] by journalist Sandipan Deb, in *Mint* of the Hindustan Times group, dated 4 April:

> When several thousand agitators demanded freedom for Sayeedi at Kolkata, not a single political party uttered a squeak. Not Trinamool, not the Left Front. Everyone loves a Muslim vote bank, and that vote bank in West Bengal has shifted from the Left Front to Trinamool in the last some years ... Banerjee wants to keep that bank with her, and the Left wants to get it back. So, silence is the best policy in the matter of a convicted Islamist fundamentalist war criminal. Meanwhile, in the month following Sayeedi's sentencing, Jamaat supporters in Bangladesh have attacked more than 300 Hindu temples, homes and shops. Silence is the best policy there too.

Garga Chatterjee, at the time a researcher at the Massachusetts Institute of Technology, expressed grave concern about the direction politics was taking in Bengal in his article, 'A Dangerous Connivance', published in the *Hindu*, dated 6 April.

> The rally thundered that West Bengal would be 'cleansed' of supporters of war crimes trial and the present Prime Minister of Bangladesh. They promised that political forces supporting Shahbag would be 'beaten with broom-sticks' if they came asking for Muslim votes.... They expressed solidarity with the anti-Shahbag 'movement' in Bangladesh. This assertion is worrisome, as the anti-Shahbag forces in Bangladesh have initiated a wave of violent attacks on Hindus, Buddhists and secular individuals, and the destruction of Hindu and Buddhist homes, businesses and places of worship.[6]

In the same article, Chatterjee cited another example of 'double standards':

> On March 21, a group of small magazine publishers, human rights workers, theatre artists and peace activists were disallowed from marching to the Deputy High Commission of Bangladesh to express their support to the war-crimes trial efforts. The police had 'orders'; some marchers were detained. A month earlier, the same police provided security cover to an anti-Shahbag march and later to the marchers when they submitted a memorandum to the Deputy High Commission demanding the acquittal of convicted war criminals.

Chatterjee warned, 'When the political class acts as tactical facilitators or tactical spectators to apologists of one the largest mass-murders ever, the demise of Kolkata as a centre of culture is a natural corollary. A combination of circumstances can cause an uncontrollable unravelling. Bengal's experience with sectarian politics is distinctly bitter.'

That Chatterjee himself would turn out to be a principal propagator of 'sectarian politics' of a different kind in a few years is a story which we will come to later.

Amid the leftist and secular camp's silence on Islamic fundamentalism, the saffron camp hijacked the issue of violation of human rights of the

Hindus in Bangladesh, which, in any case, had turned into an issue of international concern. It was a legitimate issue, remaining under-discussed if not entirely undiscussed in Kolkata, 'India's cultural capital', where people so easily relate to the pain of the oppressed in faraway lands. They felt deeply for Vietnam during the 1960s, for instance, when graffiti on walls proudly proclaimed *'Tomar naam amar naam Vietnam Vietnam'* (Vietnam is your name, Vietnam is my name); or when the Maoists in Bengal claimed *'Cheener chairman amader chairman'* (China's chairman is our chairman) during the late 1960s and early 1970s, or during the second Iraq War, when *'Markin samrajyobad Iraq-Afghanistan theke haat othao'* (Keep your hands off Iraq and Afghanistan, American imperialism) was splashed in glowing red on white walls, keeping the common people apprised of the major developments in the world.

Bisorjon and Muharram

The Mamata Banerjee government faced a test in maintaining communal harmony in 2015 when Muharram coincided with the immersion day of Durga Puja. Bijoya Doshomi, the official concluding day of the festival, was on 22 October that year. Usually, families immerse their puja idols on Bijoya Doshomi itself. Many community pujas, however, take out immersion processions over the two following days, Ekadoshi and Dwadoshi. In 2015, Muharram – when processions displaying arms used for self-flagellation are taken out in many parts of the state – was on 24 October, the day of Dwadoshi.

One procession is a loud, colourful, cheerful and an animated spectacle of celebration to bid adieu to the goddess Durga and her children. The other is taken out in mourning, and the participants wail. In one procession both men and women participate, sing and dance. The other is men-only.

Mamata Banerjee did not deem it fit to allow both communities to take out processions on the same day. In September, she first announced sops for community pujas – discounts on electricity bills and waiver of municipal tax on puja advertisements – and then restricted the immersion schedule. Immersion was allowed on 22 October and then on 25 and 26 October. Though Muharram was on 24 October, Mamata also prohibited immersion processions on 23 October – Ekadoshi – on the grounds that the tajias (tableau) for Muharram are prepared and the processions rehearsed by many organizers on the eve of the occasion.

This decision did not elicit much criticism or political opposition, but the same challenge returned the next year, and the test got tougher in 2016. Bijoya Doshomi was on 11 October and Muharram fell on the next day, Ekadoshi. This time, Mamata decided to curb the timings for immersion on Bijoya Doshomi to facilitate rehearsals of the Muharram procession. In August, she announced that Durga idols can be immersed on Bijoya Doshomi only till 4 p.m. There would be no immersion on Ekadoshi.

Mamata Banerjee thought that as in the previous year there would not be much of a hue and cry over this. Her priority was the prevention of communal clashes, which had been on the rise in the state over the past couple of years. What she miscalculated, perhaps, was that the BJP's principal agenda in West Bengal was to right 'injustice to Hindus'. This time, first the BJP and then the RSS criticized the government's decision. Dilip Ghosh said they would explore legal options, and some other individuals dragged the government to court. Sandeep Bera, a BJP member, filed a petition in the Calcutta High Court challenging the government's decision.

Bera, a swayamsevak who hailed from Kharagpur and at that time lived in Kolkata, claimed in his petition that his family performed puja every year and that the neighbours were also part of it and that the government's order restricting immersion to 4 p.m. on Bijoya Doshomi would curb their rights. Two others too approached the high court against the government order.

The government not only lost the case but also earned sharp criticism from the court. 'There has been a clear endeavour on the part of the State Government to pamper and appease the minority section of the public at the cost of the majority section without there being any plausible justification. The reason therefore is, however, not far to seek,' justice Dipankar Dutta wrote in his order, dated 6 October.

'The administration has failed to take note of the fact that Muharram is also not the most important festival of people having faith in Islam. To put it curtly, the State Government has been irresponsibly brazen in its conduct of being partial to one community, thereby infringing upon the fundamental rights of people worshipping Maa Durga.'[7]

This was nothing less than a slap on Mamata Banerjee's face. It was also good ammunition in the hands of the saffron camp.

The judge went on to write, 'The State Government must realize that it would be dangerous to mix politics with religion. We the people of India boast of being a secular nation but actions of some State Governments are in deviation of the constitutional norms and principles. No decision ought to be taken that would have the potential of pitting one community against another. We are living in difficult times. Intolerance would rise in the event of such arbitrary decision of the State Government being put in place and enforced.'

Justice Datta allowed immersion of all family Durga pujas till 8.30 p.m. on Bijoya Doshomi, though he declined to entertain the plea filed by a community Durga puja organizer that wanted to immerse their idol on the night of Bijoya Doshomi.

Following the court order, Left and Congress leaders criticized Mamata Banerjee in no uncertain terms for her inability to maintain communal harmony. The saffron camp launched an intense campaign on social media, quoting excerpts from Justice Datta's order and claiming that the points they had been making against the Mamata Banerjee government so consistently had now been legitimized by the court.

To add to Mamata Banerjee's worries, several communal clashes took place over Muharram and Bisorjon processions in 2016. Riots broke out at Hazinagar (Naihati) in North 24 Parganas and went on for three days. Hindus and Muslims clashed at Chanchol in Malda, Chandannagar in Hooghly and Kharagpur in West Midnapore. There were minor clashes in the districts of Burdwan and Birbhum. They were low-intensity clashes in most cases, causing injuries and damage of property. But overall, social tension was increasing. Fake news started flooding social media platforms. Photos of attacks on Hindu temples and idols in Bangladesh were shared in West Bengal rather rampantly, with captions describing them as images of recent incidents in the Indian state under the Mamata Banerjee regime.

The government was getting nervous. One of the major causes of Mamata Banerjee's anxiety was that many of the persons whom the police arrested in connection with communal clashes from different districts were TMC supporters and local leaders – both Hindu and Muslim. The next year, Muharram would again fall on Ekadoshi. In 2017 Bijoya Dashami and Muharram were on 30 September and 1 October, respectively.

The Sangh Parivar decided this was the moment to push for 'an awakening' of the Hindus. Ram invoked Durga for the battle with Ravana. Now that the festivities around the worship of Durga had hit a hurdle, the Sangh invoked Ram.

Ram Navami would be their counter to Muharram. Ram Navami 2017.

Saraswati Puja vs Milad-un-Nabi

In 2016, Prophet Muhammad's birthday, known as Milad-un-Nabi, or 'Bishwo Nobi Dibos' in Bengali, fell on 13 December. In two schools, one in Howrah district and the other in Nadia, trouble had been brewing over demands that the Prophet's birthday be celebrated, especially since Saraswati Puja is also observed. The authorities were not in agreement but the protesters would not budge.

At Tehatta High School in Howrah district, trouble continued for nearly two months. A few days ahead of 13 December, a group of people, mostly outsiders to the school, started meeting the authorities of the government-aided school demanding that Nobi Dibos be celebrated in the school. The teacher-in-charge, Utpal Mallick, told them this required permission from the school management committee. This school was founded on a plot which was debottar property, land dedicated to Lord Jagannath. The school management committee did not permit celebration of Nobi Dibos, stating that no event in addition to those in the existing schedule would be allowed.

Two demonstrations were staged outside the school. Muslim clerics and maulvis came to deliver speeches. Their argument was, if Saraswati Puja was permitted on the campus, why not Nobi Dibos? Saraswati Puja, for the record, had been celebrated at the school since its foundation in 1952. Now, a group of outsiders who were allegedly using a few Muslim students of the school as a front were hell-bent on starting celebration of Milad-un-Nabi at the institution. On the thirteenth, these outsiders forcibly entered the school, along with some students of class nine and ten, set up a stage and celebrated 'Bishwo Nobi Dibos'.

The school closed down after the tension this incident provoked.

In a letter to the inspector-in-charge of Uluberia police station, dated 16 December 2016, headmaster Mallick wrote, 'I am informing you that on 13 December 2016, some students of class IX, X and outsiders influenced by some local Islamic fundamental groups forcefully entered the school campus causing communal tension, celebrated Bishwo Nobi Dibos without taking permission from the school authority and disturbed school atmosphere.' He wrote that the management was compelled to close the school indefinitely because teachers and the teaching staff felt insecure about coming to a communally tense locality.

The school reopened after about a week, following prolonged negotiations between the local administration, the school authorities and the local Muslim leaders. It was decided that a section of the students would be allowed to celebrate Nobi Dibos for fifteen minutes and that the date would be chosen by the school authorities. This celebration did not happen, however. This time the school education department objected. So, trouble reemerged as the date of Saraswati Puja neared. The Puja day fell on 1 February. Those who had been pressing for celebrating Nobi Dibos in the school now demanded that either the Nobi Dibos would be celebrated before 1 February or Saraswati Puja would not happen at all.

On 27 January, Nihar Kanti Bhuniya, president of the school management committee, sent a letter to the inspector-in-charge at Uluberia police station, saying: 'Some students and Islamic fundamentalists are going to celebrate Bishwo Nobi Dibos on the campus of Tehatta High School, Uluberia, Howrah, on 28.01.2017 without taking any permission from the SMC [school management committee].' He sought the urgent help of the police to restore normalcy at the school.

Next day, clashes broke out in front of the school between a Muslim mob and the police and Rapid Action Force. On 29 January, the school education department ordered indefinite closure of the school.

This sparked another round of tension and, this time, on 31 January, several hundred Hindu students carrying a three-foot-high Saraswati idol marched about eight kilometres to the national highway and put up a blockade on the road. They demanded immediate reopening of the school so that Saraswati Puja could be performed the next day.

The police dispersed the mob with a lathi charge. Photos of students, including girls, being caned by the police, were published in some newspapers and a few web portals, which went viral on social media. The most popular caption accompanying the photos was: 'In Mamata's Bengal, students are beaten up for seeking to perform Saraswati Puja. It's the writ of the Islamic fundamentalists that's running the state. Another step towards West Bangladesh.'

Anatomy of a Few Riots

> I hail from Chandrakona Road in West Midnapore. A few days ago, a dispute arose between a Toto [e-rickshaw] driver and the driver of a Maruti over parking. In a very short time, heated arguments made way for a fight. The place was a Toto stand. Many Toto drivers were present there. Some of them came to the aid of their friend. There was no one there at that time to stand by the Maruti driver. He ran away and came back with his driver friends from the Taxi stand. A riot broke out. The Toto driver was a Muslim and the Maruti driver a Hindu. Thereafter, Hindus came in large numbers but no one was there. Many fruit shops were around, owned mostly by Muslims. The shops were first vandalized and then set afire. Next on target was the house of a Muslims garment merchant who lived in a Hindu-dominated area. His shop encountered the same fate. Muslims were not sitting quiet either. Houses of Hindus who lived in Muslim-dominated areas came under attack. When some panic-stricken Hindu women and children ran into the neighbouring Santal village in search of shelter, the tribal people came out in large numbers with their bows and arrows.[8]

The text above is a Facebook post written on 3 June 2016 by Jubi Saha, a Jadavpur University student. The riot took place on 28 May, a day after Mamata Banerjee was sworn in for the second term. It took heavy deployment of police forces for a week for the situation at Chandrakona to normalize.

Bengal was at a crossroads.

Twenty-seven incidents of communal riots were reported in West Bengal in 2015, claiming five lives and causing injury to eighty-four. This was eleven incidents more than in 2014, according to a report of the National Crime Records Bureau (NCRB). Two riots had already taken place in 2016. The first one happened at Kaliachak, an area bordering Bangladesh in Malda district. On the 3 January 2016, a Muslim mob gathered to protest Hindu Mahasabha leader Kamalesh Tewari's remarks against Prophet Muhammad, made a month ago in Uttar Pradesh. A section of the agitators turned violent and attacked the Kaliachak police station, setting fire to two dozen vehicles. Thereafter the mob went on to ravage a few Hindu households in the nearby area.[9]

The police smelt a plot right from the beginning.[10] The manner in which the protest was called, against an incident that took place in Uttar Pradesh a month ago, and the way the agitators, without any provocation, attacked the police station and burned down documents hinted at a conspiracy. Investigation was soon directed towards rackets involving illegal poppy cultivation and smuggling of fake Indian currency notes. Police acted cautiously and without drawing much attention, but one by one they nabbed nearly all the accused – all of them Muslim. A crackdown on illegal poppy cultivation and rackets dealing in fake Indian currency notes was launched jointly by the National Investigation Agency, Narcotics Control Bureau, a Special Task Force of the Kolkata Police and the CID. Between 1 and 9 February, central and state agencies destroyed illegal poppy fields on 1,016 acres of land under the Kaliachak police station jurisdiction.

The second riot happened in March 2016, at Ilambazar in Birbhum district. A third-year undergraduate student, a Hindu, made an objectionable Facebook post on Prophet Muhammad.[11] Though the police arrested him on the very same day, clashes broke out the day after, when a Muslim mob gathered at the police station and demanded that the accused be handed over to them. They wanted to hang him right there. As the mob tried to vandalize the police station, the policemen fired tear gas shells, chased down the protesters and allegedly entered a mosque and dragged people – who argued they were praying – out of the mosque. This led to a flare-up, with Muslim protesters blocking the national highway. In the ensuing clash between the police and the Muslim mob a youth died, allegedly in police firing, while several others were injured and properties destroyed.

Following the Chandrakona riots in 2016, communal clashes broke out at Hazinagar in Naihati area of North 24 Parganas district in October. Aniruddha Ghosal's report in the *Indian Express*[12] said the trigger was a low-intensity bomb allegedly thrown at a Muharram procession. The report quoted a Muslim tailor as saying that tension had been prevailing in the area for the past few months over a Hindu group's insistence on changing the route of their Durga idol immersion procession. The new route they proposed would cross a mosque. A report in *The Hindu*[13] pointed out the same root cause. It said that a sudden change of the route of a Durga immersion procession, allegedly at the insistence of a group of Hindu Jagran Manch members, had led to a communal flare-up in 2014. The recent riot was an outcome of the same tension prevailing since that time.

Now, changing the route of a religious procession was a dangerous proposition. All religious processions have routes that have been traditionally followed. New routes are allowed only after thorough consideration of multiple aspects. Hindu processions do pass through Muslim-dominated localities, and Muslim processions through Hindu-majority areas; but these routes have been in place for years and they have usually settled down after many a trial and error. But it was not Hindu organizations alone playing with fire.

At Dhulagori, also called Dhulagarh, along the border of Sankrail and Panchla assembly constituencies, tension had been brewing since 10 December 2016. What this author gathered, speaking to a senior police officer posted in Howrah district, was that when a group of Muslim youths were putting up the Islamic flag at Narayantala area, members of a local club, Annapurna Byayam Samiti, as also some other local Hindu residents, objected to the flag arguing that it was Pakistan's national flag. The Muslim youths were stopped from putting up the flags, which was part of their preparation for the 13 December procession on the occasion of Nobi Dibos. The police arrived on the spot without delay and defused the tension by clarifying that the flags were not Pakistan's.

However, according to Dynt's well-researched documentary on Dhulagarh,[14] a meeting took place at the neighbouring Natibpur village on the night of 12 December, when some local Muslim youths urged a local TMC leader to ensure that the procession scheduled the next day could pass through Narayantala. Originally, the procession was to start from Natibpur, and the police had fixed Munshipara as the area it would pass through before entering Dhulagori. The organizers of the Nobi Dibos procession had assured the leader of 'cent-percent Muslim vote' if the procession was allowed through Narayantala. The leader gave them the go-ahead. Police denied them permission, but the procession was taken out anyway. Clashes broke out soon after the procession crossed the Byayam Samiti at Narayantala.

The riots went on for two days, with both Hindus and Muslims suffering loss of property. The saffron camp, using Mamata's silence to portray it as her consent to the Muslim atrocities against Hindus in West Bengal, got #Dhulagarh to trend on social media platforms.

Then, on 2 July 2017, a tasteless Facebook post – a morphed photo uploaded by a Hindu boy – triggered tensions in the Muslim-dominated Baduria area, in North 24 Parganas district. The next day was the Ulto Rath Jatra[15] of the Hindus. Within hours, as protesters turned violent, the residence of the boy who created the Facebook post – a class-eleven student – was torched. The house stood bang opposite a mosque, Milan Masjid. The boy lived with his uncles. They had all left their home in the evening of 2 July. Around night, a massive mob of Muslims put Baduria police station under siege. The mob was demanding that police bring before the crowd the class-eleven student who had created the blasphemous Facebook post.

The police had sought help from some of the prominent Muslim personalities of the area. One of them, Abdul Matin, secretary of an Islamic social organization, Sunnat-al-Jamayaat, that ran several madrasas in Baduria and surrounding areas, went to the police station and addressed the mob. Some of the video footage of the siege of the police station that emerged on Facebook over the following days showed Matin trying to pacify the crowd. 'We must abide by the Constitution. We cannot take the law into our own hands. Moreover, we cannot do anything that harms anyone except the culprit. The RSS is conspiring across India to fuel trouble. We must not fall into that trap. Taking the law into our own hands will be nothing less than harakiri,' Matin told the gathering.[16]

The mob wasn't impressed.

Finally, after much persuasion, Matin and Abdur Kayum, who was a lecturer at Alia University in Kolkata, managed to send the mob back with the promise of launching a blockade of the main road if the police failed to arrest the boy within twenty-four hours.

The police nabbed the boy, who had fled his home by then, at 3 a.m. on Monday. He was taken out of the area for his own safety.

From early in the morning on 3 July, Matin, Kayum and Mohammad Kamrujjaman (who headed Minority Youth Forum), kept issuing statements through social media, urging Muslims to refrain from staging any blockade of the road, as the accused was already arrested and it was the day of Ulto Roth Jatra. Md. Yahiya, president of Bengal Imams' Association, issued a similar appeal. All these appeals fell on deaf ears. Trouble spread to Baduria's neighbouring Basirhat and Deganga police station areas. The *raths* came under attack at two places, one each in jurisdictions of Baduria and Basirhat police stations, resulting in clashes in which several dozen houses and shops belonging to Hindus were vandalized and gutted. About two dozen people suffered injuries. Nearly a dozen police vehicles outside Baduria police station had been torched by the agitating Muslims. They were mostly angry about the police not handing over the accused to them.

So, if the leaders of the Muslim community were preaching peace, who fomented trouble by deliberately blocking the route of the Rath Jatra even after the culprit had been arrested? As this author spoke to Muslim leaders of different political affiliations, a sub-plot emerged – infighting in the TMC. The story that was told, almost in consensus, was that a TMC minority wing leader, Haji Montu, who was a rival of the TMC's Baduria civic body chief Tushar Singha, wanted to discredit the civic chief. Haji, at that time, was the president of TMC's minority cell in Baduria and working president of the party's district unit minority cell. Allegedly, he floated a rumour that the police had taken the boy to a safe place and that the boy would be released once the tension fizzled out. The TMC leader reportedly encouraged road blockades and assured protesters that he would 'manage' the administration. When this author asked Haji Montu for his response to these allegations, he rubbished it all as 'a grand political conspiracy'. It was difficult for the author to independently ascertain who was telling the truth.

However, the narrative got a little more intriguing when Republic TV on 7 July released recordings from a sting operation in which Haji Montu was seen blaming the municipal chairman for inaction. Among other things, he called Singha 'communal' and blamed him for his preoccupation with minting money through illegal means and for allowing things to spiral out of control by not visiting the locality where the boy lived. 'What did Tushar Singha do? He was merely standing next to Matin-saab when the latter was speaking. How much did the chairman speak? Could he at all? He doesn't have that thing in him,' Haji was heard telling the journalist, blissfully unaware of the spy camera in action. 'The tension could have been defused had he visited the home of the boy and apologized to the people on the minor's behalf, keeping the boy's family standing next to him. That would have solved it. But he didn't attempt it,' Haji said.

For the record, videos of the gherao of the police station showed Singha, with folded hands, tendering an apology on behalf of the boy, his family and the entire Hindu community, saying that the incident had the Hindus hanging their heads in shame, and insisting that no Hindu would approve of the boy's act.

The situation at Baduria, Basirhat and Deganga continued to be tense, despite deployment of Border Security Force personnel and the shutting down of internet services. Tension and sporadic violence continued; there were clashes on 5 July, resulting in grievous injuries to several. Kartik Ghosh, fifty-five, who was knifed by a group of unidentified Muslim youths, died at R.G. Kar hospital in Kolkata the next day. The news triggered another round of clashes in Basirhat on 6 July. By this time, Hindu organizations had started to mobilize their forces.

Hindu Milan Mandir, a wing of the Bharat Sevashram Sangh, became the centre of Hindu mobilization. Activists of the VHP and the Hindu Samhati had swung into action. Indigenous weapons were probably used – this author saw a creative 'slingshot bow', made of PVC pipes and rubber that could shoot an arrow up to 300 meters and could fit into a trouser pocket. On 6 June, Muslim neighbourhoods came under attack, and a Hindu mob vandalized the residence of the local TMC MLA, Dipendu Biswas, who was a Hindu, accusing him of siding with the Muslims.

Soon after the news of Ghosh's death broke, BJP leaders, including state unit president Dilip Ghosh, alleged that Ghosh was a member of their party. BJP leaders staged a demonstration at R.G. Kar hospital after authorities disallowed them from entering the ICU where Ghosh's body was still kept. BJP leaders Locket Chatterjee and Sayantan Basu claimed that they had come to offer homage to Ghosh, but the administration did not allow them in. Later, Dilip Ghosh too tried to enter the hospital but was stopped.

Another group of BJP leaders, including Roopa Ganguly and Samik Bhattacharya, were on their way to Basirhat but the police did not let them enter the area. In Kolkata, BJP leaders claimed Ghosh's family wished to take the body to Basirhat for cremation, but the police were denying them permission. Dilip Ghosh alleged that the police agreed to hand over the body to the family only on condition that they would conduct the cremation in Kolkata. This was a gross injustice towards the grieving family and amounted to blatant disregard for their sentiments, Ghosh alleged.

Kartik Ghosh's sons, however, refuted all of BJP's claims. 'Neither was my father a member or even a supporter of the BJP nor did the police press for cremation in Kolkata. The administration has been cooperative,' Prabhashis Ghosh told journalists.[17]

Haji Montu, gradually got sidelined in the TMC. And tellingly, after another two years, in mid-2019, Montu would switch over to the BJP.

SIX

The Bengal Plan

Sangh Signals Green

THE CHAIN OF COMMUNALLY charged incidents led to West Bengal becoming a significant item on the central agenda of the RSS. In March 2017, Akhil Bharatiya Pratinidhi Sabha, the highest decision-making body of the RSS, passed a resolution under the heading of 'Grave concerns over the unabated rise in violence by Jihadi elements in West Bengal.'[1]

The resolution said, 'The Akhil Bharatiya Pratinidhi Sabha (ABPS) expresses grave concern over the unabated rise in violence by Jihadi elements in West Bengal, encouragement to the anti-national elements by the state government due to its Muslim vote-bank politics, and declining Hindu population in the state.' It touched upon the Kaliachak incident, claimed that Hindus came under attack from fundamentalist elements in Katwa, Kaligram, Ilambazar and Metiabruz, and said that a large number of Hindus were being 'forced to flee from the border areas under the pressure of fundamentalist forces'.

It also referred to the Khagragarh blast, in which the NIA investigation had unearthed the involvement of JMB sleeper cells, to the Dhulagarh riots and the Tehatta high school controversy. Talking about the administration's 'planned crackdown' on schools run by various RSS-affiliated organizations – 'the schools which are instilling the spirit of patriotism' – they alleged that the government was 'turning a blind eye towards thousands of institutions like the notorious Simulia madrasa (of the Khagragarh blast connection) where Jihadi and fundamentalist training is being imparted.'

The resolution did not overlook the controversy around the use of the word '*rongdhonu*' in place of '*ramdhonu*' for 'rainbow' and '*asmani*' instead of '*akashi*' for 'blue', in a Bengali text book for class six. In January 2017, these two changes triggered a major controversy in Bengal – in both the social and mainstream media. Ramdhonu and rongdhonu are both used in Bengali, though use of the former is predominant in West Bengal and use of the latter in Bangladesh. In West Bengal, rongdhonu had become limited to poetry and song and, in most cases, only those pursuing literature were acquainted with its use. Linguist Pabitra Sarkar, former vice-chancellor of Kolkata's Rabindra Bharati University, had traced its origin back to the East Pakistan years of Bangladesh, when the words Ram and Indra were being dropped from Bengali words – in an attempt that can be described as 'de-Hinduization' or 'Islamization'.[2] Likewise, asmani and akashi are both used in Bengali, but asmani is more popular in Bangladesh, whereas in West Bengal the word is mostly heard in faqiri (Sufi) songs.

Incidentally, these changes took place at a time when the government in Bangladesh was facing widespread allegations of Islamizing school text books – dropping works by Hindu and secular writers and replacing Bengali words with those of Arabic-origin, for example – under the influence of Muslim fundamentalists.

Speaking on the context of West Bengal, the ABPS resolution alleged, 'Original Bangla words in the textbooks are being distorted under the influence of fundamentalist elements.'

Then the resolution addressed their core issue: demography. This author had earlier heard an RSS leader summing up their main issue in a crisp and powerful sentence before attendees of a '*bouddhik* session' during a camp in North 24 Parganas district. He had said: 'For West Bengal, demography is destiny.' The ABPS resolution elaborated on the idea:

> At the time of Partition, the Hindu majority area of Bengal came into existence as West Bengal. Thereafter, due to their continuous persecution and atrocities in East Pakistan, present Bangladesh, large numbers of Hindus were forced to seek refuge in West Bengal. It is surprising that despite the large influx of Hindus displaced from Bangladesh to West Bengal, the Hindu population of the state, which constituted 78.45 per cent in 1951, has declined to 70.54 per cent as per census of 2011. This is a matter of serious concern to the unity and integrity of the country.

Finally, the ABPS called upon the people of the country to raise their voice against the Mamata Banerjee government. It was the government they were at war with in West Bengal. 'The ABPS strongly condemns the extremist violence and the Muslim appeasement policy by the state government and calls upon the countrymen to create awareness against this Jihadi violence and communal politics of the state government.'

Soon, Mamata Banerjee got a new moniker, popularized by the saffron warriors on social media: Jihadi Didi.

Jai Shree Ram!

5 April 2017: The top leaders of the BJP's Bengal unit, including Dilip Ghosh, had dropped several hints that there would be 'a show' on Ram Navami. Journalists got similar hints from members of the Vishwa Hindu Parishad and the Bajrang Dal. Even so, when the day came everybody was caught unawares. Thousands of young men with saffron headbands on, marched or took out bike rallies in dozens of places across every district of West Bengal, including in the heart of Kolkata, and in Mamata Banerjee's own constituency, carrying idols of Ram, Laxman, Sita and Hanuman in tableaus. They brandished swords, tridents and other sharp-edged weapons, dancing to loud music that was known in Bengal as 'DJ Music', shouting '*Jai Shree Ram!*' and '*Ramlala ki Jai!*' from time to time.

West Bengal had never witnessed such a grand celebration of Ram Navami. Thus the Sangh Parivar announced its growing clout in the state with a bang.

Ram Navami, pronounced as Ram Nabomi in Bengal, had traditionally been a marginal event in the state. Most of the schools in the state did not observe a holiday for Ram Nabomi. Public celebrations took place mostly in pockets dominated by migrants from Bihar and Uttar Pradesh in the industrial towns of the state. Some Bengali households celebrated it in their homes.

Now, Dilip Ghosh himself led the show in Kharagpur, an industrial town where Ram Navami is traditionally celebrated by the local akhadas, known for their culture of physical training. That day, Ghosh was sometimes seen playing with two sticks, sometimes wielding a mace and sometimes flaunting a sword.

Preparations for mega processions across the state started from end-2016. The VHP, Bajrang Dal and Hindu Jagran Manch, chosen as the main Sangh Parivar outfits for organizing Ram Navami celebrations in the state, coordinated with the many akhadas, as also with the Bharat Sevashram Sangh and its chain of Hindu Milan Mandirs, which had been taking out processions on Ram Nabomi traditionally, though on a small scale. The Sangh Parivar's target was to increase the number of such processions and strengthen the old ones. Wherever possible, processions would be merged to make them large affairs. It was advised that swayamsevaks should try to form a Ram Nabomi celebration committee at as many places as possible and try to organize rallies under that banner. The RSS itself, as also the VHP, Bajrang Dal and Hindu Jagran Manch, would do the work of organizing the celebrations and, on the day of the event, BJP leaders would join the rallies with their followers.

Mamata Banerjee had wished people on the occasion of Ram Nabomi early that morning on social media, just the way she wished her people on dozens of other religious and important occasions in India. As the day progressed, it became evident that the saffron camp had used the occasion, quite successfully, as a show of strength in the state. In some rallies in Birbhum and Purulia districts, even school children were seen with swords and daggers in their hands. By evening, Mamata started taking digs at the BJP for politicizing a religious festival. She also alleged that armed processions were taken out without permission from the police and lambasted the saffron camp, particularly for handing weapons to children.

Dilip Ghosh could not care less. He said no one required permission for taking out Ram Nabomi processions in 'the land of Ram'. Ghosh, in his usual style, threw Mamata Banerjee an open challenge. 'Ram belongs to the whole world. He is behind the entire creation. We believe in this. Ram does not belong to those who are scared of him. A battle between the Ramzada (Ram's children) and the Haramzada (illegitimate born) is being fought out here. It's a test to show who are on the side of Ram and who are against,' he said in Kharagpur, as the procession there came to an end.[3] He still had a sword in his hand as he spoke to the media.

About a month later, Dilip Ghosh announced that the next such display of weapons would take place on Bijoya Doshomi, when *shastra pujan* would be performed. He even announced distribution of trishuls among women ahead of Bijoya Doshomi. This announcement triggered another controversy, as Durga Puja had until now nothing to do with shastra pujan, even though some traditional household pujas included worship of some of the weapons in the goddess's hands. Shastra pujan is more associated with Dusserah.

Mamata Banerjee was furious. Briefing the media at the state secretariat, she warned the RSS–BJP against 'playing with fire' and said she would not allow any procession with weapons on Bijoya Doshomi. 'They'll come from outside Bengal and teach us how to behave at our festivals?' she was quoted as saying in a report in the *Telegraph* on 18 September 2017.

Joy Bangla!

The saffron camp invoked the slogan 'Jai Shree Ram' to instil 'confidence' among the Hindus who, members of the saffron camp thought, needed to be protected from 'jihadi aggression'[4]. The slogan inadvertently stoked Bengali ethnic/regionalist sentiments, with a section of Bengalis considering 'Jai Shree Ram' and Ram Navami as symbolizing the saffron camp's attempted imposition of 'conservative, north Indian culture' on a 'liberal Bengali society'. Some of these people invoked 'Joy Bangla' (victory to Bengal), a key slogan of the Bangladesh Liberation War (1970–71), and a secular slogan, as they called it, to counter 'Jai Shree Ram'. Some others used the cry 'Joy Maa Kali', arguing that Bengal belonged to Kali. Whether or not Ram was alien to Bengal became the subject matter of a heated debate on social media as well as mainstream media.

Bengali ethno-regionalism, nationalism, sub-nationalism or ethno-nationalism – whatever name one may call it by – has a history. 'Deshbondhu' Chittaranjan Das, in many of his speeches during the first half of the 1920s, had primarily addressed the Bengali-speaking people. His insistence was on the notion that the linguistic unity of the Bengali people was greater than any other divide they faced. In *Banglar Kotha,* which was actually delivered as a speech in 1921, Das said, 'He may be a Hindu, a Muslim or a Christian; but a Bengali is a Bengali. He has a distinct shape, a distinct character and a distinct religion.'[5] He even insisted that Bengali was a distinct nationality.

In the 1930s, an organization named Bengali Protection League emerged in Kolkata; it began to highlight issues facing Bengali Hindus and Muslims. The Hindi-speaking Hindus and Urdu-speaking Muslims were harming the interests of the Bengali people, it alleged. In 1942, during the days when a heightened communal atmosphere reigned over Bengal, Nazrul Islam, the 'bidrohi kobi' (rebel poet), wrote, '*Bangla Bangalir hok. Banglar joy hok. Bangalir joy hok*' (Let Bengal be the Bengalis'. Let Bengal be victorious. Let the Bengali be victorious).

Ahead of Bengal's second Partition in 1947, Subhas Bose's elder brother and comrade-in-arms, Sarat Chandra Bose, who was in his own right one of the stalwarts of Bengal politics at the time, was one of the proponents of the United Bengal theory. Along with East Bengal-based Krishak Praja Praty's A.K. Fazlul Haq, he opposed the creation of Pakistan and sought to carve out an independent nation for the Bengali-speaking people of both the east and west Bengal. The Bose-Haq initiative failed to withstand the stormy days of heightened communal divide, when both Hindu and Muslim hardliners were bent on partitioning Bengal along religious lines if neither could get the whole of it.

On 31 December 1948, while delivering his presidential address at the East Pakistan Literary Conference, poet Muhammad Shahidullah said, 'It is true that we are Hindus and Muslims; but it is a higher truth that we are Bengalis. This is no ideological talk, this is the reality. Mother Nature by herself has left such an impression of *Bangaliyana* (Bengaliness) on our appearance and language that the garland-sandal-paste or the skullcap-lungi-beard cannot hide it.'[6]

Four years later, on 21 February 1952, four students of Dhaka University – Rafiq, Salam, Barkat and Jabbar – fell to police bullets while demonstrating, defying prohibitory orders, to protest attempts to impose Urdu on the Bengali-speaking people. In 1999, at Bangladesh's initiative, UNESCO adopted 21 February as the International Mother Tongue Day.

If in eastern Bengal a language movement was shaping a political discourse against the imposition of Urdu, in Manbhum, erstwhile Bengal's western-most district that had been conceded to Bihar after Independence, a movement against imposition of Hindi took shape in 1948 after the Bihar government instructed that Hindi would be compulsory from the primary level in schools. The Bengali department at the zilla school in the district was abolished, installation of signboards in Hindi became mandatory in schools and business establishments, and Hindi was declared as the official language of the district.[7]

This language movement ultimately forced the Union government to bifurcate Manbhum. This resulted in the creation of the district of Purulia, comprising Manbhum's Bengali-speaking population, which was acceded to West Bengal in 1956. A similar language movement developed in 1960 in the Barak valley of Assam against the imposition of Assamese on the Bengali-speaking people of the area. This movement ultimately led to the death of eleven, including a woman, in police firing near Silchar station on 19 May 1961, following which Bengali was recognized as an official language in Barak.

The story of Bengalis in Assam did not end there, as from the mid-1960s, the notorious Bongal Kheda (expel the Bengalis) movement, a jingoistic drive to ethnically cleanse the Brahmaputra valley of Bengalis, drove thousands of Bengali-speaking people out of Assam, or to the Barak valley in lower Assam. In reaction, a Bengali rights group emerged in West Bengal and Tripura in the early 1970s. Named Aamra Bangali (We, the

Bengali), it was the political wing of the socio-religious movement called Ananda Marg.

Amra Bangali mainly had its base in the districts of West Bengal bordering Bihar and Assam. They even managed to win some panchayats in Bengal and an assembly seat in Tripura. The movement, however, never appealed to the larger mass of Bengalis in West Bengal, and Amra Bangali remained a fringe outfit. Another round of Bengali rights activism started at the beginning of the twenty-first century, with writer Sunil Gangopadhyay and other academics and intellectuals launching a movement to ensure that Bengali is made mandatory on every signboard in the state. The movement remained confined mostly to Kolkata, where activists wrote in Bangla the names of shops on some signboards where the language was missing. But this movement too fizzled out in a few years.

The Ram Navami celebrations of 2017 revived all dormant sentiments of Bengali ethno-regionalism. The following text from a Facebook post of writer-blogger Saikat Bandyopadhyay, dated 8 April 2017,[8] may give readers an idea of the nature of this sentiment against 'Hindi-aggression'. The post was shared more than 500 times from his social media profile alone, leaving aside the many shares by means of copy-pasting and sharing on WhatsApp. Here is an excerpted translation from the original Bengali text:

> ...You, your father, grandfather, had so long considered it a trouble whenever they saw monkeys on the trees, you chased them out, you mocked at *Panchalis*. Now, in atonement, learn worshipping the monkey... Also know of the next step: *Bangaali pantha aur machhli kha kha key adha Mussalman aur adha Kerestan hoye gelo* (the Bengalis have become half-Muslims and half-Christians consuming meat and fish). Boycott Michael Madhusudan and Nazrul. Instead of celebrating Tagore and Nazrul's birth anniversaries, listen to *Jai Jagdeesh hare* while chewing *Pan Parag*. Spit wherever you want. Stop calling the *Ramchhagol* as *Ramchhagol*,[9] instead greet each other with Ram-Ram... And yes, speak Hindi for sure. Because the religion of Uttar Pradesh is the religion of India and the language of Uttar Pradesh is the language of the Bengali people.

Ramayana and Ram have, of course, been part of Bengal's public culture. *Sriram Panchali* by Krittibas Ojha, better known as *Krittibasi Ramayan* is one of the most influential renditions of the Ramayana in any regional language. It was composed during the first half of the fifteenth century, about a century before Goswami Tulsidas's *Sriramcharitmanas*, written in Awadhi. It is in the *Krittibasi Ramayan* that Ram's untimely invocation of Devi Durga in the month of Ashwin – the present timing of the Puja – is introduced in the narrative of the Ramayana.

Chaitanya Mahaprabhu (1486–1534) worshipped both Ram and Krishna. The iconic 'Hare Krishna' chant that Chaitanya coined also includes 'Hare Ram'. Ram is also worshipped as Roghunath in Bengal. There are many large towns with Ram in their name – Srirampur, Ramrajatala, Ramnagar, Rampurhat, Ramjibanpur, Ramgarh – and many villages too share these names. Ram is also a common prefix and suffix in Bengali names. To scare off ghosts, children often utter, '*Bhoot amar poot, petni amar jhi, Ram-Lokkhon bukey achhe korbi amar ki?*' (Ghosts are kids to me, as I have Ram and Laxman in my heart.)

Nevertheless, Ram has not been vital in the religious practices of the Bengali Hindus. He is not a household deity. According to Nrishingha Prasad Bhaduri,[10] an eminent Indologist, Ram entered Bengal's religious scene in the fifteenth and the sixteenth centuries, with the advent of the Bhakti movement led by Chaitanya. 'It is interesting to note that, though Chaitanya worshipped both Ram and Krishna and his influence played a key role in the spread of Lord Krishna's popularity across the state and among all sects of Bengali Hindus, worship of Ram never gained popularity. Chaitanya himself is far more accepted as a human avatar of God than Ram,' Bhaduri said, in an interview with this author.

The word Ram is often used in Bengali as a superlative – as, for example, in *Ram-pantha* (a complete idiot), *Ram-pyadani* (beating up black and blue), *Ram-kunre* (super lazy), *Ram-da* (a large cutlass), *Ram-konjus* (extremely miserly), *Ram-paka* (ultra-precocious) and so on. Chicken is often called *Ram-pakhi*. Film and literary critic Sanjoy Mukhopadhyay told this author that the Bengali language has traditionally witnessed a more secular, rather than religious, use of the word Ram.[11] One of Bengal's most iconic works of literature during the era of Renaissance, *Meghnad Bodh* (The Killing of Meghnad) by Michael Madhusudan Dutt, portrays Ravan as the hero. The poet reserves all his sympathies for Ravan and Indrajit. Despite being hard to comprehend for its Sanskritized Bengali and the use of blank verse, *Meghnad Bodh's* influence on the intellectuals of that time, including Ishwar Chandra Vidyasagar, had ensured its immortality. Two other adaptations from the stories of Ramayana by iconic literatures – Sukumar Ray's *Lokkhoner Shoktishel* and Abanindranath Tagore's *Khudi Ramlila* – are full of humour and satire but are completely devoid of devotion.

Bengal, in the truest sense, has been the land of Kali, Krishna and Shiv. They have innumerable temples dedicated to them in every locality and are also household deities. The biggest religious influence on Bengali culture (literature, art, music) has been through the Vaishnavite poems and songs centred on the love of Radha and Krishna, and through Shyama Sangeet, the songs dedicated to Kali. Swami Vivekananda had quite aptly captured the religious profile of the Bengali Hindus when he said: 'In this land, old Shiv is idling, Maa Kali is savouring mutton and Bansidhari is playing his flute… that old Shiv will play his damru, Kali will savour meat and Bansidhari will keep playing his flute – in this land, forever.'[12]

Kali, the dreaded, meat-and-wine-loving slayer of demons, has of course been the most influential of all deities. Nature, i.e., the abundance of ponds and rivers, gave Bengali Hindus fish; and religion, the Kalikula Shaktism school of Hinduism,[13] gave them meat. When someone is stepping out of the home, members of a devout Hindu family generally utter 'Durga-Durga'. People most commonly swear in the name of Kali – '*Maa Kali-r dibbyi kete bolchhi.*' Durga Puja and Kali Puja are the biggest Hindu religious festivals of Bengal, along with Doljatra. There are so many avatars of Kali alone – Shyama, Chhinnomosta, Bhoirobi, Brohmomoyee, Bhobotarini, Roksha Kali, Shmoshan Kali, Bhodrokali, Mohakali, Rotontikali, Korunamoyee Kali, Johura Kali, and so on – that Kali Puja in different forms goes on almost throughout the year. One theory about the etymology of Kolkata says that it came from Kalikshetra. It is no wonder that Gunter Grass's *Show Your Tongue*,[14] a self-illustrated book of essays composed during his stay in Bengal during 1987-88, refers directly to Kali.

Different Hindu practices peacefully coexisted in Bengal for centuries. Many *shakto* families have weekly vegetarian days. But with the saffron camp's boastful launch of Ram Navami, there were voices of 'apprehension' ringing out loud on social media and public forums. Besides, a whisper campaign had started against the Bengali calendar itself. Bengalis traditionally celebrate new year's day twice – on Poyila Boishakh, usually on 14 April, and on 1 January, the new year's day of the English calendar. However, this time, anonymous write-ups were circulating on social media urging Bengalis to embrace the Hindu Nav Varsh (usually in March) because the Bengali calendar was apparently developed by Akbar and was a deviation from the real Hindu calendar. This too triggered a backlash.

In May 2017, while travelling in a local train, this author overheard a conversation between a few middle-aged officer-goers:

> 'They start with imposing their Ram Navami on our Basanti Puja, they end with taking away our meat and fish.'
>
> 'This is a festival of the Hindi-speakers' display of strength in Bengal.'
>
> 'Cow-belt has reached Bengal.'

Many Bengalis who felt threatened by 'north Indian aggression' started highlighting the distinctiveness of Bengali Hindu practices from that of 'theirs': Bengalis worship Gonesh on Poyla Boishakh, the first day of the Bengali calendar, but Ganesh Chaturthi has never been an event here; the Bishwokorma in Bengal is young and mustachioed, the Vishwakarma in the north and the south is elderly, white-bearded; while north Indian Hindus fast during Navratri, Bengalis feast on the occasion of Durga Puja, held at the same time; Hindus in the Hindi heartland chant *'Ram naam satya hai'* while carrying the dead but Hindus in Bengal chant *'Bolo hori, hori bol'* in funeral processions. Hori, or Hari, is, of course, Krishna. The Dusserah on Vijaya Dashami, the burning of Ravana's effigy, is a practice mostly alien to Bengal. On Bijoya Doshomi, Bengali married women paint each other's face red with vermillion; men hug and wish each other '*Shubho Bijoya*', and families exchange sweets.

The already-growing anti-Hindi sentiment and trivialization of north Indian people and practices found a trigger for escalation in September 2017, when some north Indian Hindus trolled Bengali video-blogger Saptarshi Chakraborty, who runs the YouTube channel Bong Eats, for sharing a 'Durga Puja Special Egg Roll Recipe'. Those trolling the blogger said advertising non-vegetarian food during the fasting days of Navratri was a great sin and hurt their religious sentiments. It snowballed into a major controversy quite soon. Hate statements were exchanged.

Saptarshi Chakraborty's response to the trolls, two lines especially, went viral on social media. He wrote a blog post on medium.com, dated 11 September,[15] from which some lines were quoted in mainstream media reports. Elaborating on the hate messages he received, he wrote: 'Most of this hatred is targeted towards Bengalis and Bengal. We, as well as other people in India who do not speak Hindi and have religious rituals and a culture different from the mainstream north Indian Hindus, have always been looked at with a mixture of suspicion and contempt.' And then, he added, 'Our mother is not a submissive cow! She is a fire-spewing, demon-killing, badass woman who knows how to have fun.'

A section of the educated Bengali youth, mostly urban – with an assistant professor of statistics, Garga Chatterjee, leading the pack – started using Joy Bangla to counter Jai Shree Ram. There were others too taking up the slogan. On social media, especially Facebook, which is much more popular in West Bengal than other platforms, the use of #JoyBangla became more frequent with every passing day. Some of these scattered voices would then consolidate into an organization, Bangla Pokkho (On Bengal's Side), which had a roaring royal Bengal tiger on their flag. They took inspiration from the 'linguistic nationalism' of Bangladesh, and from the Tamil, Kannadiga and Maratha people.

Bangla Pokkho started from where the other Bengali ethnic movements left off. Garga Chatterjee and his followers often referred to Hindi-speaking people as '*Hindi jontu* (animal)' or '*gutkha jontu*'. Its members – Hindus and Muslims, from the folds of the TMC and the Left – argued that Bengal was never part of 'Hindustan' and that Bengalis, including stalwart litterateurs of the nineteenth and the twentieth centuries, traditionally referred to north Indian people as Hindustani. 'We are Bengali, we are Bharatiya and we are Indian. But we are not Hindustani,'[16] Chatterjee started announcing at Bangla Pokkho street-corner meetings, using the megaphone.

Connecting Bengal

The BJP was prepared for such a Bengali regionalist movement to emerge. According to a BJP organizer who did not want to be named, Shiv Prakash, the BJP's national joint-general secretary (organization) who was looking after Bengal, told the state unit leaders in 2016 that Mamata Banerjee would resort to Bengali sub-nationalism once they pushed for Hindutva. From this perspective, the BJP state organization was rearranged. In the 2011 assembly elections, thirty-two of the 289 candidates had been Hindi-speaking, and the majority of them got tickets in Kolkata and the industrial towns. The BJP put up the highest number of Hindi-speaking candidates among all the parties. Now, Hindi-speaking leaders of the state unit, such as Ritesh Tiwari, Raj Kamal Pathak and Prabhakar Tewari, were gradually moved out of prominence.

In another move to appease Bengali sentiments, the RSS tried cozying up to Pranab Mukherjee, whose presidential tenure was to end in July 2017. Advaita Charan Dutta met him in Delhi in mid-2017, when Mukherjee invited Dutta to visit his home during Durga puja. In October, four RSS leaders, including Dutta, attended the Puja at Mukherjee's Birbhum residence. These exchanges would finally lead to Mukherjee accepting the RSS's invitation to be the chief guest at their flagship annual event in Nagpur in June 2018. By honouring the tallest Bengali politician of recent times, the RSS drew significant public attention, if not sympathy.

Besides, a prolonged campaign was planned to highlight how Hindutva was an integral part of Bengal's cultural heritage. It was decided that a set of organizations working in collaboration with the BJP and the RSS would arrange a series of small-, medium- and large-scale events to generate discussion around Bengali icons.

In this ideological battle, they had a two-fold approach, according a state-level leader of the BJP who spoke to this author on condition of anonymity. The first was to deny Bengali ethno-regionalism any superiority over Bharatiya nationalism; and second, to emphasize that Bengal was the place of birth of Bharatiya nationalism. Bengalis would be told that they need not feel threatened by the popularization of Bharatiya culture; rather, Bengal should be proud that this Bharatiya nationalism is their contribution to the rest of the India; that Bankim Chandra penned 'Bande Mataram' and that Sister Nivedita planned a tour of India carrying the image of Bharat Mata that was created by Abanindranath Tagore. Where else should people be prouder about shouting 'Bande Mataram' and 'Bharat Mata ki jai'?[17]

The first such event was organized in October 2017. Rantidev Sengupta, a veteran Bengali journalist who had been working in close association with the RSS over the past few years, was the chief organizer of the event, in the capacity of being the general secretary of the Sister Nivedita Mission Trust. The Trust organized a talk on the occasion of the 150th birth anniversary of Nivedita, Swami Vivekananda's Irish disciple who had a profound influence on Bengal's extremist revolutionaries of the *Ognijug*, or age of fire. Nivedita's role in India's struggle for freedom is unforgettable. She, among other things, introduced Bengali revolutionaries to the autobiography of Mazzini, which contained a chapter on guerrilla warfare. Talks around Nivedita would always resonate in Bengal.

Now, Mohan Bhagwat was to deliver a speech on her. From the dais on 3 October, Bhagwat said: 'All diverse languages and practices should coexist, but under the unifying idea of Bharat Mata. All diversities must be subservient to nationalism.'[18]

The second major event was Amit Shah's. He was to speak on Bankim Chandra. This event was organized by New Delhi-based BJP think-tank Syama Prasad Mookerjee Research Foundation (SPMRF), one of the main organizations to whom the BJP had entrusted the task of connecting with the Bengali intelligentsia – especially the bhodrolok. Its helmsman, Anirban Ganguly, a Jadavpur University alumnus who lived in Delhi and was a member of the BJP's central policy research wing, was to work together with the nominated Rajya Sabha MP Swapan Dasgupta, a columnist. The two would coordinate with Shiv Prakash and RSS ideologues in Bengal.

The SPMRF was to hold a series of discussions in towns across Bengal, highlighting nineteenth and twentieth century Bengali nationalist icons – Bankim Chandra Chattopadhyay, Sister Nivedita and Kazi Nazrul Islam, among others. The BJP had to be established before the public as the true torchbearer of the legacy of Bengal's nineteenth and twentieth century icons.

The invitees for Shah's speech were chosen carefully — a large number were college and university teachers, including six former vice-chancellors. The task of SPMRF was to build a network of intellectuals to revive talks around Bengal's Hindu nationalist icons of the pre-Independence era. An SPMRF organizer once told this author that the best way to establish relations with academics and researchers of certain repute was to hold events on personalities in whom all Bengalis took pride.

Ahead of Shah's event, Bengal BJP's senior leaders systematically approached prominent public intellectuals to drop off invitations. Actor Soumitra Chatterjee, former Supreme Court judge Ashok Kumar Ganguly, former Naxalite-turned-writer Santosh Rana, theatre actors Rudraprasad Sengupta, Chandan Sen and Manoj Mitra, singer Amar Paul and painter Samir Aich, among others were invited for the function. None of them turned up. The only popular writer who came was Buddhadeb Guha, who was never previously seen around politicians of any colour and hardly ever spoke on socio-political issues.

The auditorium, however, was full on 27 June 2018 as Shah took the stage. There was no space unoccupied in the auditorium and there were many standing outside. The others on the dais included Netaji researcher Purabi Roy and former vice-chancellor of Gour Banga University Achintya Biswas. Biswas had been close to the RSS for some time.

The image of Bharat Mata on the stage was not the one usually seen at Sangh Parivar events in the rest of the country. The one here was the iconic Bharat Mata painted by Abanindranath Tagore in 1905. Shah was also presented a framed picture of Kali.

In his speech, Shah said the Partition of India could have been avoided if the Congress had adopted 'Bande Mataram' in its entirety as the national song. 'Congress's politics of appeasement was expressed through its incomplete acceptance of 'Bande Mataram' in 1937, and it led to the path to Partition. They divided the song and divided the nation,' he said, and continued, 'Bande Mataram does not belong to any particular religion or language. It unified India. Congress made a blunder by linking the song with religion. I am forced to draw its reference because we must take lessons from the mistakes of the past.'

In a more significant remark for the state, Shah announced: 'The song was an expression of India's national revivalism. Our nationalism is cultural nationalism and Bankim Chandra is the fountainhead.'[19]

The audience erupted in applause. One after another, the audience was shouting, 'Bande Ma-ta-ram!'

SEVEN

The Sangh Spreads Its Wings

MAMATA BANERJEE WAS NOT fighting the BJP alone; she was fighting the entire Sangh Parivar. A network of about three dozen socio-religious organizations affiliated to the RSS worked in different parts of the state, among different constituencies of the people, and in the sectors of health, education, religion and self-sustenance. There were villages where the BJP had no or nominal presence, but organizations belonging to the Sangh Parivar had engagements with the people.

Since these organizations mostly work as or through NGOs, they even managed to get state government-run organizations collaborating with them. For instance, even after Mamata Banerjee virtually declared a war on the RSS, the department of science and technology and biotechnology of the state government sponsored a four-day workshop, titled 'Daily Life Mathematics', organized by a unit of the RSS's science wing. Consumer Affairs Minister Sadhan Pandey ended up consenting to attend a programme by Akhil Bharatiya Grahak Panchayat, the consumer affairs wing of the RSS, while TMC MLAs and panchayat pradhan (chief) attended an event co-organized by the RSS's MSME wing, Laghu Udyog Bharati, in South 24 Parganas district.

Understandably, when Shree Hari Satsang Samiti and Friends of Tribal Society (often called Vanvandhu Parishad) pushed for expansion in 2013 and started setting up Ekal Schools and Sanskar Kendras in tribal villages and organized musicals on Krishna and Ram, especially in north Bengal and the south-western region, grassroots-level TMC leaders did not take them seriously. It took some time before Mamata Banerjee warned the people of the state against the one-teacher Ekal School programme. Even then her knowledge of the organization was scanty, as she kept calling them as 'Ekkel' and 'Akkel'.

'You should know that they have formed an organization named Ekkel or Akkel ... BJP, RSS, Bajrang Dal ... in the name of that Ekkel, they are appointing teachers in tribal areas. They have so much money ... they pay Rs 20,000 as salary. They sit on the veranda and teach the kids about the RSS in the name of imparting education. Don't trust them. This Ekkel NGO belongs to the BJP. They are misleading you,' she said at a rally in Alipurduar on 9 January 2018.[1]

But by that time the Ekal movement in the state had gained momentum.

Who's Who of RSS in Bengal

The RSS has no formal membership. Attending a shakha (literally a branch) – the lowest organizational unit of the RSS that gathers daily at an open space in the morning or evening – is the only way to join it. The participants are called swayamsevak, meaning volunteer. They participate in games, physical exercises, group discussions and chorus singing before ending their hour-long sessions with prayers offered to motherland and respects paid to the bhagwa dhwaj, the saffron flag, the ultimate guru that the swayamsevak is dedicated to.

The ganvesh (uniform) is not mandatory for the shakha but is a must on special occasions. Shakhas with more than thirty or forty attendees are often divided into groups, called gata, for the convenience of exercise, games and group discussion. For those who cannot make it to the shakha every day, there are the weekly and monthly gatherings, called milan and mandali, respectively.

'At the core of the activities of the shakha is 'character building', which is to create the basis of nation-building, the saha-prant pracharak of the

RSS in south Bengal, Bidyut Mukherjee, explained to this author.[2] The swayamsevaks are indoctrinated into devotion, nationalism and social dedication. Discipline is of utmost importance. Swayamsevaks with a greater degree of dedication become functionaries. The ones devoted enough to give all their time to the outfit, and stay away from marriage and other engagements, are adopted as pracharaks. They live in the Sangh offices, eat vegetarian food and get their monthly expenses covered by the Sangh. However, before becoming a pracharak the candidate must prove his abilities and dedication by serving at least two terms as a vistarak or a whole-timer for a limited period (usually for some months to a year). In most cases, pracharaks are appointed when in their early twenties and chosen from among those who attended shakhas from their school days.

The next level of involvement after attending a shakha is participation in the prathmik shiksha varg or initial training camp – known as ITC in Sangh parlance. These are seven-to-ten-day camps held at the district level annually. Members of the pranta karyakarini (state executive) and zilla karyakarini conduct various classes at these camps. After this, the next stepping stone is the OTC or officers' training camp held at the state level. There are three categories of OTC camps. First-year OTC is the state-level camp, second-year OTC the regional level camp, and third-year OTC the national-level camp. The first two types of camps are of twenty days' duration, while the third is a twenty-five-day camp, held in Nagpur.

Attending an ITC is not among the easiest of ways to spend a week. The following set of advisories given to applicants in October 2016 by the RSS's Barrackpore district unit[3] for the seven-day ITC gives an idea about what it takes:[4]

(a) Come prepared with the complete uniform.
(b) Bring along exercise books and pens, a plate and glass, an extra half-pant and t-shirt, shaving kit, personal belongings of daily requirement, bed sheet, mattress and mosquito net.
(c) Do not bring Bermuda and lungi.
(d) Get a health check-up done. Do not come with any illness.

(e) Do not bring costly wrist watch, gold chain, mobile phone and camera.

(f) Do not bring excess cash.

(g) If you bring a mobile phone, it has to be deposited with the camp authority right at the beginning and will be returned only after the end of the camp.

(f) If it becomes necessary to contact family members, phones of camp officials can be used, after permission is granted by the camp in-charge.

Testing of leadership skills starts from the gata, or group, level. One participant is appointed as a gatanayak (group leader) and another as a shikshak (instructor). The shakha-level leadership consists of the karyavaha (secretary) and mukhya shikshak (chief instructor), the latter being the de facto head of a shakha. A few shakhas make a mandal (panchayat). A few mandals make a nagar in the municipal areas and a khand in rural areas.

Ideally, a mandal's range of operations should correspond with a gram panchayat area and a khand's with a community development block. But in Bengal, there was no mandal between the shakha and khand in most places because there were not enough shakhas in the state yet, as compared to the number of shakhas in other states where the Sangh's activities had taken deep root. However, populous municipal towns, such as Siliguri in north Bengal, were divided into upanagars or sub-towns (such as Binay upanagar, Sushrut upanagar, etc., in Siliguri). The same was done in populous community development blocks. The Chinsurah-Mogra block in Hooghly district consisted of the Bandel and Mogra khands.

Above khand are the zilla (district), vibhag (division), prant (state) and kshetra (regional) levels. Large administrative districts were divided into two organizational districts. The administrative district of Hooghly was divided into Hooghly and Tarakeswar organizational districts, while the neighbouring administrative district of Howrah was divided into Howrah mahanagar (urban) and Howrah rural organizational districts.

The organizational districts of Hooghly, Tarakeshwar and Howrah rural made the Hooghly-Howrah vibhag, which operated under the Dakshin Banga prant.

North Bengal, which at one time was a division under the West Bengal prant, was made a separate organizational state or prant after 2000. In north Bengal, districts like Alipurduars, where RSS's growth was fairly exponential during the Mamata Banerjee regime, many places had mandal-level formations between the RSS shakha and khand/nagar levels. There must be more than two shakhas within one panchayat area for a mandal to be formed.

The Pracharaks

From the nagar/khand level, the leadership is made of sanghachalak, karyavaha and pracharak. However, in West Bengal, only the district-headquarter towns had nagar pracharaks. As this author understood from observing the functioning of the organization, the sarsanghchalak is the helmsman at the topmost level and the sarkaryavaha the second-in-command. At the base level of shakha, the mukhya shikshak is the de facto head. The karyavaha plays the most important role at the nagar/khand level. At the levels of district, division, state and region, the pracharak is the key person, along with the karyavaha.

A pracharak is available round the clock and coordinates the work of different levels of committees and sectors, including that conducted by affiliate organizations. New pracharaks are usually appointed first as nagar and khand pracharak. For instance, the Suri nagar pracharak in Birbhum district in 2019 was Arindam Pal, a man in his twenties, who hailed from Tarakeshwar in Hooghly district.

From nagar to kshetra, the role of the sanghchalak is more that of a guide than an organizer. Several swayamsevaks this author interviewed described the RSS as a 'pracharak-based organization'. For example, the Hooghly-Howrah Vibhag pracharak, Ashis Mandal, was the de facto head of the RSS in this division, and he worked through the zilla pracharaks of Hooghly, Arambag and Howrah rural. Around 2018–19, Asansol zilla

Pracharak Palash Dolui and Bardhaman (Burdwan) zilla pracharak Tarun Bera reported to the Bardhaman vibhag pracharak Paritosh Saha, the key organizer in Burdwan. The vibhag pracharaks report to the prant pracharak. There may be several pracharaks in a district, working in various capacities, but all have to report to the zilla pracharak. Similarly, all pracharaks in a state are to be guided by the prant pracharak.

Some of the pracharaks are 'loaned' to affiliate organizations, but the RSS can always recall them or depute them to some other organization. This effectively means that a pracharak is supposed to work in different organizations of diverse interests, while his loyalty would remain towards the RSS.

Right from the beginning of the RSS activities in Bengal, pracharaks were sent from Nagpur at regular intervals. According to some of the veteran RSS functionaries this author interviewed, Eknath Ranade came to West Bengal as the eastern zonal pracharak in 1949, shortly after the nationwide ban on the RSS was lifted. The state already had three pracharaks – Ramprasad Das (possibly the first pracharak from the state), Keshab Chandra Chakraborty and Sukumar Banerjee.[5] Bansilal Sonee, who became a pracharak in 1949, had come to Kolkata from his home in Jharkhand to study at Vidyasagar College and got deeply involved in the Sangh's activities.

A batch of swayamsevaks was sent from Nagpur in 1950. They included Amal Kumar Basu, Keshav Rao Dikshit and Prabhakar Lakhe. Vasantrao Bhatt, who was sent in 1956, rose through the ranks rapidly. Dharmchand Nahar, a Jain from Rajasthan, came to Kolkata in 1960, became a pracharak in 1965 and served the RSS in the state for thirty years in various capacities, including as state sharirik pramukh or physical chief. Balakrishna Naik worked as a pracharak in various capacities during the 1970s and 1980s. Shrikrishna Mothlag and Vijayganesh Kulkarni were sent in the 1980s. Mothlag later served as Paschimbanga prant pracharak and also as an invited member of the RSS's national executive. Kulkarni is most remembered for his role as the organizing secretary of Vidya Bharati West Bengal. K.S. Sudarshan, predecessor of Mohan Bhagwat as sarsanghchalak, had his base in Kolkata for more than a decade.

Some of these non-Bengali-speaking pracharaks could boast of quite a remarkable achievement – that of being considered worthy of 'pure Bengali' nomenclature, with a 'da' suffixed to their name. Balkrishna Naik became known in Bengal as Keshto-da. For the uninitiated, Keshto is the common Bengali nickname for Krishna. After serving the RSS in Bengal in various capacities, he was sent to the VHP. As of 2019, he was one of the VHP's national vice-presidents. Dharmchand Nahar became known as Dharmo-da. Vasantrao Bhatt became known as 'Bosonto-da', and so widely that even Hindi-speaking swayamsevaks and pracharaks used to call him by that moniker.

Bhatt, who became a pracharak in 1947 and had his first assignment in Jabalpur, was sent to Hooghly district in 1956. Bengal became his home thereafter. He was appointed as the prant pracharak in 1960. During the late 1970s, he was given responsibility of the eastern India unit of the Vanvasi Kalyan Ashram, whose all-India organizing secretary he later became. RSS men consider him as the 'Bhagirath' of Purvanchal Kalyan Ashram. He died at Keshav Bhavan in Kolkata in 2013.

Keshavrao Dikshit, who was originally from Aurangabad in Maharashtra, came to Bengal in 1950 as a pracharak and has made this state his home since. He also served as prant pracharak. Dikshit had special sentiments for Mookerjee. He was already in Bengal and in the thick of things at the RSS when the formation of the Jana Sangh was initiated. As of August 2020, Dikshit is quite active. When this author saw him at Keshav Bhavan in 2014, Dikshit still had his characteristic straight walk. He was even then addressing indoor gatherings and participants at training camps. He was regularly attending events even outside Kolkata – for instance, he went for the inauguration of the RSS's Hooghly district office in November 2016. He was ninety-three at the time. In March 2019, Dikshit travelled down to West Midnapore to visit the residences of several Sangh functionaries. On 23 June 2019, the ninety-six-year-old Dikshit was at Keoratala crematorium in Kolkata to pay floral tributes to Syama Prasad Mookerjee on his death anniversary.

Bansilal Sonee, who was present during Golwalkar's meeting with Mookerjee in Kolkata in 1950,[6] has served in the RSS in various capacities, including as north Bengal pracharak. He was later sent to the BJP at the turn of the new century. He served as a member of the BJP's national executive and later had a key role in building the party's base in Assam, until he came back to Kolkata, serving the RSS again.

During the period 2014–2020, among the most important RSS functionaries in West Bengal were three national executive members – Vadla Bhagaiyah, Advaita Charan Dutta and Pradip Joshi. Among the state-level leaders, Bidyut Mukherjee, Jisnu Basu, Atul Kumar Biswas and Jaladhar Mahato were the most prominent, if we exclude those leaders loaned to other organizations. Bhagaiyah, who served as all-India bauddhik pramukh for several years before being appointed all-India saha-sarkaryavaha or joint general secretary in 2015, had been based in Kolkata for years. Dutta, after serving as eastern zonal pracharak, was appointed as akhil bharat saha-pracharak pramukh (national co-in-charge of affairs related to the whole-timers) in 2015. Joshi replaced Dutta as purba kshetra (West Bengal, Odisha, Sikkim and Andaman) pracharak. At the state level, in 2015, Bidyut Mukherjee replaced Ramapada Pal as south Bengal prant pracharak; Jisnu Basu was elevated from prachar pramukh to secretary of south Bengal; and Jaladhar Mahato was appointed as north Bengal prant pracharak.

Focus Areas

The RSS's activities focused on three regions in West Bengal: two of them were the under-developed regions of the state – north Bengal and the western part, known as Paschimanchal; while the third consisted of the areas bordering Bangladesh, stretching from Cooch Behar in the north to the Sunderbans in the south. It is due to the relative backwardness of these regions that separate government departments overseen by independent ministers look after north Bengal, Paschimanchal and Sunderbans. The north Bengal districts together have eight of the state's forty-two Lok Sabha seats. The Paschimanchal districts too have eight seats. The Sunderbans area is represented by two Lok Sabha seats, one each in South 24 Parganas and North 24 Parganas. The population in all three regions is dominated by the backwards classes – SCs, STs and OBCs.

Different Sangh Parivar outfits worked in different sectors and focused on different localities within these areas. Their members remained in touch with the people through wide-ranging social and religious works. Ahead of the elections, the members undertook jagran (awakening) campaign and helped build a wave of nationalism and Hindu pride in these regions.

The list of Sangh Parivar organizations active in Bengal during 2013–2020 is as follows:

1. Vishwa Hindu Parishad (VHP)
2. Bajrang Dal (VHP's youth wing for men)
3. Durga Vahini (VHP's youth wing for women)
4. Hindu Jagran Manch (HJM)
5. Hindu Yuva Vahini (HJM's youth wing)
6. Vanvasi Kalyan Ashram (works among the tribal people)
7. Arogya Bharati (traditional medicine wing)
8. Bharatiya Kisan Sangh (farmers' wing)
9. Bharatiya Mazdoor Sangh (trade union wing)
10. Sahakara Bharati (cooperative wing)
11. Samskar Bharati (cultural wing)
12. Vijnana Bharati (science wing)
13. Shakti (women's wing of Vijnana Bharati)
14. Vidya Bharati (education wing)
15. Arogya Foundation of India (part of Ekal Abhiyan)
16. Friends of Tribal Society (also known as Vanvandhu Parishad, part of Ekal Abhiyan)
17. Shree Hari Satsang Samiti (part of Ekal Abhiyan)
18. National Medicos Organization (allopathy wing)
19. Bangiya Shikshak O Shikshakarmi Sangha (high school teachers' organization)

20. Bangiya Naba Unmesh Prathamik Sikshak Sangha (primary school teachers' organization)
21. Akhil Bharatiya Vidyarthi Parishad (ABVP, the students' wing)
22. Sewa Bharati (social work wing)
23. Kreeda Bharati (sports wing)
24. Prajna Pravah (think-tank or intellectual wing)
25. Bastuhara Sahayata Samiti (refugee wing)
26. Laghu Udyog Bharati (MSME wing)
27. Rashtra Sevika Samiti (women's wing of the RSS)
28. Bharat Vikash Parishad
29. Akhil Bharatiya Adhivakta Parishad (works in Bengal under the banner of Nationalist Lawyers' Forum)
30. Rashtriya Kala Manch (art wing of ABVP)
31. Saksham (RSS wing for the differently abled)

These organizations worked in coordination. For instance, at Sompara in Shaktipur area in Murshidabad district, Vivekananda Bidya Bikash Parishad runs a Saraswati Shishu Mandir (formal school), and Sewa Bharati runs a Sanskar Kendra (informal pre-primary school). On Janmashtami, the RSS's Dharmajagran Samanvay (religious awakening coordination) wing involves the students of both schools in a 'dress as Krishna' competition. The Rakhi Bandhan celebration in an open field in 2017 saw nearly 300 mothers of students from both schools attending. Matukeshwar Paul of the RSS's Parivar Pravodhan (family awakening) wing was the chief speaker. At Amtala in South 24 Parganas district, an eye camp was conducted at Manjusree Villa on 23 November 2014. It was organized by Rashtra Sevika Samiti, in collaboration with Bastuhara Sahayata Samiti and supported by Amtala Nagarik Adhikar Raksha Samiti. In north Bengal, two outfits, named Alipurduar Ganobibaho Samiti and Sebayan Paschimbanga, worked in close coordination with the VHP and Shree Hari Satsang Samiti to organize mass weddings for the tribal people.

There were other organizations in the Parivar fold busy taking their ideology to the people. On 24 February 2013, Kolkata Sankhanaad Samarasata Mission celebrated Sant Rabidas Jayanti at Sukanta Sadan, Barrackpore, at which mostly members from the Balmiki Samaj were present. The saha-sarkaryavaha (national joint-general secretary) of the RSS, Krishna Gopal, who would become the Sangh's pointsman for the BJP at the national level after a little more than a year, was also present. The Mission's annual activities included contests for memorizing the Gita and free distribution of the book at various religious events. During the event at Barrackpore, Krishna Gopal said that Ambedkar, along with his followers, had embraced Buddhism after realizing that Hindus were not ready to denounce untouchability, and this had exposed Dalits to the lure of Islam or Christianity. Ambedkar essentially wanted to save India from Islamization, Krishna Gopal argued.[7]

The most remarkable incident at the event, however, took place when Parimal Nayek, a sweeper at the Kolkata Municipal Corporation, donated five *cottah* (3600 sq. ft.) of land to the Mission. Upon this, Pradyumna Kumar Choubey, a Brahmin and the president of the Mission, touched the feet of Nayek, a Dalit. The principal call of the gathering was to build a Hindu society free from untouchability.

Another organization was the Shree Burrabazar Kumarsabha Pustakalay, which confers the Dr Hedgewar Prajna Samman, in recognition of scholarship, every year. In 2014, Akhil Bharat Itihas Sankolan Yojna's national president, Satish Chandra Mittal, got the award. Krishna Gopal was the main speaker at the event. In 2015, Mohan Bhagwat came to Kolkata to present the award to Dina Nath Batra of Shiksha Sanskriti Utthan Nyas. Murali Manohar Joshi was the main speaker.

From 2013 onwards, numerous newly-founded social and 'apolitical' organizations popped up in various parts of the state. They included Manabadhikar Raksha Mancha, Sachetan Nagarik Mancha and Bangiya Jatiyatabadi Parishad. Their agenda was common – to campaign for Hindutva and the protection of Hindus from 'discriminatory politics'.

In the following portion of this chapter we discuss in brief the workings of some of the prominent RSS-affiliated organizations in the state. All these organizations had a basic, two-pronged strategy – the general promotion of Indian traditions, culture and the spirit of Hindu nationalism, and the addressing of specific issues concerning the sectors in which they were working.

Ekal Abhiyan

On the picturesque banks of the river Jayanti, which forms a natural border between India and Bhutan, a one-teacher school was established by Friends of Tribal Society at a Shiva temple in Hatipota village, in the buffer zone of Buxa Tiger Reserve, in 2015. This place lay in the Kumargram area of Alipurduar district. The villagers here mostly depended on the nearby Rahimabad Tea Estate, which remained open on and off. Collecting and crushing stones from the Jayanti riverbed – illegally – was their primary source of income.

In the front yard of the Shiva temple, a lady in her mid-twenties taught the students all subjects. The school was informal; it better fit the description of a coaching centre for students between the age group of six and fourteen. In addition to being taught lessons out of text books, the students were also taught Indian culture and heritage – such as saying 'pranaam' to their parents every morning, respecting the teachers and elders, honouring the national flag, Bharat Mata, the national anthem, 'Bande Mataram', cows and Indian icons such as Shivaji, Rana Pratap Singh and Syama Prasad Mookerjee.

Saraswati Bandana, for instance, is integral to the routine of Ekal schools. The school started with eleven students, but by 2017 the number had doubled. The nearest government school was about four kilometers away. Those who had enrolled there did not turn up regularly. Running Ekal schools did not require a great amount of money –quite contrary to Mamata Banerjee's claim that teachers used to get a salary of Rs 20,000, they actually got paid about Rs 1,000–Rs 1,200 per month. The annual cost of each school ran into Rs 20,000, according the Ekal campaign's annual report for 2016-17.[8] Funds mostly came from NRIs.

Back at Hatipota, after the school became popular, Shree Hari Satsang Samiti set up a Sanskar Kendra for the adults of the village. The Sanskar Kendras usually start with a bhajan mandali – weekly gatherings to listen to bhajan. Once the bhajans or Hari Katha (tales of Hari) musicals ensured a regular audience, the Satsang Samiti volunteers started lecturing the villagers on Indian society and culture, against alcoholism and other moral issues. One of the aims of these Sanskar Kendras is the inclusion of the tribal people into the mainstream Hindu fold. Many of these people still considered Sarna/Sari[9] as their religion. Evidently, this was on the wane with the increasing influence of Brahmanical Hindu practices on the community. The Satsang Samiti also arranged mass marriages for impoverished families, took school children pandal-hopping during Durga Puja and organized yajnas.

With time, two more organizations entered the scene. Arogya Foundation of India organized free medical check-ups and distributed medicines a few times a year. Health and hygiene tips were given to the villagers. Ekal Gramotthan Foundation encouraged villagers, and actually helped them, to plant fruit trees on the little excess land they had using vermicompost fertilizer produced from cow dung. These house-orchards were called poshan vatika (garden of nutrition). This campaign encouraging fruit cultivation was focused on reducing anaemia among women.

These four organizations together make the Ekal Abhiyan, one of the Sangh Parivar projects with the potential to create a tremendous social impact on the local residents as a result of its holistic approach involving four major aspects of life – education, income generation, culture/religion and health. Organizers describe the programme as 'the largest Indian grassroots movement that focuses on holistic development of rural and tribal villages using the Ekal school as a nucleus.'

By 2017, the Sangh Parivar had a firm footing in Hatipota and its neighbouring villages in the Rydak gram panchayat area. Realizing the rising influence of the RSS in the locality, the state government in April 2017 planned a home-stay-based tourism circuit involving twelve villages in Jalpaiguri and Alipurduars districts. One of the villages was Hatipota.

TMC leader Sourav Chakraborty told this author that they tried to close down a few schools for preaching communal enmity, but new ones were opened in other areas. 'Also, closing down a free coaching centre is a sensitive issue and needs to be dealt with care,' said Chakraborty,[10] who was then the president of the TMC's Jalpaiguri unit. Alipurduar was part of Jalpaiguri.

'Our motto is to encourage people to live an eco-friendly way of life,' said Pradip Musaddi, one of the organizers of the Ekal movement in Malda district, when this author spoke to him over the phone.

In Malda, one of Bengal's three Muslim-majority districts, the Gramothan Resource Centre run by Ekal Gramotthan Foundation at Bhalukbona village in tribal-dominated Habibpur was the centre of many activities. It had been developing at its research centre pesticides made from cow's urine and fertilizer from cow dung. The institute, situated on a twenty-six-bigha plot of land was using about five bighas for paddy cultivation, completely avoiding chemical fertilizers and pesticides. Farmers from the neighbouring villages were often invited to have a first-hand look at how organic farming works.

The institution ran a free dispensary, provided computer training to the local school children and conducted tailoring classes for the local women. Those who did not have the money to buy a tailoring machine after the end of the course were provided the amount by the institution, on condition that Rs 500 would be refunded every month for twelve months.

One of the most interesting services of this centre was its mobile computer training facility. A bus with twenty seats was fitted with eleven computers for trainees. Two or three teachers attended to them. The bus visited every village for two hours a day, twice a week, for three months. Students were taught basic computer usage, and at the end of the course were provided certificates from 'Spoken Tutorial', a Mumbai-based project funded by the ministry of human resource development and developed by IIT-Bombay. The vehicle visited four villages every day, covering twelve villages a week. Since the course ran for three months, the Ekal on Wheels could serve about forty-eight villages a year and train forty-four students from every village every year.

It was around this centre that the Ekal Abhiyan intensified its influence in Malda district's tribal-dominated belts. Incidental or not, it was only at Habibpur that the BJP, or any political party in Malda district for that matter, managed not only to put up a fight against the ruling TMC but actually trounced Mamata Banerjee's party in the rural, parliamentary and assembly bye-elections held during 2018 and 2019.

Nationally, during 2017–18, the Ekal campaign managed to develop 789 gardens of nutrition or poshan vatikas, 153 of them in Malda district alone. Of the roughly 300 tribal-dominated villages in Malda district, as many as 210 had Ekal schools by the beginning of 2019.

Overall, in Bengal, 3,567 Ekal Vidyalayas had 87,861 students as of June 2019. There were nearly the same number of Sanskar Kendras. The number of schools had been 2,936 as on 30 June 2016.[11] In 2013, the number of schools stood at 2,281.

Vidya Bharati

A thin book in the hands of the headmaster described Maharshi Kanada as the 'world's first atomic scientist' and Rishi Bhardwaj as the 'father of aeronautics'. Varahamihira 'could predict the future using astrology', it said. Afghanistan, it said, got its name from the Sanskrit word '*upaganasthan*'.

This was one of the books of the Bodhmala series, in Bengali, taught in the formal schools run by Vivekananda Bidya Bikash Parishad (VBBP), the south Bengal chapter of the RSS's education wing, Vidya Bharati Akhil Bharatiya Shiksha Sansthan, or Vidya Bharati in short. The Bodhamala series on India's history, heritage and culture is taught in addition to the state government-approved curriculum. The two books this author read sitting in the room of Anil Kanrar, the pradhan acharya, or headmaster, at the Saradha Shishu Tirtha, Tantiberia, were taught to students of classes three and four. This school had 1,150 students and thirty teachers in 2017.

One of the books placed Hedgewar, Golwalkar and Deendayal Upadhyaya among the 'great men' of India since the ancient times. Another claimed that eating before bathing harmed one's health. Another said the cow is considered a mother 'because gods live in her body'.

Though not part of the government curriculum, this series of books is so vital to Vidya Bharati schools that not only the students but also the teachers are required to take centrally-conducted tests every year on this series of books alone.

'We equally stress on curricular and co-curricular activities, aiming at comprehensive development of the children, including moral, cultural and physical (development),' headmaster Kanrar said.

The Bodhamala series of books was at the centre of a controversy at that time. In the state assembly, education minister Partha Chatterjee had said that the government was considering shutting down 125 RSS-inspired schools for 'deviating' from the state's curriculum and operating without the required 'no-objection certificate'.[12] The state education department carried out inspections at Vidya Bharati-run schools twice during 2016. School inspectors were accompanied by police. Partha Ghosh, Vidya Bharati's north Bengal in-charge, alleged[13] that the headmasters were asked about the curriculum, about the management committee members and their associations with the RSS, and about whether RSS funded these schools or received any financial benefit from the operation of the schools.

Kanrar was unapologetic. 'We follow the government's syllabus without any deviation. How could providing students with some additional knowledge and awareness be wrong? We teach the students to touch the feet of their parents every morning. We instil values in them. Education is a mission.'

Schools run by the VBBP are named Sarada Shishu Tirtha, Sarada Shishu Mandir, Saraswati Shishu Mandir and Saraswati Shishu Tirtha. The pre-primary sections are called Arun (3+), Uday (4+) and Prabhat (5+). Three framed images are put up at the venue of all VBBP programmes – they are images of the Om sign, goddess Saraswati and Bharat Mata. In the morning, the schools begin with a thirty-to-forty-five-minute session that includes Saraswati Bandana, yoga, and moral and spiritual lessons. Chanting slokas from the Gita and the Gayatri mantra is part of the routine. Students are allowed to have their tiffin only after chanting the 'bhojanam mantra'.

Besides the syllabus of the West Bengal Board of Secondary Education, three additional subjects are taught – Vedic mathematics and Sanskrit from class two, and India's tradition and culture from class four. The teachers are mostly those who adhere to the ideology of the RSS and are engaged with the organization in various capacities. There is the example of Tarakdas Sarkar, who, from being a pradhan acharya, or headmaster, of a Vidya Bharati-run school, became a pracharak of the RSS and went on to become the organizing secretary of Vivekananda Bidya Bikash Parishad.

Education did not come free. The admission fee ranged from Rs 1,000 to Rs 2,500, and monthly fees between Rs 100 and Rs 400. Being un-aided, no mid-day meal was offered. But these schools still attracted more students than the government-run primary schools.

As of 2017, there were 326 such schools in the state ,[14] with a total of 66,090 students and 3,193 teachers. Only seventeen of these schools were added between 2011 and 2017. The Mamata Banerjee government's planned crackdown, however, came after the Left accused it of letting RSS-run schools mushroom in the state. Education Minister Partha Chatterjee's statement in the assembly that 'schools are not the places for wielding sticks' refers to the fact that the schools run by VBBP doubled as venues for shakhas and training camps of the RSS, VHP, Bajrang Dal, Durga Vahini and Hindu Jagaran Manch; they were also venues for health camps and any disaster relief work required in the nearby areas.

This author spoke to a few people whose children attended a VBBP school at Tantiberia. They said they found nothing objectionable in the school's books. They were all pleased with the standard of teaching and with how discipline was taught and maintained.

This author even met a few Muslims who sent their children to the Saraswati Shishu Mandir at Balibela in the Goghat area of Hooghly district. Founded in 1992 with only seventeen students in a mud hut, the school in 2017 had 427 students in eight classes – pre-primary sections Arun, Uday and Prabhat, and classes one to five. It had eighteen teachers (acharyas) and three non-teaching staff. Bijoy Chandra Roy, a swayamsevak since 1981, had been the headmaster since the inception of the school. In 2017 he was in his early fifties and lived in the school, which had two double-storeyed buildings. A third building was nearing completion.

The atmosphere at the Balibela school was tense. Roy said that the local MLA, the TMC's Manas Majumdar, had held a meeting outside the school premises barely a few days ago and warned the school authorities against spreading hatred.

Majumdar readily admitted to this: 'Yes, I addressed a meeting. It was to make people aware of the heinous, divisive plan of those who run the school. Senior RSS pracharaks stay at the school while visiting Goghat and its adjoining areas. It hosts the RSS's training sessions. Why are they using a school as a breeding ground of communal hatred?'

Some of the Muslims whose children were in this school, however, did not agree with Majumdar's charges. Sheikh Sariful Hosen, a trader, slammed Narendra Modi for his 'divisive politics', sitting inside the headmaster's room where photos of Hedgewar and Golwalkar hung on the walls. Roy, the headmaster, was sitting next to him. Hosen's son, Hasibul, studied in class five and his daughter, Amrin Khatun, in the pre-primary section called Uday (for students aged four-plus). He had only praise for the school and its headmaster. 'As long as my children are in good hands, it does not matter to us if they also take part in Saraswati Bandana.'

Bajrang Dal

One by one, three young boys, aged about eighteen, emerged out of a narrow, muddy trench about twenty feet long, covered with heaps of leaves, shouting 'Jai Shree Ram' as they crawled out. They ran towards a mango tree, climbed a rope hanging from it, and climbing laterally with the help of a second rope using hands and feet, moved to a coconut tree about thirty feet away. The second rope hung about forty feet above the ground. Anyone who fell would be badly hurt, but none did. It was the fourth day of the camp and the participants had had quite a lot of practice in the first three days alone. After getting down from the coconut tree, the boys ran towards a triangular structure made of bamboo poles. It was about thirty feet high. They climbed up and down the structure, negotiated another structure in the same way, and then walked on a single, horizontally-placed bamboo pole, balancing carefully with their outstretched arms, as if walking the tightrope.

They shouted 'Jai Shree Ram' all the while. They displayed enviable fitness. And the audience – the trainers and the other participants, all in the uniform of white shirt, blue shorts and saffron scarf – encouraged them with cries of 'Jai Shree Ram'.

The 'trench' and the bamboo structures had been created by the participants themselves on 17 December 2017, the day the six-day Yuva Shaurya (valour of youth) Training Camp of Bajrang Dal's south Bengal chapter started. It was on the premises of a secondary school run by an NGO affiliated to the Vishwa Hindu Parishad at Jalaberia, Kultali block, in the Sunderbans region of South 24 Parganas district. The school had a two-storeyed structure attached to a single-storeyed one, and a playground and a temple in its compound.

The 156 participants, aged between fifteen and thirty-five, were predominantly from the lower castes and lower-income groups from various districts in south Bengal. The participants bore the expenses for their transport and uniforms and also paid Rs 350 each for food. They were chosen from among the attendees of one-day camps held earlier in each of the districts. Some of those training at Jalaberia would be chosen for the regional-level camp.

'Everyone receiving training will go back to their native areas and work on establishing local akhadas for imparting basic physical training to the local youth,' explained Sourish Mukherjee, spokesperson for south Bengal VHP, who was also present at the camp.

The neighbourhood had a mixed religious population. Round the clock, a five-member team stood alert as 'sentries' (guards) at the entrance to the school. Kushal Kundu, a resident of Murshidabad and the VHP's assistant secretary for south Bengal, was in charge of the camp. He told this author: 'The aim is to ensure that Hindus are prepared to defend themselves in the face of aggression from members of other religious communities, besides keeping a civilian workforce ready for helping the army in case of external aggression.'

An indoor session followed the physical training session. This was again followed by sessions on wielding the lathi and dummy swords, loading and unloading of rifles and use of the nunchaku, a martial arts weapon consisting of two sticks joined at their ends by a short length of chain.

The schedule was tight indeed – one physical session after another, punctuated by sessions for intellectual and spiritual development, and prayers. The day started at 5 a.m. and ended at 10.30 p.m. Participants slept on heaps of straw on concrete floors, washed their own clothes and dishes and cleaned the campus and toilets every day. The food was basic – muri-ghughni[15] for breakfast, rice, dal and vegetables for lunch, muri-chanachur in the evening and bread/rice, dal and vegetables for dinner.

Sagar Adhikari, a man in his early thirties, had come from Kalyani in Nadia district, shutting his small business for a week. 'The cause of protecting my religion is of greater importance than a week's earnings,' he said passionately.

Sachindranath Singha, the VHP's eastern regional organizing secretary, addressed an intellectual and spiritual development session on the inaugural day. On 21 December, the penultimate day of the camp, Sohan Singh Solanky, national co-convener of the VHP, arrived to address the participants at a closed-door 'intellectual session'. It ran for about an hour, after which there was a break for lunch, followed by another session by Solanki, during which he answered participants' questions.

In the evening session, Solanki told the participants: 'Bharat is the only country considered mother. You'll never hear someone saying Mother America, Mother Pakistan or Mother China. It's only Mother India. We are her children. It is for her that we shall live, die, and also kill if necessary.'

Everybody applauded with cries of 'Jai Shree Ram!'

These camps were one of Bajrang Dal's many activities. In the south-western districts of Purulia and Birbhum, Bajrang Dal, by 2018, had emerged as one of the principal forces of the saffron camp. One of its primary ways of building public contact was by carrying out campaigns against what they called 'love jihad', distributing leaflets outside school and college campuses warning against it. 'Love jihad', also called 'Romeo jihad', describes an alleged religious war waged by Muslim men who marry non-Muslim women feigning love, only to get her converted to Islam, thus fulfilling their religious duty. To succeed in this war of drawing the woman into his trap of fake love, the Muslim man/boy is provided with attractive clothes, motorbikes, smartphones and money for rendezvous with the woman at restaurants.

This concept was, in a sense, southern India's export to the rest of the country. In Karnataka, right-wing Hindu groups had started building conversations around this subject around 2005 and developed it into a full-fledged controversy by 2009.[16] In Kerala, some Catholic priests raised alarm bells in 2009, alleging planned and organized conversion by Muslims using the lure of romantic love.

From the beginning of the second decade of this century, campaigns against 'love jihad' have taken centre stage in the Hindu right-wing agendas in north India, influencing social conversations and impacting the lives of men and women who found life partners in someone outside their own religion. In West Bengal, the VHP and Bajrang Dal, especially the latter, started raising the issue since 2014–15. Later, Durga Vahini, the female counterpart of Bajrang Dal, would also be used to carry out a campaign against 'love jihad' among their friends and classmates in their school or college.

Another of Bajrang Dal's main means of capturing the allegiance of the local people was to set up Hanuman temples, or to simply place a Hanuman idol under a tree in a street corner. In some cases, Bajrang Dal directly initiated the foundation of such temples. In some other cases, committees were formed, involving the local residents, to build these temples. More than 100 temples were constructed locally in different districts of the state between 2015 and 2019. This activity saw a peak between February and April 2019, during the run-up to the Lok Sabha elections.

The month of April 2019 witnessed the inauguration of at least one temple in each of Bengal's twenty-three districts. The single day of 19 April saw temples inaugurated in Paschim Kumorpur (Contai, East Midnapore), Shakharibazar Madan Mohan Tala (Bishnupur, Bankura), Khamarberia (Onda, Bankura), Chanditala in Ganta (Anandapur, West Midnapore), Mahakalpalli (Siliguri, Darjeeling), Radhanagar (Krishnanagar, Nadia) Bhabanipur (Kharagpur, West Midnapore) and Asansol (West Burdwan), among other places. Calls of 'Jai Bajrangbali', 'Jai Shree Ram' and 'Bharat Mata Ki Jai' rent the air.

Bajrang Dal's political impact was first observed in 2018 in Purulia district. Balarampur on the Ayodhya hills was the heartland of the TMC's base in Purulia. The district unit president and minister, Shantiram Mahato, was an MLA from Balarampur. The zilla parishad sabhadhipati (chairperson), Trinamool's Shrishtidhar Mahato, also hailed from Balarampur. Even under the TMC's hegemony, Bajrang Dal continued to grow since 2016, under the leadership of a youth named Birinchi Kumar. It celebrated Independence day, Republic day, Akhand Bharat Divas, Janmashtami, Dol Jatra and Hanuman Jayanti, among other Hindu or nationalistic observances. The 2017 Ram Navami celebration was massive, and the 2018 edition was even bigger. This time, weapons were brandished. A communal clash also broke out when the procession made a bid to pass through a Muslim-dominated village.

The TMC initially did not consider the Bajrang Dal for a threat, but the Hindutva activists who ran a high-pitched campaign against 'jihadi-appeasement of the Mamata Banerjee government', also started doubling up as BJP workers as the 2018 panchayat elections neared. In the elections, the TMC was routed from Balarampur and received jolts in many other parts of the district. In Balrampur, the BJP won both the zilla parishad seats, bagged all the seven gram panchayats and seventeen of the twenty seats in the panchayat samiti. Gopinath Goswami, a retired government employee, who had been associated with the Vishwa Hindu Parishad and sang kirtan at religious programmes and had never been involved in politics at all, emerged a giant killer. He defeated the zilla parishad sabhadhipati, Shrishtidhar Mahato. Birinchi Kumar won a seat as a BJP candidate in the Balarampur panchayat samiti. After the electoral success, both Goswami and Kumar were candid in admitting that it was the Sangh Parivar that had fought the elections in Balarampur.

'What is the BJP here without the Bajrang Dal? We decided everything. We chose the candidates and we carried out the campaign. We took the TMC head on. I am a Bajrang Dal man. I will be with the BJP as long I am asked to continue,' Kumar said to this author on the phone.

'The RSS said politics needed people like me. So, I am here,' Goswami said.

Vanvasi Kalyan Ashram

Banking on the goodwill created by the Saraswati Shishu Mandir at Keshiyari in West Midnapore district since 1992, Vanvasi Kalyan Ashram started opening Shishu Sanskar Kendras, their one-teacher coaching centres for students aged three to eight, in the Shishu Mandir's neighbouring panchayats, from 2002-03. By 2009, there were a dozen or so Shishu Sanskar Kendras in the Keshiyari block. Four were in and around Kukai village, in the Lalua gram panchayat area.

The workings of these Shishu Sanskar Kendras were similar to those of the schools run by the Ekal Abhiyan. The schools had about thirty students each from two or three adjoining villages. They were taught health and hygiene, singing, recitation, mathematics, dance, drawing, tradition, ethics and etiquette. They were told about tribal and national heroes, and tribal and national culture and heritage. Worship of images of Bharat Mata, Saraswati and Ram were integral to the classes, which were conducted for about two to three hours every evening. Students paid a nominal monthly fee; funds for the school largely came from sponsors. The annual cost of running such schools, including the minimal honorarium paid to the teachers, came to about Rs 8,000.

In 2009, Kalyan Ashram decided on expansion. A shishu mela (children's fair) was organized at Kukai on Children's Day on 14 November for the students of the Shishu Shikha Kendras and their guardians. Five volunteers of the Kalyan Ashram's Yuva Samiti came from Kolkata, bringing gifts. The saffron flag of the ashram was hoisted to kick off the celebrations, to chants of 'Bharat Mata Ki Jai'. There were games and contests for the students, who were gifted writing slates, chalk and toffees. The event ended with a picnic, with tribal song and dance performances. Over 250 people had participated in the mela.

The local residents had not come across such an event before. They started showing interest in the activities of the Kalyan Ashram, which decided to organize shishu melas in different parts of the state from the next year. The 2010 edition was held at Sonakhali in the Sunderbans area. The mela was back in Keshiyari in 2011 for its third edition. This time, 180 students from six Shishu Sanskar Kendras attended the day-long contests and festivities. The number of volunteers coming from Kolkata rose to sixty-three.

With time, other village development activities, such as construction of reservoirs for storing rainwater, were initiated. The standard size of these reservoirs was 10 feet (depth) by 100 feet (length) by 70 feet (breadth). Farmers were told that the reservoirs would help them during a weak monsoon, and that during a year of good monsoon the water could be used for a second crop. In most parts of Keshiyari, a second crop is rare on account of the lack of irrigation infrastructure. Between April and August 2014, ninety such reservoirs were built in south Bengal with the active participation of farmers. About a dozen of them were in Keshiyari. In most cases, Kalyan Ashram supplied the farmers with excavators.

At the February 2014 annual meeting of the Akhil Bhartiya Vanvasi Kalyan Ashram in Sikkim, it was decided to launch a pan-India village-development project. Veteran RSS pracharak Prakash Kamath was appointed as the all-India gram pramukh. The Bengal chapter too was asked to initiate gram vikas programmes. The first village identified was Pathar-Huri, about 10 km from Kukai, falling within Lalua's neighbouring panchayat of Kusumpur in Keshiary. Kalyan Ashram had already done some ground work here. It ran a Sanskar Kendra and had built reservoirs-on-field.

For the new project, described as the Jal-Jan-Jameen-Jaanwar-Jangal model, a team of fifteen volunteers was created, with ten from Kolkata and five from the local towns of Keshiyari and Kharagpur, said one of the members of the team of volunteers who did not wish to be identified. Primary work started with a medical camp at Pathar-Huri on 31 August 2014. A group of ninety-five volunteers came from Kolkata, including doctors, professionals, students and businessmen. The medical team included three general physicians, two ophthalmologists, two yoga experts and some medical students. A total of 380 villagers underwent a general health checkup. Simultaneously, a survey was conducted at sixty households about their source of income, cattle, fuel and water sources. A faculty member from IIT Kharagpur's agriculture department attended the camp, though in his individual capacity. He advised the villagers on various agricultural techniques, including the use of organic manure and water management.

The families that showed interest in VKA's proposition were later provided with or helped to buy biogas plants and three or four non-milch cows. Cowsheds were cemented to avoid waste of cow dung and cow urine. Manure pits were dug and biogas plants installed. The plants had the capacity to provide fuel for two hours of cooking per day. This was supposed to relieve the families of the task of gathering wood for their kitchens. The residue from the bio-gas plants was being promoted as organic manure. The villagers were also provided saplings of mango, guava, jamun, bel, neem, lemon, papaya, banana, tamarind and sahajana. These would be grown using organic manure. Each farmer was given about three dozen of saplings of different fruit trees.

As things changed in the village and its neighbourhood, bit by bit, Kalyan Ashram started bringing farmers from other districts – as also young urban enthusiasts – to show them how this experiment had started yielding results and promised a better future.

By 2018, Kalyan Ashram's initiatives had started taking the shape of a movement in parts of Keshiyari. The number of Shishu Shiksha Kendras had increased. And the BJP's popularity grew rapidly. Swayamsevaks of the RSS's jagran (awareness/campaign) wing gave momentum to the anti-TMC campaign, especially on the issue of corruption at the panchayat level, before the 2018 panchayat elections. The BJP captured both the Lalua and Kusumpur panchayats.

After the 2019 Lok Sabha elections at end-May 2019, the TMC office at Kukai village was put under lock and key by local BJP supporters. Most of these villages where VKA worked in Keshiyari did not have RSS shakhas, and the TMC never suspected that VKA's activities could be a threat to them.

Keshiary was only one of the centres for VKA's wholistic village development experiment. Work was progressing across the state. Headed by

Purbanchal Kalyan Ashram's secretary Biswanath Dey, organizing secretary Sushil Soren and joint-organizing secretary Mahadeb Gorai, Shishu Sanskar Kendras started mushrooming in south Bengal by 2013. In October that year, Purvanchal Kalyan Ashram claimed that they ran about 400 Sanskar Kendras in south Bengal. Nearly 300 of them had been established since the fall of the Left regime in May 2011. By 2018, the number of Sanskar Kendras in south Bengal exceeded 500.

Again, Sanskar Kendras were only one of VKA's projects. Another key activity was the running of hostels for tribal students from economically deprived backgrounds, who studied in government-run schools between classes five and ten. The hostels bear all their expenses, including education, food and clothing, till completion of their schooling. The funds are arranged through sponsorships. In Purulia, there were five such hostels for boys and one for girls, each accommodating thirty to forty students. There was one each in Birbhum and South 24 Parganas districts. These schools had pictures of Durga, Saraswati, Bharat Mata, Ram and sometimes Bajrang Bali in the rooms and had tulsi manchas in their compound.

The hostels served another purpose – as night shelter for the teams of doctors from Kolkata and its suburbs visiting the rural pockets to participate in free health camps. It was around October–November 2011 that Kalyan Ashram had built a team of volunteers comprising doctors and medical students. By the end of 2015, the team had conducted more than 100 medical camps in the districts of Purulia, Bankura, Birbhum, Jhargram and West Midnapore, almost always in villages in the vicinity of the hostels.

Explaining how medical camps helped the organizations spread their influence in new areas, *Van Samvad*, a Hindi publication of Purvanchal Kalyan Ashram of 2018,[17] narrated a story from Purulia district, without specifying the exact location. When a woman volunteer living in one of the remote villages told her neighbours that doctors from Kolkata would conduct a free health checkup and medicine distribution camp at their village, no one took her seriously. People even made fun of her. But when, in a few days, the camp indeed took place and patients identified for cataract surgery were taken to Kolkata for the procedure, the volunteer's social prestige and influence rose. This, in turn, helped the volunteer organize other types of programmes, such as the Shishu Shiksha Kendra.

Vishwa Hindu Parishad

The VHP, the Sangh Parivar organization with the largest mass base after the BJP, played one of the most important roles in using Hindutva as a political tool against the Mamata Banerjee government. Spearheaded by Sachindranath Singha, the eastern India organizing secretary (later all-India assistant secretary) – the undisputed 'boss' of the VHP in Bengal – the organization built up public contacts through social and religious work, helping orchestrate a surge in Hindu nationalist sentiments.

The VHP pushed for an expansion of its activities in West Bengal in 2011–2012. Praveen Togadia and Ashok Singhal came to Nabadwip in April 2013 for the Vijay Mahamantra Jap Shibir. Togadia paid a visit the next month again, attending an event at Taldi in the Sunderbans area on 26 May. He shared the dais with the RSS's south Bengal sanghachalak Atul Kumar Biswas and the VHP's Sachindranath Singha. Togadia lambasted the Mamata Banerjee government for the riots in the Tangra and Kultali areas in the same district. However, in January 2015, after Togadia's presence in Birbhum coincided with the VHP's ghar-wapsi programme to 'reconvert' tribal Christians to Hinduism in another part of the same district, the Mamata Banerjee government banned Togadia's entry to the state altogether, and issued a circular in April to this effect.

It did not have much of an impact on the VHP's expansion plan, though. From holding religious events and protests against atrocities on Hindus in Bangladesh and West Bengal, to organizing picnics, quiz competitions on Indian history, debates on contemporary issues, music and conch-shell-blowing contests for women, kabaddi tournaments for boys and girls, and health camps – VHP and its affiliated organizations multiplied their public contacts in the state within a very short period of time.

The VHP functions through a range of organizations attached to its wings: seva (social service), dharma prachar (religious campaign), samajik samarasata (social harmony) and dharmacharya sampark (contact with religious gurus) wings. The samajik samarasta wing worked towards reducing caste conflict. Caste unity is essential to Hindu unity, the Sangh Parivar believed. The seva wing's activities are categorized under the sectors of education, healthcare, child welfare, orphanages, women's empowerment, rural livelihood, socio-cultural activity and disaster relief. Its social work is mainly run through trusts. In March 2015, the VHP Bengal unit claimed to be running 160 seva works across Bengal. Of them, 121 were permanent seva projects in the field of educational, health and self-reliance.

The dharmacharya sampark wing maintained contact with the priests of various temples and spiritual gurus. The heads of several ashrams of the Bharat Sevashram Sangh (BSS) and its chain of Hindu Milan Mandirs worked in close collaboration with the VHP. One of them was Kolkata-based Swami Gurupadananda, who headed the countrywide chain of Hindu Milan Mandirs. BSS founder Swami Pranavananda's photograph and quotations can be seen at many events of the VHP and its affiliated-organizations. In Hooghly district, the VHP's Hooghly-Chinsurah 'prakhand'[18]had teachers of the Pranab Kanya Sangha, which has been running a primary school in Chinsurah town for years, closely associating with such events as Janmashtami and Raksha Bandhan, which involved children and, naturally, their mothers.

The VHP did not limit its religious campaigns to activities around Ram and Hanuman. Leaving the task of popularizing Ram and Hanuman to the Bajrang Dal and Hindu Jagran Manch, the VHP also focused on Krishna and Shiva (Shib, for the Bengalis). Janmashtami, Jhulan, Doljatra and Shibratri provided chances for better public engagement in this part of the country, where Ram and Hanuman have not been popular as deities. Krishna – Krishno as the Bengalis pronounce it – and Shib had not become 'political', and they were popular across Bengal.

The following set of directives issued by VHP's south Bengal unit for grassroots-level organizers for Shibratri in February 2018 throws some light on the way they went about their religious campaign.[19]

1. Organize the celebrations in Khands and Prakhands. It is better if mass committees are formed for conducting the celebrations.

2. Gather at Shiva temples at your own village or a neighbouring one.
3. It would be good if flags with Om Namah Shivay printed on them are hoisted at houses and public places.
4. Try to arrange for Prasad for the devotees.
5. Men and women volunteers need to be arranged.
6. After the programme, attempts should be made to build a permanent relationship with the organizers (of the temples).
7. Send photos of these activities to the state headquarters using WhatsApp.
8. We must strive to organize celebrations at as many places as possible.
9. We should try to ensure the prevalence of a religious atmosphere.
10. Saints and socially established personalities should be urged to remind people of the danger the society is facing and that the Hindus needed to be united to get out of the crises.

In March 2018, more than a hundred processions were taken out in various parts of the state on the occasion of Doljatra. In September, the VHP's district-level organizers were asked to ensure the celebration of Janmashtami in every community development block. The celebrations would include processions, religious talks, naam sankirtan, distribution of bhog/prasad and sports like handi bhango – the game of human pyramids breaking an (earthen) pot strung at a great elevation. Janmashtami celebrations finally took place for three days at about 750 locations, with about 100 processions taken out, according the VHP's claim.[20] At many places, these events were carried out under the banner of mass committees, such as the Krishna Bhavna Samiti at Konnagar in Hooghly district.

From the end of 2018, VHP started holding Hindu sammelans in different districts. On 9 December, a conference by the name of Biswa Shanti Yajna O Birat Hindu Sammelan was held at Islampur State Farm Colony in Uttar Dinajpur district. On 17 December, another, called Swami Shraddhananda Bolidan Dibos O Birat Hindu Sammmelan, was held at Egra, East Midnapore district. Similar conferences were held on 8 December at Balarampur in Purulia district and at Helabattla Milani Maidan at Barasat in North 24 Parganas district. It appeared from the speeches at these conferences, captured in video clippings circulated online, that the purpose of these gatherings was twofold – to bring a religious bent to the Bengali psyche, and to unite Hindus to 'save Bengal from the jihadi elements, nurtured and protected by the Mamata Banerjee government'.

Akhil Bharatiya Vidyarthi Parishad (ABVP)

The Akhil Bharatiya Vidyarthi Parishad, or ABVP, started its activities in West Bengal in 1951. Since then and up to 2014, they only won elections in one or two colleges, on and off. But given that the state, by the end of the Left regime in 2011, had more than 400 colleges, winning one or two meant nothing more than a marginal presence. The ABVP presence had largely been limited to the areas bordering Bangladesh. Its main contribution lay in supplying the RSS and BJP with a flow of organizers.

It was in 2015 that the ABVP's presence was felt in the state for the first time. It had gone on an expansion drive at the end of 2012, and the college elections held in 2013 and 2014 revealed that left-wing student organizations had lost ground. After Modi came to power, the ABVP's activities stepped up and, in 2015, it managed to win elections in three colleges – one each in Kolkata, Purulia and Cooch Behar districts. They also won several seats in a few more colleges.

The same year, the ABVP conducted four training camps in four parts of the state – Cooch Behar and Raiganj in north Bengal and Kharagpur and Kolkata in south Bengal. More than 700 ABVP organizers attended these camps. More than eighty attendees offered to 'dedicate one year to the country' by working as vistaraks, or whole-timers for a limited-period, living away from home.

The ABVP took a two-pronged approach to draw students into its fold. The first was a high-voltage campaign on nationalism, and the other consisted of protesting and resisting the highhandedness of the TMC's student-wing leaders and their corrupt practices, especially during college admission time. By the end of 2018, the ABVP had formed units in about 400 colleges, including Industrial Training Institutes and polytechnic colleges.

While clashes between supporters of the Trinamool Chhatra Prarishad (TMCP) and the ABVP started making news quite frequently, the 20 September 2018 incident at Darivit high school in the Islampur area of Uttar Dinajpur district brought the organization to prominence across the state. The ABVP had been active at Darivit over the past few years. When students and their parents started expressing their resentment at the lack of teachers in the school for Bengali and science subjects, a few former students of the school who had now become ABVP organizers joined the current students in their protest. Meanwhile, the education department announced the filling up of two vacancies – for Sanskrit and Urdu.

These appointments added fuel to the fire, and the agitating students and their guardians did not allow the newly appointed teachers to join the school. But these teachers, who were freshers, had to join, as per government norms. So the education department sought the help of police to ensure the teachers could complete their joining formalities. The tension on the campus kept escalating and, on 20 September, things came to a head. There are no reliable accounts of how exactly it happened, apart from a minor scuffle between the police and agitators on the campus, but in the presence of police, two ex-students, Tapas Barman and Rajesh Sarkar, died of bullet wounds.

The students and their guardians blamed the police for opening fire. The police denied the charge. It was no big deal to prove whether the police opened fire or not. This could be done by simply carrying out ballistic examinations of the bullets found in the bodies of the deceased. But there was no news of any ballistic examination even after one year of the incident.

Politically, the Sangh Parivar wanted to use this development to create a turning point in Bengal politics. 'Students wanted teachers for Bengali but were given one for Urdu. This is nothing but Mamata Banerjee's attempt to Islamize West Bengal,' was the common statement that came from all ABVP leaders in Bengal – from Saptarshi Sarkar to Subir Haldar – as also from the state's senior BJP leaders.

'Two students agitating to study in their mother language were killed in police firing – what can be worse? This is our topmost issue in Bengal at present,' the south Bengal secretary of the RSS, Jisnu Basu, said.[21]

Their propaganda instantly triggered a political debate. Md. Salim, the local CPM MP, accused the saffron camp of distorting facts. 'The fact was that students were demanding teachers for science subjects and Bengali, as the positions were lying vacant. Instead, they got teachers for Urdu and Sanskrit. Whether the appointing authority played a practical joke on the students remains to be known, but the RSS is giving a direct twist to the tale and is doing it blatantly. No ABVP, BJP or RSS leader mentioned the appointment of the Sanskrit teacher and none of them mentioned that the students were also demanding teachers for science subjects,' Salim alleged.

The saffron camp, nevertheless, launched a statewide campaign against the Mamata Banerjee government's planned 'imposition of Urdu on Bengali'. Social media platforms were flooded with their version of the story. Over the following months, it was around Darivit that the Sangh Parivar's work on polarization of north Bengal progressed, especially in the districts of Uttar Dinajpur, Dakshin Dinajpur and Malda.

By early 2019, the ABVP had opened units in more than 400 colleges in the state, growing fivefold in five years, with Kishore Burman and Apangshu Sekhar Sil as the key organizers. After Burman was sent to Delhi with greater responsibilities, Sil replaced him as Bengal ABVP's organizing secretary. Sil had served several years in the northeast, including as coordinator for the ABVP's SEIL (Students' Experience in Interstate Living) project for several years before being sent to West Bengal.

Sewa Bharati

Vivekananda Vikash Parishad (VVP) was a newly registered NGO in 1989 when it started operating a free homoeopathy dispensary at Hetedoba village in Ichhapur gram panchayat, barely a few kilometers outside the Durgapur municipal area in Burdwan district. After lying low till 2010, running two dispensaries and four Shishu Sanskar Kendras in the villages of Hetedoba,

Benachiti and Ichhapur, the NGO's activities got a fillip in 2011, when it opened a computer training centre, Ichhapur Computer Academy, for local students and the youth, on 12 January – Vivekananda's birthday. This was followed up with a tailoring training centre for the local women.

The following days witnessed steady growth in the activities of VVP, a unit of Sewa Bharati, the social work wing of the RSS, which functions in West Bengal under the banner of Samaj Seba Bharati, an umbrella of numerous organizations working in the sectors of education, health and self-reliance.

Centring on Ichhapur – a medium-sized village with a population of 1,092 in 2011, of whom 517 and 316 belonged to the ST and SC communities, respectively – Vivekananda Vikash Parishad's activities spread fast in the panchayat area comprising nineteen villages. By January 2016, the organization was running twenty projects in the villages of Ichhapur, Patsawra, Banguri, Nildanga, Amlauki, Hetedoba and Benachiti. By July 2019, it was running forty-two in Ichhapur panchayat and in some slum areas in the Durgapur Municipal Corporation. They included twelve Shishu Sanskar Kendras and six coaching centres (for students from classes 8 to 12, with about 250 students.

Some villages had two Sanskar Kendras – one for students from pre-primary to class four, and the other for students from classes five to seven. There was a Matri Mandali for the mothers of the students. In mid-2019 the Matri Mandali in Ichhapur had about eighteen members who met every week, practised yoga together and discussed social issues. The guardians of the students were invited to three annual meetings to discuss their children's progress. Annual cultural programmes, sports and picnics were other ways of getting the family members involved.

'We call them Sanskar Kendras because we do not merely provide coaching to the students but we focus on complete personality development,' Manoj Chatterjee, the RSS's south Bengal sewa pramukh (chief) who looked after VVP's activities, told this author.

The Parishad also provided self-defence training to the local girls. By mid-2019, their judo and karate classes had about twenty girls. Homeopathy dispensaries had grown from one to four and 'neurotherapy centres' from one to two. Five self-help groups had been initiated – three in Banguri village alone – involving women who made toys and various kinds of bags. A five-year painting course was launched, upon the completion of which the Parishad provided certificates. It also arranged for students to appear for the painting exams of Allahabad University.

As part of a larger programme, Sewa Bharati had put together a dedicated medical team comprising members of Arogya Bharati, ayurveda wing of the RSS, and National Medicos Organization, its allopathy wing, to conduct health camps at facilities run by Ekal Abhiyan, Vanvasi Kalyan Ashram, Vidya Bharati and other Sangh Parivar organizations.

Organizations similar to Vivekananda Vikash Parishad were functioning across the state. The Asansol-based Swadesh Vikash Kendra, which operated in Andal, Barabani and Burnpur in present-day West Burdwan district, ran sewing centres named Nivedita Selai Kendra, Saraswati Selai Kendra and Maa Durga Selai Kendra in Barabani, apart from Sanskar Kendras. At Bhebiya, in Hasnabad area of North 24 Parganas district, Dr Hedgewar Gram Vikash Samiti has been working since 2002.

They organize eye camps and do free cataract surgeries. They also rewarded the better ones among the local students. During these 'talent honour programmes', they always had the parents of the children saying a few words. Images of Bharat Mata and Saraswati always adorn their venues. Maa Sarada Gram Vikas Samiti, which worked at Tarakeshwar in Hooghly district, established a Dharma Jagaran Kendra, Swami Vivekananda Shishu Sanskar Kendra, Dr Hegdewar Charitable Clinic and also a library. At Canning in South 24 Parganas, Annapurna Gram Vikas Samiti ran the Bhagini Nivedita Shishu Sanskar Kendra, a library, a bhajan mandali and a vermicompost training centre.

Akhil Bharatiya Rashtriya Shaikshik Mahasangha (ABRSM)

Bangiya Shikshak O Shikshakarmi Sangha, an organization for high school teachers, had a little over 1,000 members in 2011, when the change of regime took place in the state. It grew to 2,000 members by the end of

2013. By December 2016, membership rose to 3,500, and by 2017, it had district committee formations in nineteen of the state's twenty-three districts. And their district conferences began to draw the attention of the Bengali press. The Birbhum district conference in November 2017 had seen the attendance of more than 200 teachers, according to a report in the Bengali daily *Ei Samay*[22]. The organization grew faster in the north Bengal districts of Cooch Behar, Alipurduar, North Dinajpur, South Dinajpur and Jalpaiguri, where block-level conferences had been held by 2019.

It was one of the three teachers' organizations in the state affiliated to the Akhil Bharatiya Rashtriya Shaikshik Mahasangha (ABRSM), the teachers' wing of the RSS. The two other organizations were Bangiya Naba Unmesh Prathamik Sikshak Sangha, for primary school teachers, and Jatiyatabadi Adhyapak O Gobeshok Sangha, for college and university teachers and research scholars. All of them witnessed a spike in membership, with the ABRSM's state organizing secretary Alok Chattopadhyay playing the key role, and they gradually became more influential than the teachers' cell of the Bengal BJP.

Members of these organizations had a role in influencing the opinions of the guardians of their pupils. On Guru Purnima, they would organize programmes to felicitate senior and retired teachers. Guruvandan karyakram was observed in July, on the birthday of Vyasa. Talks on the Indian tradition of respecting the guru, teachers, parents and elders were a given on such occasions. These outfits also organized protests. In north Bengal, especially, different units of these teachers' organizations conducted blood donation camps to protest the killings at Darivit high school campus. In some schools, such as the ones in Cooch Behar district, their organizations for primary school teachers took up issues on behalf of the non-teaching staff and also the matter of child-care leave for female teachers.

There was another impact of these school units – orders of the state government or school authorities that could become controversial were spotted and brought to the limelight. For instance, the June 2019 circular of the state minority affairs department seeking information on schools with more than 70 per cent students belonging to the minority communities – so that dining halls for mid-day meals could be built in those schools – had been leaked on social media by members of the Bangiya Naba Unmesh Prathamik Sikshak Sangha's Cooch Behar district unit.

This stirred a major controversy, with the BJP alleging that the government was discriminating between children on religious grounds by building dining halls only for schools in Muslim-dominated areas. 'The West Bengal government has issued a circular whereby it has directed the school authorities where 70 per cent or more students are from the Muslim community to reserve a dining hall with seating arrangements for them. Why this discrimination between the students on the basis of religion? Is there some other mala fide motive behind this segregation? Another conspiracy?', Dilip Ghosh tweeted that very night. The next day, CPM MLA Sujan Chakraborty met Mamata Banerjee in her room in the state assembly to press for an investigation.

The government later defended the circular, clarifying that dining halls were being built from the education department's budget in most of the schools and that the gaps between budget allocation and fund requirement was being filled by diverting a portion of funds from the allocation to the minority affairs department. 'And, in any case, it is not for the use of the minority community students alone; the dining halls are for the use of all students,' minority affairs minister Giasuddin Molla said[23]. But the controversy continued, with the BJP and the RSS-backed teachers' organizations claiming that the government was backtracking after the alarm had been raised.

On 4 July 2019, the secretary of the RSS in south Bengal, Jisnu Basu, attended the annual general meeting of Bangiya Naba Unmesh Prathamik Sikshak Sangh. He explained how the teachers needed to defend and propagate the new education policy of the Central government.

Sahakara Bharati

The Sahakara Bharati, the cooperative wing of the RSS, started activities in West Bengal in 2001, but could not make much of a headway because of the Left's dominance in Bengal's cooperative movement. It was decided in 2016 that the organization would be revived and strengthened across the state, focusing on weavers, fishermen, farmers, milkmen and small tea producers, besides producers of natural honey, Tulaipanji rice, incense sticks, organic soaps, and other such items.

The first state conference was held in Adyapith auditorium in Kolkata on 24 June 2017. A total of 454 delegates from all districts of the state attended the two-day conference to elect its state executive committee. The delegates included 126 women. Senior RSS functionaries, including Advaita Charan Dutta (akhil Bharatiya saha pracharak pramukh), Uday Joshi (all-India general secretary of Sahakar Bharati), Vijay Debangan (all-India organizing secretary of Sahakar Bharati), Sunilpada Goswami, (member of the RSS national executive committee) and Pradip Joshi (eastern India pracharak of the RSS). Dutta launched the outfit's magazine, *Samobay Probah.*

During the following months, Bibekananda Patra, the newly elected organizing secretary of Sahakar Bharati, who was a pracharak and lived at Keshav Bhavan, the RSS's south Bengal headquarters, went on a tour of the districts. Often, he had meetings in different blocks on successive dates with the local people to help establish self-help groups and cooperative societies. He travelled extensively in the state: across Jhargram, Purulia, Bankura, Cooch Behar, Alipurduars and Jalpaiguri. Almost every such meeting witnessed participation of 100 to 250 local residents, predominantly women.

By November 2017, the first district committee was set up in Purulia. Fifteen Samobay Krishi Unnayan Samitis (agricultural cooperative societies) and self-help groups participated in a conference, whose main theme was, 'Corruption and Political Interference-free Cooperatives'. By this time, the Trinamool Congress had captured large numbers of cooperative societies from the control of the Left. Activities of the Sahakar Bharati surged following the conference.

The first women's conference was held in September 2018. In November, the dairy wing held a convention in Murshidabad district, which, significantly, has the state's highest concentration of Muslims (67.2 per cent in 2011), with the plan of forming dairy cooperatives. In north Bengal's tea belt, the organization initiated cooperative societies for small tea growers, who produce nearly 45 per cent of West Bengal's and Assam's total tea output but earn too little. Bharatiya Kshudra Cha Chashi Sangha was formed in 2018 to specifically address their concerns. More than 100 small growers who owned three to twenty bighas of land each came together to form the Rajganj Shree Lakshmi Small Tea Growers & Agro Industrial Co-operative Society Ltd. Land had been purchased by early 2019. 'There is a provision in Tea Board of India's rules for 40 per cent subsidy for processing units put up for self-help groups and cooperatives if more than 50 per cent of the members are from the tribal population. In our case, about 70 per cent of the members are from the tribal community,' Bibekananda Patra told this author.

By June 2019, the organization got eighteen cooperatives registered in West Bengal, and paperwork for another five dozen were under preparation. Some of these were Sankalpa Bharati Parisheba Co-operative Society (Pandapara, Jalpaiguri), Matribhumi Multipurpose Co-operative Society Ltd, (Tamluk, Purba Medinipur), Bangalpur Mahila Co-operative Society Ltd. (Bagnan, Howrah), Rajganj (Talma) Tea and Agro Processing Co-operative and Rajganj Shree Lakshmi Small Tea Growers & Agro Industrial Co-operative Society Ltd (North Dinajpur).

Kreeda Bharati

The sports wing of the RSS made its presence felt once a year – on International Yoga Day, its flagship event – when it organized yoga sessions on the streets in most of the prominent towns of West Bengal. Through the rest of the year, the organization maintained a low profile, but quietly increased its public contacts by establishing relations with sports and cultural clubs, yoga and martial art training centres and coaching centres for wrestling, kabaddi and archery, across the state. It tied up with clubs – both in rural and urban areas – to organize special yoga and karate training camps, and helped these centres hold competitions in indigenous sports.

Often, its units would not function under the banner of Kreeda Bharati. Its volunteers tried to open one- or two-teacher coaching centres at the village level using some nondescript banners. Sometimes, it convinced locally-known sports personalities to start such centres for football, karate, yoga and kabaddi.

With Madhumoy Nath, a pracharak, and Bibhas Majumdar as the key organizers, Kreeda Bharati spread its network across Bengal's rural belt, as also in some slum areas in towns, tying up with formal schools, with Shishu Sanskar Kendras and hostels run by the various Sangh Parivar outfits, and with rural and suburban clubs to make their sports events more popular. In the process it expanded its own reach of public contact. Pictures of Bharat Mata and the saffron flag could always be seen at these sports venues.

To encourage the popularity of sports, mothers of successful sports personalities are given the Veer Jijamata award, named after the mother of the Maratha warrior Shivaji. In 2018, the Veer Jijamata awards were given to: Shipra Ghosh, mother of the 2017 Commonwealth Games medallist in weightlifting, Kaustav Ghosh; and Bimala Biswas, mother of mountaineer Debashis Biswas. The same awards were also given at felicitation ceremonies held at the district level and, in some places, at the block level. During the events, references to Shivaji and his brand of Hindu patriotism naturally featured in the discussions.

Hindu Jagran Manch

The formation of the Manch in Bengal was initiated in 2011, and the HJM's south Bengal chapter was officially established the next year, with the veteran Somen Das as president, Swarup Dutta as general secretary and Dilip Ghosh as organizing secretary.

It straightaway focused on bringing out Ram Nabomi processions in new areas. 'We built the organization around Ram Nabomi,' Dilip Ghosh told this author.[24] 'Ram is a Kshatriya. He epitomizes the Hindu fighting spirit. Hindus need to overcome fear to prevent Muslim dominance in politics and the virtual takeover of the administration by them.'

After Dilip Ghosh went to the BJP, Tapas Barik took charge as the HJM organizing secretary in the state. Ashutosh Mandal became its president in 2017. By that time, the HJM had its units in nearly all of West Bengal's 343 administrative blocks, and in some cases even had panchayat-level units.

Young men and boys were drawn into the organization through its youth wing, Hindu Yuva Vahini, and such events as Bharat Mata Puja, Akhand Bharat Sankalp Divas (around 15 August) and Rashtra Suraksha Divas (on 13 December, commemorating the 2001 attack on the Indian parliament), blood donation camps or the creation of Hanuman temples.

The HJM had a two-pronged approach towards creating its grassroots-level network. One was to campaign on general ideological issues, and the other was to build local-level movements concerning local issues. From August 2016, the HJM tried to organize a movement against cow slaughter at Rasapunja area, within the jurisdiction of Bishnupur police station in South 24 Parganas district. They got the local residents to petition the local and state administration to enforce the West Bengal Animal Slaughter Control Act. In 2016, at Baruipur in South 24 Parganas, members of the Majerhat Bot-tola Club were encouraged and assisted to take out a Bijoya Doshomi procession on the day of Muharram, deliberately ignoring Chief Minister Mamata Banerjee's appeal to community puja organizers to avoid Durga immersion processions on that particular day.

At Gaighata in North 24 Parganas, the HJM members had built a rapport with several local clubs over the issue of campaigning against 'love jihad'. When, in June 2018, a Hindu girl, a resident of Aamkola village, eloped with her Muslim boyfriend, a resident of Angulkata village, the HJM members stood by the Hindu family to trace their daughter, even though she had recently turned eighteen. The HJM organizers gathered members of several local clubs to search for the Muslim youth, though in vain.

Every few months the HJM organized major events in Kolkata – essentially to simply announce their presence. In January 2016, they organized protests in Kolkata against the lawlessness displayed by Muslim mobs in Kaliachak in Malda district when they attacked the local police station. In June 2016, a protest rally was organized from College Street in north Kolkata to Esplanade in central Kolkata where, on Rani Rashmoni Road, the HJM held a public meeting, protesting atrocities against the Hindus in Bangladesh. In November the same year, a procession was taken out in Kolkata demanding protection of the fundamental rights of the Hindus in West Bengal.

In December 2017, a protest was organized in Kolkata against the male and female leads in the Bengali film *Rong Beronger Korhi* being named Ram and Sita. The grounds for the protest was that the movie showed this couple separating. Their names must be changed, the protesters demanded. On the 28 July 2018, the HJM staged a demonstration in front of Hare Street police station in Kolkata to protest the resolution passed in the state assembly to rename the state as Bangla. They alleged that it was an attempt to dilute and relegate to the backburner the legacy of Syama Prasad Mookerjee.

Each HJM-backed rally grew larger than the previous one and, by the beginning of 2019, the HJM had block-level committees in almost all of north Bengal and in many parts of south Bengal.

The HJM organized a number of Hindu sammelans in many districts of the state during 2017 and 2018, but their biggest show in the state took place on 15 December 2018 at Shahid Minar ground in Kolkata. From the dais of the Virat Hindu Sammelan, Hindutva leaders from Bengal as well as from outside the state, including RSS pracharak Suman Kumar, the eastern region organizing secretary of the HJM, and Sadhvi Saraswati of Sanatan Dharma Prachar Seva Samiti, lambasted the Bangladesh government for failing to protect the Hindu minorities, took digs at Mamata Banerjee for 'trying to turn West Bengal into West Bangladesh' and sought expulsion of all illegal Muslim Bangladeshi immigrants from the state.

Due to Dilip Ghosh's stint at the HJM before joining the BJP, HJM members and organizers worked closely with the BJP's grassroots-level organizers. Nishith Dutta, who worked closely with Dilip Ghosh at the Hindu Jagaran Manch during 2013-14, gradually became a member of the state BJP's cooperative cell, even as he continued as an organizer at the HJM. He also headed the RSS-backed Ganga Samagra Abhiyan's south Bengal chapter. BJP's cooperative cell also had Mrinal Kanjilal as a member since 2017. Kanjilal, who had served as a pracharak for over four decades, had been the spokesperson of the Hindu Jagran Manch south Bengal chapter till 2017, when Dilip Ghosh brought him into the BJP to edit the party's Bengali mouthpiece *Kamol Barta*.

EIGHT

Changing Equations

The Rise and Rise of Dilip Ghosh

HE CALLED JADAVPUR UNIVERSITY'S women students 'behaya' or shameless,[1] threatened to pull its professors by their collars and throw them out of the campus;[2] he asked whether the Nobel laureate economist Amartya Sen had made any noteworthy contributions at all;[3] he suggested that intellectuals should be beaten with shoes. Sometimes he urged people to tie policemen to trees,[4] or to tear down their uniforms, and on one occasion threatened that the law-keepers would be skinned alive for their partial actions.[5] He warned TMC workers he would rub salt all over their body after skinning them alive[6] and even threatened to set Mamata Banerjee's house on fire.[7]

He was variously called a loudmouth, a loose cannon, someone who had earned notoriety with his hate speeches, and a person of unparalleled nuisance value. Dilip Ghosh was a man who was being talked about. He was not the only loudmouth in Bengal politics. There were loudmouths in the TMC and the CPM, too. Anubrata Mondal, the TMC's Birbhum district president, had publicly asked supporters to hurl bombs at the police if they tried to come to the aid of independent candidates in the rural elections.

Later, when the controversy snowballed, Mondal said it was a 'slip of the tongue'. In most cases, however, the loudmouths in the districts used to apologize after a rebuke from the state leadership.

But Dilip Ghosh was at the top in his organization. He was leading the verbal duel, 'the battle of nerves', as BJP leaders often called it. Here was a fearless leader who could talk to the TMC, his eyes looking into their eyes; he was the one who would never apologize, even if he said that police stations should be bombed.

Barely a few days after the 2016 assembly elections, he led the gherao of the office of the superintendent of police at West Midnapore. From the dais, he issued a warning to the TMC: 'We too are good at fighting. Half the people here have RSS training. It's no big deal for me to break two or three necks with my bare hands. I am daring them to put all policemen off duty for a week and we will see who has drunk how much of their mother's milk. The sound of breaking bones will travel down to Kalighat. We do not want that though.'[8]

He then assured party workers and supporters of the backing from the Central government and the party. 'State leaders have reached every spot where violence took place since the elections. We are the only Opposition party who are still on the road. We are on the road and we will be on the road. Don't fear. The whole country is with you. The Central government is with you. The state unit president is with you.'

He kept his word. He was on the road. He spent much more time in the districts than at the party headquarters in Kolkata. His convoy came under attack from TMC workers several times. He was shown black flags. TMC supporters shouted 'go back' slogans at him, encircling his car. On one occasion, TMC workers were seen among a crowd pushing Ghosh. His car was vandalized a few times. But he withstood all these attacks. He addressed scheduled public meetings even after the police had denied permission for them. He led protest rallies defying the administration. In a very short span of time, his attitude created a follower group much wider than any other Bengal BJP veteran's. His events were drawing bigger crowds and his speeches received louder applause as he continued with his '*gorom gorom boktrita*' (inflammatory speeches).

Interacting with journalists at the state unit headquarters a little after the police registered a case against him for 'hate speech', he displayed absolute nonchalance, '*Ami to sob somoy gorom gorom e boli* (I always deliver inflammatory speeches). *Gorom gorom ekhon dorkar achhe* (It is the need of the hour). I find it ridiculous that the police who fail to protect our workers from the TMC's hooliganism would register a case against me for hate speech. I am merely speaking. But the TMC is acting!'

Sometime in July 2017, after leading a protest march in Kolkata against communal violence in the Basirhat sub-division of North 24 Parganas, Ghosh said: 'Look at our bearded intellectuals. Some Akhlaq[9] has died somewhere. We do not know whether he was run over or bitten by a dog. But for him, here at Dharmatala, their eyes are flooding with tears.'

About Amartya Sen, he said, 'He is very upset that he was removed from the vice-chancellor's post at Nalanda. What's his achievement? But these types of people are now Bengal's pride – the people who have no spine or character.'[10]

His attacks on intellectuals had become commonplace, but he was never in any dilemma about it. 'What intellectuals! What kind of intellectuals are they? They are harming the society. Instead of nation building, all these intellectuals are engaged in promoting anti-national activities. They need to be thoroughly exposed. People should have no regard for them whatsoever.'[11]

This author once asked Ghosh if his anti-intellectual attitude came from the fact that most of Bengal's prominent public intellectuals or opinionmakers are essentially opposed to the saffron camp. He instantly said yes. 'We have come to power (in India) despite vehement opposition from the media and the Leftist intellectuals. Why should we worship them?'

To journalists, he always spoke his mind. For journalists following politics, covering Dilip Ghosh was easy. He never tried to be politically correct and he never spoke off the record. Journalists hardly ever received a rebuttal or rejoinder from him for quoting him on any matter, a controversy of any magnitude.[12] Also, he returned missed calls. It was not long after he took charge of the state unit that this author once asked him what he felt about frequently courting controversy with his speeches.

His answer was candid: 'You people do not give us coverage otherwise. I say a few loud things and then you create a hullabaloo. You all show my speeches. You now follow me everywhere. All my meetings get media coverage. If this is what it takes to draw media attention, I can do it.'

He also argued that the morale of Opposition workers needed to be kept high and this would not be possible without speaking 'rough and tough', the way Mamata Banerjee preferred to describe herself.

By 2018, '*Pher Belagam Dilip*' (Dilip crosses the line again), '*Pher Kukotha Dilip-er*' (Dilip continues with his abuses) were among the frequently seen headlines in Bengali newspapers.

Nevertheless, he had emerged as the most popular Opposition leader in Bengal.

Enter Mukul Roy

Mukul Roy's return to the TMC – after his cold war with the party throughout 2015 – did not ensure him a comfortable life. Roy started cozying up to Mamata Banerjee from December 2015. In February 2016, she formalized Roy's return to the party by appointing him as one of the vice-presidents. This post, however, was in no way close to the positions he had held in the party barely a year and a half ago. He began to work towards regaining his earlier stature in the party, but that was not to be. A new 'number two' was rising in the party – the nephew, Mamata Banerjee's heir apparent. Roy made up his mind about what he would do after he was denied an opportunity to speak from the dais of the party's annual mega show of martyrs' day, on 21 July 2017.

In August that year, Mukul Roy's breakfast with Arun Jaitley at the latter's residence stirred much speculation. Roy told the media that he met Jaitley as the chairman of the parliamentary committee on travel, tourism and culture, a post to which his party had nominated him in 2016, a few months after he was reinstated in the leadership. His party did not buy this argument. Mamata Banerjee removed Roy from the post late in August. On 16 September, she reconstituted the TMC national and state committees. There was no significant change, apart from abolition of the post of national vice-president. Mukul Roy had no post in the party again. He had been shown the door.

The rest happened rapidly. On 25 September 2017, Roy announced his resignation from the TMC, and on 11 October resigned from the Rajya Sabha. On 3 November, he was at the BJP central office in New Delhi. After a closed-door meeting with Amit Shah, Ravi Shankar Prasad formally welcomed him into the party at a press meet, in the presence of Kailash Vijayvargiya, the BJP's Bengal 'observer'.

'With his kind of very experienced political activism, I am quite sure his coming to the BJP would help the party expand its footprint in Bengal,' Prasad said, after introducing Roy as 'a founder-member of the Trinamool Congress, who toiled for the expansion of the party and helped it come to power.'

The BJP did not offer him any post initially, but Roy's prominence among the BJP state unit leaders was made evident. He was merely a primary member, but a room had been allotted to him at the BJP's state unit office. Only three other leaders had their own rooms – state president Dilip Ghosh, his predecessor-cum-national secretary Rahul Sinha and state general secretary (organization) Subrato Chattopadhyay.

Roy embarked on a tour of various pockets across the state soon after, most of the times being accompanied by central leaders Kailash Vijayavargiya, Shiv Prakash and Dilip Ghosh. In December 2017, when asked about Roy's role in the party, Dilip Ghosh told journalists in Kolkata: 'He's guiding us.'

A Contest for the Runner-up

So, who was the Trinamool Congress's principal opponent? The answers were different for different periods. Until May 2018.

The Basirhat assembly bye-election in September 2014 saw the BJP winning, but in February 2015 they came third in the Bongaon Lok Sabha bye-election and second in the Krishnaganj assembly by-poll. Municipal elections held in 2015 exposed the BJP's organizational weakness, as their tally stood fourth, winning only ninety-seven of the 2,094 municipal wards, against the TMC's 1,428, the Left's 242 and the Congress's 187. The party painted yet another dismal picture in the 2016 assembly elections, with the BJP's vote share coming down to 10.16 per cent from 16.8 per cent in the 2014 Lok Sabha elections. It managed only three of the 294 assembly seats in the 2016 state election.

The bye-elections to one assembly and two Lok Sabha seats in November 2016 again saw a lacklustre performance by the party. In Cooch Behar Lok Sabha constituency, The TMC received 59.03 per cent of the vote; the BJP came second, with 28.32 per cent of the vote, while the Left and the Congress were wiped out, securing only 6.49 per cent and 2.49 per cent votes, respectively. In the Tamluk Lok Sabha constituency, which the TMC won by a mammoth margin of 4.97 lakh votes, bagging a 59.76 per cent vote share, the Left came second, with 21.62 per cent of votes, while the BJP's share stood at 15.06 per cent. In the Manteswar assembly seat, the TMC's vote share was as high as 77.59 per cent. The Left came second, but its vote share of 10.63 per cent was narrowly above the BJP's share.

The two assembly bye-elections held in 2017 presented contradictory pictures. In April, the BJP surprised Bengal's political circles by securing 30.97 per cent of the vote in the Kanthi assembly segment (part of Tamluk Lok Sabha constituency). The TMC won comfortably, securing 55.89 per cent of the vote. The Left candidate had his deposit forfeited, as he got only a 10.21 per cent vote share. However, in December, the Left came second at Sabang, with a vote share of 20.26 per cent. And the BJP, despite fielding a former CPM heavyweight in the district, ended with a vote share of only 18.67 per cent.

The February 2018 bye-elections to one Lok Sabha and one assembly seat indicated that the Left's fortunes were declining steadily. They stood slightly behind the BJP in Noapara assembly segment but way behind the BJP in the Uluberia Lok Sabha constituency. The crucial question was, where would the downward spiralling of the Left's vote share stop?

The rural elections in May 2018 were poised to be the acid test. Not for the TMC. They faced no threat. It was a battle for the runner-up.

Building Organization – the 'Gujarat Model'

Amit Shah is credited with introducing three organizational positions/structures in the BJP that were novel to any political organization, perhaps across India. By and large, booth committees[13] are considered the lowest possible organizational tier for a political party. Shah introduced another tier below the booth committee – 'panna pramukh'or 'panna prabhari', literally meaning 'page in-charge', a person effectively in charge of a page in the voters' list, usually comprising about sixty names. The panna pramukh would keep in touch with these sixty voters and ensure that all of them went to vote. This was first introduced in Gujarat sometime before the 2012 assembly elections.[14]

The second introduction, shakti kendra, was a tier above the booth committee. Overseeing five to seven booth committees, shakti kendras are an intermediary stage between the booth and mandal committees. The creation of shakti kendras started in Gujarat at the end of 2012 and was a full-fledged exercise by early 2013.

The third introduction was that of the vistarak (bistarok in Bengali), an idea borrowed from the RSS, launched at national level in the beginning of 2017. As in the RSS, vistaraks are whole-timers for a limited-period (six months to a year), who are to be deputed to a district other than their home districts. They received a monthly stipend from the party for their basic expenses, and were also provided with motorbikes and smartphones.

Having an organizational network that reached down to each page of the voters' list was a new high for a political party. For a comparison, in West Bengal, the CPM, which held influence for more than half a century, had branch committees as its lowest organizational structure. Branch committees used to oversee about three or four booths each. Each booth usually had 600 to 1,300 voters in Bengal. The CPM used to form booth committees ahead of every election but they were dissolved once the polls were over. Above its branch committees, the CPM had the local committee, zonal committee (congruent with assembly seats), district committee, state committee and state secretariat.

The TMC, until coming to power in 2011, had its anchal committees (congruent with gram panchayats) and ward committees (in municipal areas) as its lowest organizational tier. Each anchal or gram panchayat comprised seven to twenty-three booths. Above the anchal were the block (congruent with assembly seats) and district committees. The TMC focused on forming committees in all of the state's (roughly) 78,000 booths only after its 2009 Lok Sabha election success.

The Bengal BJP's organization had been in disarray. Up to 2014, it mostly had the district and mandal committees below the state committee. Not all mandal committees were functional. Moreover, the BJP's mandal committees in Bengal mostly covered one municipality or one community development block, an area consisting of 210–260 booths. The area under a mandal committee in Bengal was three times the size of the BJP's mandal areas in states where the party had a traditional base, as in Gujarat and Madhya Pradesh.[15] There was no committee in more than two-thirds of the state's 78,000 booths.

The first thing Amit Shah focused on after the party's disappointing performance in the 2016 assembly elections was to reshape the Bengal BJP organizationally. Work on this began at the two-day 'chintan baithak' at Diamond Harbour. Kailash Vijayvargiya and Shiv Prakash lectured the state leadership for two days, starting 17 December 2016. The two put all their energies into convincing the state unit leaders about the necessity of strengthening the organizational structure. More posts needed to be created and more grassroots-level supporters and organizers needed to be engaged and assigned new responsibilities. All the state unit members were asked to spend three days in the districts and engage with grassroots-level organizers. These visits were to be completed by 31 December.

There was another notable development. Kailash Vijayvargiya told the state unit leaders in no uncertain terms that Mamata Banerjee was the party's prime concern. 'Rahul Gandhi has no acceptance in the Congress. There is no gain worrying about him. However, Mamata is consistently provoking the regional powers against Modi-ji. We, therefore, need to corner Mamata politically,' Vijayvargiya told the attendees in a closed-door meeting, according to a state unit member who spoke to this author on condition of anonymity.[16]

By early 2017, the state BJP organization was divided into five zones – north Bengal, Rarh (south-western), Nabadwip (south-central), Hooghly-Midnapore (southern) and Kolkata. Each zone was to have a committee which would be convened by a state executive member. At the next level of organization were the district committees. Some of them were partitioned into two and some into three. Overall, the district committees were shaped to correspond with Lok Sabha constituencies. This was done in phases. As a result, while the state had twenty-three districts, the BJP created thirty-eight organizational districts.

At the next level, the mandal committees were split into two to three mandals each. Whereas previously, mandal committees looked after 210–270 booths, after 2017 they had only sixty to ninety booths under them. Thereby the number of mandals rose, from 464 in 2016 to over 1,200 by 2018, according to Dilip Ghosh.

The other focus was on creating shakti kendras, comprising five to nine booths. For this purpose, vistaraks were appointed. The BJP state leadership was asked to find one vistarak each for the state's 294 assembly and 42 Lok Sabha seats. They would have to take responsibility in a district other than their own district of residence and live in the new place for several months building booth-level organization and shakti kendras. The party would provide for their monthly expenses. Finding dedicated workers who would live in a different district from their own for months together doing organizational work as whole-timers – that too, for a minimal monthly payment – was not easy. By early 2018, only 200 vistaraks had been identified. A good number of them were also swayamsevaks and ABVP members.

Vijayvargiya and Shiv Prakash, along with state leaders Dilip Ghosh and Subrato Chattopadhyay and the general secretaries, travelled Bengal's length and breadth to build the shakti kendras and reorganize mandal committees. They knew that reaching the level of panna (or prishtha) pramukh would take time, as the party did not have functional committees in a majority of the state's polling booths. Under these circumstances, shakti kendras could hold the key to organizational strengthening at the grassroots level.

The new structure required more organizers and office bearers – many more than the state BJP unit could supply. The RSS played a key role in these times of building the organization – guiding the state BJP with ideas and aiding them with manpower, most crucially, with skilled organizers with a clean background, that is, with no taint of corruption. The Left workers who had joined the BJP deserting their respective parties also came of great help. 'Left workers knew booth management; they were into it for years. Our workers were never as involved in the elections as to engage in booth-level vote management,' an RSS organizer-turned BJP leader in Jhargram district told this author while explaining the party's speedy growth in a very short span of time.

It was, however, the swayamsevaks who were shaping the Bengal BJP organization at various levels. Till the 2016 assembly elections, the state unit had three pracharaks – Dilip Ghosh, Amalendu Chattopadhyay (general secretary organization) and Subrato Chattopadhyay, joint general secretary (organization). After the elections, Amalendu Chattopadhyay was called back to the RSS and Subrato Chattopadhyay stepped into his shoes. Amalendu's removal was soon compensated with the induction of Deepanjan Guha, Hooghly district unit secretary of the RSS, in the state committee. He was given the crucial post of secretary (office), popularly called office secretary. So, Dilip Ghosh would lead from the front and Subrato Chattopadhyay and Deepanjan Guha would wield the keys of the organization staying away from the limelight. Shyamapada Mandal, a former pracharak from Birbhum district, was appointed as one of the secretaries of the state unit. Later, Guha was made Bengal BJP's 'training in-charge', and Mandal was appointed as his deputy. Mrinal Kanjilal, who served as a pracharak for years, came to the BJP as editor of *Kamol Barta* (lotus news), the party's weekly publication in Bengali.

Among the five general secretaries appointed in mid-2017, new entrants Sayantan Basu, Debashree Chaudhuri and Raju Banerjee had their roots in the ABVP. Chaudhuri's association with the RSS started during her school days as a member of Rashtra Sevika Samiti. Pratap Banerjee, who had been part of the state leadership since the 1990s, had undergone the RSS's third-year OTC training. Another general secretary, Sanjay Singh, had been with the BJP since the 1990s and a Howrah Municipal Corporation councillor for ten years. He, too, loved to call himself 'a proud swayamsevak'. Debjit Sarkar, who was appointed as the youth wing president in 2017, had been associated with the RSS from the time he was a student of class eight.

In the districts, the first round of change had come soon after Dilip Ghosh took charge in December 2015, when the presidents of twenty district units were changed. Changes kept happening thereafter. Shamit Das, the RSS's Midnapore district unit secretary, was made the BJP's Midnapore district unit president. The party's Jhargram district unit president Sukhamay Satpati came from a family of swayamsevaks.

The 150-odd vistaraks who had been identified till October 2017 underwent the first round of training in Kolkata on 31 October 2017. This was conducted by Shiv Prakash, Dilip Ghosh, Subrato Chattopadhyay, Deepanjan Guha and Shyamapada Mondal – all of them 'RSS men'. Next year, in 2018, two more organizers would be sent to the Bengal unit – Kishore Barman, a pracharak from the ABVP, as joint-general secretary (organization), and Arvind Menon, a pracharak-turned-BJP leader from Madhya Pradesh, as co-in-charge. In 2019, pracharak Amitabha Chakraborty would join the team as another joint-general secretary (organization).

Rural Polls – TMC's Self-goal

The panchayat elections were due in the middle of 2018, but the political tempo began to rise early that year, especially with the Trinamool Congress leaders, one after another, publicly setting the goal of making the panchayats free from any Opposition. That the TMC would sweep the elections was beyond doubt. But they wanted everything – every seat, every board. 'Birodhi-mukto (Opposition-free) panchayat' was their motto.

On 5 February, while presiding over the party's political workshop for north Bengal at the Siliguri stadium, Mamata Banerjee said, 'I will request the students and youths to put up such a fight in every district, every block and every village during the coming panchayat elections that opponents who are shedding crocodile tears find no place in future even to weep politically.'

Taking her message one step further, her nephew Abhishek Banerjee told the workers that the opponents would have to be subdued in each booth. Taking the cue, other leaders spread the message. On March 26, Transport Minister Suvendu Adhikary stoked a controversy by announcing that Rs 5 crore each would be granted to the panchayats where no Opposition party member would be elected.

The BJP started its ground work in end-2017 by organizing gheraos of TMC-run panchayats, alleging corruption. These agitations often resulted in physical clashes. On 24 February 2018, during the party's state-level workshop on the panchayat elections, in the presence of Kailash Vijayvargiya and Shiv Prakash, Dilip Ghosh gave grassroots-level leaders and organizers some vocal tonic: 'We have to contest as TMC's chief opponent. We have to contest to win. The people are scared to speak up but we have to give them a voice. We have to gherao the panchayats and declare the thieves as thieves. Take their names. Yes, name the pradhan, sabhapati and zilla parishad member and call them and their entire family a band of thieves. We will not get the police and the administration by our side but we will have to contest and win. You must have the courage to do that.'[17]

Ghosh then explained why the Left and the Congress stood no chance against the TMC despite their performance being better than the BJP's in the 2016 assembly elections: 'The Left and the Congress will not be able to put up a fight. Even if they try, they will fail because they will not get outside support. They will quit. No leader (from outside) will come to stand by them. But our national leaders and ministers will come and stand by us. So, we have to make the lotus the symbol of resistance against the TMC.'

And then, he pitched his speech higher: 'We must know that we have to be prepared to go from the police, court and hospital to the crematorium. I am telling you, the battle will end at crematoriums, and only those who have the guts will fight.'

He took a pause, a look at the media persons, who had been allowed in to cover the inaugural session, and said, 'Yes, I am reiterating my words, in the presence of the media, that they [TMC] should know that the battle will not end at the [polling] booths; we will drag it up to the crematoriums. We are preparing for the battle with this mindset.'[18]

At the same meeting, Mukul Roy was appointed convener of BJP's panchayat election committee. This was his first responsibility in the BJP after joining the party in November 2017.

'Making the panchayats Opposition-free is the motto of Mamata Banerjee. We know they will first try to block Opposition parties from filing nominations and then force those who submitted nominations to withdraw their candidature. She loves to get walkovers,' said Roy, 'But turning her dream into nightmare is our motto.'

On 31 March, the state election commissioner, Amarendra Kumar Singh, announced that the elections would be held on 1, 3 and 5 May and that the results would be announced on 8 May. Nearly 5.08 crore voters would decide the fate of candidates in 48,656 gram panchayat, 9,217 panchayat samiti and 825 zilla parishad seats. All the Opposition parties objected to the schedule. They had all been demanding at least a 45-day window for campaigning from the time of announcement of the dates. This schedule left them with less than a month for campaigning. Besides, there was no clarity as to whether Central paramilitary forces would be deputed to man the polling booths – a demand that all Opposition parties made. Singh, at his press briefing, had declined to take questions.

In an unprecedented show of bulldozing the Opposition, the TMC's four-stage scheme unfolded. In the first stage, Opposition party nominees were not to be allowed to submit their nomination papers, for which 9 April was the last date. They were threatened in their localities to stay away from the elections. Not trusting the effectiveness of its threats, the TMC had its workers surround block development offices (BDO) – where the nominations for gram panchayat and panchayat samiti elections are submitted – to ensure no Opposition party worker managed to even enter the premises. In many places, the police did not come to the rescue of the Opposition parties. The BJP approached the High Court of Calcutta but did not get much relief. On 9 April, in particular, the state witnessed unique scenes. Television channels showed TMC supporters encircling almost all block development and sub-divisional offices across the state to ensure the Opposition party nominees got no chance to enter the buildings at all.

As if this was not enough, the state election commission turned itself into a laughing stock after its volte face – it issued a notification on the night of 9 April, extending the deadline for filing nominations from 11 a.m. to 3 p.m. on 10 April, only to revoke the notification early in the morning of the tenth.

The legal battle dragged on, with the BJP and the CPM petitioning the Calcutta High Court. On the field, the TMC was busy unfolding the second phase of their grand scheme – forcing Opposition candidates who managed to submit nominations to withdraw their candidature. Their family members were intimidated. This yielded fruit at many places. For example, in Birbhum zilla parishad, nominations were filed in only one of the forty-two seats by any of the TMC's opponents. This was unbelievable. Never in the history of Bengal had a whole zilla parishad been won uncontested. One of the primary reasons is that zilla parishad nominations are submitted at the district magistrate's office. Being a high-security zone in the district, it is difficult for ruling party hooligans to block entry of Opposition nominees to the DM's office. But the TMC's district unit chief Anubrata Mandal made it possible. The BJP's Chitralekha Roy, the one person who battled a sea of hurdles to submit her nomination, finally gave in. She withdrew her nomination on 12 April.

By 16 April, when the nomination withdrawals were all done, it turned out that of the 48,636 seats at the gram panchayat level, elections were to be held in only 31,812 or 65 per cent of the seats. Of the 9,217 seats of panchayat samilty, elections were to be held in only 6,158, roughly two-thirds of the total seats. The rest were taken. The highest number of candidates put up by any Opposition party was the BJP's 34,507 for the total of 58,692 seats.

The TMC was bent on giving the Opposition no space. As the legal battle dragged on for a month, moving from one bench to another and from one court to another, the state government brought forward a new demand: it wanted the polling to be over before the month of Ramzan starting on 16 May, leaving no option but for the poll panel to conduct the elections on a single day, as the Election Commission was dependent on the state for manpower and infrastructural assistance. Due to the tradition of violence in the state, polls are generally conducted in Bengal in phases so that security personnel may travel from one region to another, ensuring that all booths identified as 'sensitive' could be put under adequate security. The government and the TMC leaders argued that security would not be a big deal because elections would not be held in nearly one third of the seats. The TMC had indeed made the Election Commission's task easier.

The Opposition lambasted the ruling TMC and the Election Commission (for not moving court against the state government). Muslim politicians, including the Congress's Abdul Mannan and the CPM's Md. Salim, condemned Mamata's attempt to play with religious sentiments in her electoral game plan. 'I remember so many elections during the month of Ramzan over the past few decades that I have lost count,' Mannan said, when this author telephoned him for his reaction.

On 14 May, the day of polling, unfolded the third phase of TMC's programme – violence and rigging. Of the 38,507 polling stations, most did not have adequate security. The policemen on guard were visibly in no mood to risk their own lives. Voters complained before TV channels that they were being asked not to turn up at the polling booths. Bombs were hurled in front of the booths to scare away those who had gathered the courage to arrive. The Opposition parties' polling agents were driven out of polling booths and the presiding officers 'taken into confidence'. Twelve persons died in the violence that happened that day, including four TMC workers.

Perhaps even this mockery of democracy was not enough for the TMC. So violence returned on the day of counting. Bombs were hurled at counting centres; Opposition party representatives were driven out of many counting centres or were allegedly forced to sign papers.

The final results, including uncontested victories, revealed that the TMC won 793 of 824 zilla parishad seats and the BJP 22. Of the 9,214 seats of the panchayat samiti, the TMC won 8,062, while the BJP won 769. And in gram panchayats, the TMC won 38,338 of the 48,636 seats. The BJP won 5,779, way ahead of the CPM's tally of 1,483 seats and the Congress's 1,066. Independents, mostly TMC rebels, won the rest.

The results formally announced the BJP as the TMC's principal challenger in West Bengal. There were no more doubts.

The TMC still had no idea what this clean sweep of the panchayats would cost them.

NINE

Battle for Bengal

National Register of Citizens

30 JULY 2018: MUKUL Chandra Bairagya, working president of Sarva Bharatiya Namashudra Vikash Parishad, an organization of Dalit refugees from Bangladesh, received a call from the office of Mamata Banerjee within hours of the publication of the second and final draft of the National Register of Citizens (NRC) that excluded nearly four million people living in Assam from citizenship. The news that had spread from Assam was that the majority of those excluded from the list were Bengalis, predominantly Hindus who had migrated from Bangladesh. Adding fuel to the fire, the BJP's Bengal unit chief, Dilip Ghosh, announced – on the very day of the publication of the NRC list on 30 July – that a similar exercise would be carried out in West Bengal to weed out all infiltrators.

Now the chief minister's office informed Bairagya that Banerjee was keen on meeting him and other leaders of the organization on 6 August. They readily agreed. They had previously sent as many as forty letters to the chief minister's office over the past four years, seeking an appointment with her, but never got a response.

During 2016–2018, Bairagya and the fortnightly newspaper he published, *Shudra Samachar*, had been spitting venom on other Dalit organizations, who campaigned for forging Dalit–Muslim unity against what they called the 'Brahmanical Hindutva brigade'. This prompted several Dalit activists in Bengal to dub Bairagya as an agent of the RSS, a charge that Bairagyo kept denying.

Earlier referred to as Chandals during the nineteenth and the twentieth centuries and treated as untouchables, the Namasudras had a long history of bitter struggle against the Hindu upper castes. According to the 1901 census, Namasudras were the third largest Hindu caste in Bengal. They historically hailed from the districts of Backerganj, Faridpur, Jessore, Noakhali and Khulna, all currently in Bangladesh. According to the census report of 1901, '(In East Bengal), principal caste is the Namashudra or Chandal, whose home is in the swamps of the delta, and whose numbers, in spite of wholesale conversions to Muhammadanism, still exceed a million.'

If atrocities and ill-treatment by the upper castes purportedly prompted hundreds of thousands of them to embrace Islam during the late medieval period and the British rule, those who did not convert to Islam suffered extensively at the hands of the Muslims after the Partition. This prompted them to migrate to West Bengal en masse since the 1950s, in an unending flow. The 2001 census of India put the number of Namasudras in West Bengal at over 3.2 million (4 per cent of the state's population). There had been no Namasudra population in pre-Independence West Bengal but they, in 2001, formed the state's second largest Dalit group, after the Rajbongshi community of Cooch Behar in north Bengal.

The majority of the Namasudras belong to the Matua sect. The Matua movement among the Namasudras was anti-Brahmanical, and was spearheaded by Harichand Thakur (1812-1878). It was spread further by his son, Guruchand Thakur. The All-India Matua Mahasangha, the supreme body of the Matua sect, was the most influential organization among the Dalit refugees in West Bengal. The tug of war between the TMC and the BJP had almost split the Mahasangha. Mamata Thakur, who led one faction of the Mahasangha, was the TMC MP from Bongaon. She swung into action to corner her rival faction, led by her brother-in-law Manjul Krishna's younger son Shantanu, who had been hobnobbing with BJP leaders Mukul Roy and Kailash Vijayvargiya.

When this author asked Bairagya what prompted the change in his stance overnight – from lambasting the Mamata Banerjee government to agreeing to a meeting with her — he said, 'The majority of Hindus who have been excluded from Assam's NRC list are Namasudras. They (BJP) have ditched us in Assam and we strongly condemn the BJP leadership's remarks that NRC will be applied in Bengal too,' Bairagyo said.

Over the phone, he sounded agitated: 'Members of our community have been supporting the BJP all along because of the sufferings they faced at the hands of the Muslims in Bangladesh. We did not appreciate Mamata Banerjee's politics of Muslim appeasement. But maybe it is time we start resisting the BJP.'

Hurting the Hindus with a citizenship screening exercise was never on the BJP's agenda. The Assam NRC was a fallout of the Assam Accord of 1985 signed between the Congress government at the Centre and two Assamese organizations that led violent protests targeting 'Bengali immigrants' since 1979. It had no scope for religious discrimination, as the BJP would have wanted. Coincidentally, the BJP held power at the Centre when its implementation started in 2015, following a Supreme Court order.

Mamata Banerjee, meanwhile, swung into action. 'Bengalis are under threat,' she declared in Kolkata on 31 July, and sent an eight-member delegation, including MPs and MLAs, to Assam on 2 August. They were detained at Silchar airport. The Assam administration cited imposition of section 144 of the CrPC, which barred movement of more than four persons. The detained MPs told the media that the Assam administration was treating the Bengalis in a discriminatory manner.

Banerjee's meeting with the Namasudra Bikash Parishad on 6 August ended on a happy note. She accepted all their demands. She promised the formation of a Namasudra Development Board at the earliest and instructed government officers over the phone, right in front of the Namasudra Bikash Parishad delegation, to address the issues the delegation had raised.

The saffron camp was alarmed. The refugees were one of their key target constituencies. Dilip Ghosh tried to douse the fire by saying that the case of Assam, with respect to the NRC, was overseen by the Supreme Court, but the case of West Bengal would be special, and the party would ensure protection of the Hindus by enacting the Citizenship Amendment Bill. 'Hindus need not fear. Not a single Hindu will have to leave the country. We will only drive out the Muslim infiltrators,' Dilip Ghosh kept repeating at various programmes of the party.

Panic spread nevertheless among the people and in the state BJP, as one after another, Bengali dailies and TV news channels kept publishing reports on the harassment of the Bengali people in Assam, mostly Hindus. The state units of the Left, the Congress and, of course, the TMC, made it routine to brand the BJP as anti-Bengali.

To counter this combined attack, the BJP scheduled an Amit Shah rally in Kolkata on 11 August, to be organized by the party's youth wing. Along most of his route from the Kolkata airport to the venue, there were banners and placards saying, 'Go Away, Anti-Bengali BJP'. The placards did not carry the name of TMC but were in the party's trademark colours of blue and white. The venue at the Maidan too had similar posters and placards placed all around.

In his speech, Shah focused on two issues – the NRC and the Bengali identity. On the NRC, Shah insisted that infiltrators had no place in India, but that the party was committed to giving citizenship to Hindus who have migrated from Bangladesh. Hindus need not panic at all. He then he elaborated on how the BJP had been the torchbearer of the 'original culture of Bengal'.

'On my way to the venue from the airport, I saw the route covered with hoardings and placards branding us as anti-Bengali. This is an absolute lie being spread by the Trinamool Congress. How can the BJP be anti-Bengali, especially when Syama Prasad Mookerjee was the founder of our organization?' Shah asked.

'We follow the ideals of Ramakrishna Paramahamsa and Swami Vivekananda. We are in no way anti-Bengali. We simply are anti-Mamata,'

Shah said, before taking a dig at Banerjee for allegedly interfering with Hindu festivals to appease Muslims.

He went on to say, 'I want to insist that having governments in nineteen states means nothing to us until we form the government in Syama Prasad Mookerjee's land, which is Bengal. We will build a Bengal that adheres to Bengal's original culture.'

A Rath Yatra that Could Not Take Place

Mamata Banerjee had announced from the dais at the party's annual flagship event on 21 July 2018 that a mega rally would be held at the Brigade Parade Ground in January 2019 where leaders of the major regional parties opposed to the Modi-Shah regime would gather. This would ring the death knell for Modi's rule, she had said. Two days later, the BJP Bengal unit announced a mega rath jatra spanning over a month and a half and passing through all of Bengal's 294 assembly constituencies. This would take place over December 2018 and January 2019. Three 'raths' – AC buses with modern amenities and carrying national-level BJP leaders – would start from three temples in the northern, south-eastern and south-western parts of the state and travel across three zones before converging in Kolkata.

'It's a ploy to keep Mamata busy at home,' psephologist Biswanath Chakraborty, a professor of political science at Rabindra Bharati University, told this author a day after the BJP announced the event. 'The more Mamata Banerjee tries to focus on forging an anti-Modi grand alliance of regional parties, the more would the BJP try to keep her busy in Bengal. With the BJP taking out a rath jatra across the state, Mamata Banerjee would certainly have to be busy with the law and order situation.'

The proposed jatra, formally named Ganatantra Bachao Jatra (Rally to Protect Democracy), was to be the launchpad for a high-pitched campaign targeting lack of democratic space and widespread corruption under the TMC rule. It would also serve as a tool for public contact. It became popularly known among the public as rath jatra, primarily because the BJP leaders kept referring to it as rath jatra instead of by its formal name. The formal name was chosen after a great deal of discussion, especially over the argument that a rath jatra could leave Muslims feeling isolated. There was resentment against the TMC even in some Muslim-dominated areas because of their experience during the last panchayat elections. The formal name though, hardly had the desired effect on the ground.

The project created public curiosity as details about the plan started emerging in the media from October onwards. Lal Krishna Advani's 1990 rath yatra seeking the construction of a Ram temple in place of the Babri Masjid, which helped create a turnaround story for the BJP nationally, had entered only one district of the state – Purulia, the western-most one. Now, there would be three jatras over six weeks or so. Union ministers and chief ministers of various BJP-ruled states would travel in those raths, which would stop at every town with populations of more than 5,000. One mega rally would be organized along the rath routes in each of the forty-two Lok Sabha constituencies. People started talking about it, in support of it, in opposition to it, or simply out of curiosity. It was the topic of conversation on public commutes, at workplaces and in the tea stall addas.

The TMC smelled in the jatra a 'devious' plan to stoke communal tension and create law and order disturbances. So did the Left and the Congress, who dared Mamata Banerjee to prove her secular credentials by stopping the jatra from happening. In late October, the CPM state secretary, Surjya Kanta Mishra, asked at a public rally whether Mamata Banerjee was capable of playing a Lalu Prasad Yadav, who had stopped Advani's rath in Bihar. The TMC leaders, in response, said that Jyoti Basu did not stop Advani's rath from entering Bengal. Some district-level TMC leaders, such as Anubrata Mandal of Birbhum and Jyoti Priya Mallick of North 24 Parganas, swore that the raths would not be allowed to reach their destinations. Some fringe Left organizations called for blockades on the rath's routes. The BJP's Dilip Ghosh and Locket Chatterjee shot back, saying the raths would run over those who dared to come in their way.

Mamata Banerjee called the plan 'a five-star travel venture', labelled it 'Rabon (Ravan) jatra' and many other names. Sometimes she urged her party workers to carry out a pobitro jatra or 'purification rally' the day after BJP's rath jatra, following the same path. All throughout, she was keeping her cards close to her chest on the question of what the administration would do. She told party workers at a public meeting at Kanthi in East Midnapore district: 'You concern yourselves with political programmes. I will deal with the administrative part.'

Soon, the BJP got the first hint of her plan. On 29 October, state unit vice-president Jay Prakash Majumdar sent a letter to the home secretary, Atri Bhattacharya, seeking an appointment to discuss various aspects of the jatra and its routes, including security and public convenience. There was no response. Another letter was sent on 5 November; it, too, elicited no response. In mid-November, a BJP delegation met Governor Keshari Nath Tripathy; meanwhile, Mukul Roy and Dilip Ghosh were publicly saying that the jatras would happen, irrespective of whether the state administration permitted them or not. However, finally they came to the decision of getting the programme cleared by the courts so that the party would not be blamed in case of untoward incidents. There was every possibility of provocation – from various quarters – and the BJP leaders themselves were not entirely confident that the crowds travelling with the raths would remain disciplined.

By the time they moved Calcutta High Court on 30 November, a Friday, the first rally was barely a week away. The first rath was supposed to start from the Madan Mohan temple in Cooch Behar district of north Bengal on 7 December, the next Friday. The second rath was to start from Kapil Muni's ashram at Gangasagar in the south-east on 9 December, and the third from Tarapith temple in the south-west on 13 December. The preparations had been completed and the bus for the north Bengal jatra had arrived. The hearing started in Justice Tapabrata Chakraborty's court on Tuesday, 4 December. It went on the next day too. Hoping the verdict would ultimately be in their favour, BJP leaders were busy preparing for the jatra. Amit Shah was supposed to arrive on 7 December, offer puja at the Madan Mohan temple, address a gathering at Jhinaidanga – about 15 km from the town – and then flag off the first rath.

In Cooch Behar, many of us journalists stayed at the two hotels where most of the BJP leaders were put up. Mukul Roy, Arvind Menon, Kailash Vijayvargiya, Rahul Sinha and Roopa Ganguly were in one of the hotels, and Dilip Ghosh and Shiv Prakash in the other.

On 6 June, Vijayvargiya, Roy, Ganguly, Menon and Ghosh could be seen pacing up and down the corridors of the second floor, sometimes briefly resting on the sofa in a corner and chatting with journalists, or sometimes holding indoor meetings in between as the hearing continued in the high court. The bad news came in the evening. The judge did not give permission for the rally, fixed 9 January as the next day of hearing and asked for postponement of the jatra till then.

Vijayvargiya was sitting in the lobby, encircled by journalists, when the news reached him. The leaders and their assistants were all glued to the television inside their hotel rooms for updates. Vijayvargiya's expression changed the moment he heard the news. It was about 4 p.m. Not much of the day's court hours was left. After about a minute, he asked his assistant, '*Mukul-da ko phone lagao.*' His voice was stone cold. They spoke very briefly, as Roy probably told him that he was coming over. Vijayvargiya then told his assistant, in the same expressionless voice, '*JP ko phone lagao.*' JP was Jay Prakash Majumdar, state unit vice-president, who was in charge of the high court case. Majumdar was asked to approach a division bench without losing time.

The division bench accepted their appeal and fixed 12.30 p.m. the next day for hearing the matter.

Given the high court's schedule, it was very unlikely that Shah's rally could take place at all. He was still in New Delhi. He would have to take a flight after the court verdict was given. State BJP leaders kept saying that Shah had tickets booked on several flights so that he could take whichever one was next after the court delivered its order. But it all appeared very difficult. How would he address a rally 15 km from the town after sundown? The venue itself was a paddy field.

Despite all these uncertainties, more than 10,000 people had gathered at Jhinaidanga from different parts of Cooch Behar the next morning, hoping against hope that the rally would happen, even if late in the evening. The crowd was upbeat and charged. Dilip Ghosh and Arvind Menon got on the dais, spoke for a few minutes and urged the workers to go back. 'The jatra will happen. Today or tomorrow. The TMC cannot stop it,' Ghosh said, amidst a roaring cheer from the audience.

Cooch Behar, over the past couple of years, had descended into lawlessness because of rampant infighting in the Trinamool Congress, resulting in frequent incidents of physical clashes, leading to injuries and even deaths. People were fed up with the TMC's infighting in the district, where the Opposition had virtually been bulldozed. The panchayat elections here saw unprecedented terror and violence, and the TMC had managed to win without any contest in 671 of 1,966 seats of the gram panchayat and in 105 of 366 seats of the panchayat samitis. In many of the seats where the party had to face a contest, the challenge came from disgruntled TMC leaders themselves and not from opposition parties.

Did the gathering of charged BJP supporters for a meeting that was mostly unlikely to happen signal something? Did it not?

The division bench of the high court criticized the state administration on many aspects, but did not give the BJP an immediate go-ahead. It would have to submit detailed route plans before the government, which would have to confer with three BJP leaders by 12 December and convey to the BJP by 14 December its decision on whether or not permission would be given for the jatra.

The BJP had to reschedule every rally, modify the jatra routes and their duration overnight.

After the state government conveyed its decision to deny permission late in the evening on 14 December, the legal battle dragged on for another month, from one bench to another, until the state government got a verdict in its favour in the Supreme Court, on 15 January.

The timing of the verdict couldn't have been sweeter for Mamata Banerjee. It was four days before her grand 'Opposition Unity Rally' at the Brigade Parade Ground, from where leaders of most of the regional parties in the nation were to launch their common mission against Modi. She was trying to play the anchor in forging a united front of regional parties as an alternative to the Modi government. It was at her initiative that leaders of so many opposition parties with such diverse interests were gathering on a single dais. Now, she had also stopped the BJP's chariot. What other proof was required to flaunt herself as the leading force against the BJP?

Mamata Banerjee declared that 19 January 2019 would be a historic day.

The BJP decided that its leaders would take out padajatras and public meetings in all constituencies in the state. 'If you deny us travel by car, we are ready to walk the extra mile, we are ready to walk the whole distance,' Dilip Ghosh said, summing up the party's mood.

'Biyallish-a Biyallish' vs *'Unish-a Half, Ekush-a Saaf'*

The TMC started to pitch Mamata Banerjee as a prime ministerial candidate from the end of 2018. It coined the slogan '*Biyallish-a Biyallish*', meaning 'forty-two out of forty-two', indicating that the party was targeting all of West Bengal's forty-two Lok Sabha seats. Her nephew Abhishek Banerjee[1] and transport minister Suvendu Adhikary[2] – the two most prominent youth leaders of the party – repeatedly said at public meetings in different districts that the impending Lok Sabha elections provided the best chance for a Bengali to be the prime minister. If the TMC won forty-two seats, it would definitely become the third largest party after the BJP and Congress in the Lok Sabha. The TMC leaders of various ranks argued that Modi was not coming back and that a government would be formed by the regional parties in the country. With the highest number of seats among these parties, the TMC would either play the king (or queen) or kingmaker. The 19 January rally at Brigade Parade Ground was part of the same scheme.

Mamata Banerjee had been ceaselessly accusing the Modi government of being 'autocratic', 'vindictive', and 'a complete failure', referring to Modi as the 'sardar (kingpin) of black money' and what not! She targeted the Centre for the demonetization of 2016, improper implementation of the Goods and Services Tax (GST), failure to recover black money as promised, the curtailing of democratic space and the harassment of opposition leaders using various central agencies, among a range of other issues.

The leaders of almost all regional entities opposed to the Modi regime gathered in Kolkata on 19 January – and they praised Mamata Banerjee for bringing so many of them together for the first time. The TMC now started thumping its chest, telling people across Bengal, on the streets and on social media, that Mamata Banerjee had emerged as Modi's key challenger and that she would lead the toppling of the Modi-Shah rule.

As the TMC stepped up its activities to build a narrative around a Mamata Banerjee-led toppling of the Modi regime, the BJP devised a twofold strategy. On the one hand, the so-called mahagathbandhan, or grand alliance, would be ridiculed at every opportunity and its inherent contradictions exposed. On the other, the rath jatra would be pegged as the dress rehearsal for uprooting the Mamata Banerjee government in 2021. Amit Shah had set the party's target at more than half of the state's Lok Sabha seats, following which the party coined the electoral slogan of *'Unish-a Half, Ekush-a Saaf'* (halved in 2019, swept in 2021). 'Strengthen Modi's hands by giving us twenty-three seats and you will get relief from TMC's highhandedness' – was BJP's simple message.

The top brass in the saffron camp had taken the target seriously. Twenty-two seats where the party stood a chance had been identified by early 2018. It had been decided that the party would work hard on all forty-two seats, but the constituencies in focus would get additional support from outside the state and outside the party. The party's vistaraks for these twenty-two seats were invited to the Sangh Parivar's coordination meeting at Maheshwari Sadan in south Kolkata on 2 April 2018. This was attended by Krishna Gopal, Vadla Bhagaiyah and Bidyut Mukherjee from the RSS, and Ramlal, Vijayvargiya, Shiv Prakash and state unit leaders from the BJP. In September 2018, about two dozen vistaraks were taken to Gujarat for training. They were taught by BJP's Gujarat unit president Jitu Vaghani,[3] and others.

Top RSS leaders provided these organizers with guidance from time to time. South Bengal sanghchalak Atul Kumar Biswas travelled to different districts during March and April 2019, to supervise jagran work, during which he met the vistaraks of the RSS and the BJP. On 17 April, for instance, Biswas was at Nabadwip in Nadia district. He had a meeting with the RSS vistarak in Nabadwip who was an ABVP organizer out on whole-time service for one year with the RSS. He also met the BJP's vistaraks for Ranaghat Lok Sabha and Nabadwip assembly seats, besides the ABVP leadership of Nabadwip College. The subject of the discussions with these organizers was campaign strategies. On 12 May, before the last phase of the elections, the RSS's all-India co-in-charge of pracharaks, Advaita Charan Dutta, addressed a special session for the BJP's vistaraks at Maheshwari Sadan in south Kolkata. Shiv Prakash was the other key speaker.

Mamata Banerjee, who had been lambasting Modi for curbing democratic space and harassing the Opposition, was herself accused of doing the same. One thing became evident to one and all – she had decided against allowing the BJP, in particular, any space, not even for public meetings. The TMC's interruption of the BJP's planned events was unprecedented in Bengal's history of political tussles. It was made extremely difficult for the BJP to find venues, hire vehicles to transport supporters and public address systems and to get any kind of administrative permission.

On 25 January 2019, the BJP announced that Modi would address a rally at Thakurnagar in the Bongaon Lok Sabha constituency on 2 February. It was expected that the largest field at Thakurnagar would be the venue. That very evening, the pro-TMC faction of Matua Mahasangha, led by the TMC MP Mamata Thakur, submitted an application seeking permission for the use of microphones on that field for a week-long kirtan event. Permission from the sub-divisional officer came the day after. The BJP was forced to choose a smaller venue. They, in fact, chose a mustard field and prepared it for the event by applying rollers. On 3 February, the district administration in North Dinajpur and South Dinajpur denied permission for the landing of Uttar Pradesh chief minister Yogi Adityanath's helicopter. On 6 February, former Jharkhand chief minister Arjun Munda had to return from Bankura district without speaking a word after police denied permission for the rally that had been planned.

On 31 January 2019, when Amit Shah was delivering a speech at a rally in Kanthi, East Midnapore district, the windowpanes and windscreens of several dozens of buses that carried party supporters from distant areas were smashed, allegedly by TMC supporters. The broken glass from the windscreen and panes must have lined the state highway for some kilometres. Mukul Roy, who was also present at the venue, alleged that the motive behind the vandalism was to send a message to bus owners against renting their vehicles to the BJP.

Mamata Banerjee made her motto clear. In Bengali, the Kourobs' rejection of the Pandobs' demand for five villages is popular by the proverbial use of '*Bina juddhe nahi dibo suchyogro medini*' (not a grain of soil without war), made popular by poet Nabin Chandra Sen's *Palashir Juddho* in the nineteenth century. Mamata Banerjee said this, without saying it in as many words.

Modi and Shah accepted her challenge.

Time of the Turncoats

'Mujhko Hui Na Khabar, Chori Chori Choop Choop Kar
Kab pyar ki pehli nazar / Hai …
Le Gayee Le Gayee
Dil le gayee le gayee …'

This hit Bollywood number was playing repeatedly as the two mobile phones of Khagen Murmu rang incessantly. One of them had the song as its ringtone.

Was it merely a coincidence, in the light of the lyrics of the song, that Murmu had found his new love in the BJP? He had been ceremoniously inducted into the party at its central office in New Delhi on 12 March and was declared the candidate for the Malda Uttar Lok Sabha seat on 21 March. This author met Murmu on 24 March, a day after Murmu returned from Delhi.

Murmu had contested the 2014 Lok Sabha elections from Malda Uttar on a CPM ticket and was the runner-up. He was a sitting CPM MLA, having won three terms on the trot.

'It happened suddenly,' Murmu said, in between attending calls – he didn't want to upset any caller – 'The TMC put pressure on me to join them. I did not want to join the TMC and I realized that my party was not in a position to protect me from the TMC's vengeance for rejecting their offer.'

The BJP's offer came through Mukul Roy, who assured Murmu that Kailash Vijayvargiya was interested in getting him into the party. Before catching the flight to Delhi, however, Murmu did not forget to give Dilip Ghosh a call and apprise him of the development. He did not want to keep the state unit chief of his new party in the dark, especially since they knew each other from being MLAs.

This author was sitting in Murmu's tiny visitors' room on the second floor of a non-descript house in Malda town. Books, leaflets and papers were heaped on the table in the room. They included publications of the CPM, of which he had been a member for more than three decades. People telephoning him were evidently greeting him with 'Jai Shree Ram', as he was responding by repeating the same. His efforts at overcoming the unease of suddenly changing his greeting 'Lal Selam, Comrade' to 'Jai Shree Ram' were palpable.

This author had a telephonic conversation with him on 8 March 2019. There were murmurs within the state BJP unit that Murmu was in touch with them. When questioned about it, his answers indicated he was planning to switch over: 'I have been protesting against the Left-Congress alliance but the party leadership isn't heeding. If a seat-sharing proposition is agreed upon, the Left will have no candidate in Malda, as we will be supporting Congress in both seats. We fought the Congress for years. Now, if both the seats are given to them, what will happen to our party in Malda district?'

He also said a good number of local people had urged him to switch camps and keep fighting the TMC.

'However, I am yet to decide.'

When this author informed CPM central committee member Rabin Deb of Murmu's criticism of the party, Deb said that Murmu had assured the party's Malda district leadership that nothing was wrong with his relations with the party: 'If he really said this, I am hearing it only from you. He is talking rubbish and the reason is his personal interest. He would not be able to contest the Lok Sabha elections if a seat-sharing deal is ultimately struck with Congress, which is no longer our principal opponent in Malda district. The TMC and the BJP are our opponents.'

Four days later, Kailash Vijayvargiya and Mukul Roy inducted Murmu into the BJP, along with Congress MLA Dulal Bar and the suspended TMC MP Anupam Hazra.

The BJP had decided to go slow on selection of candidates so that the best possible candidate for each constituency could be chosen. They were banking on defections by known faces from the Left, Congress and TMC.

They decided to wait and watch what unfolded in these three camps over distribution of tickets. Mukul Roy would identify potential winners from among the aggrieved.

The first success came in January 2019, when the TMC MP from Bishnupur, Saumitra Khan, joined the BJP. There were murmurs in political circles since November 2018 that Khan was feeling cornered within the party, that he was unlikely to get renominated and that he was in touch with Mukul Roy, who had brought him to the TMC from the Congress five years ago. Khan's position in the TMC had started weakening with Roy's fall from grace. Khan had also fallen out with Abhishek Banerjee.

After Khan's defection, the TMC swiftly expelled the other disgruntled MP, Bolpur's Anupam Hazra. He had been publicly making sarcastic comments about his own party for quite some time. The Bolpur MP finally joined the BJP two months later, along with Khagen Murmu and Dulal Bar. About two weeks before that – on 28 February – an expelled youth leader of the TMC from Cooch Behar, Nishith Adhikari, had joined the BJP in New Delhi, courtesy Mukul Roy.

The BJP's biggest gain, however, came two days after Mumru, Hazra and Bar joined. Arjun Singh, the TMC's 'bahubali' (muscleman) MLA, who had been winning the Bhatpara assembly seat since 2001 and simultaneously managing the chairmanship of Bhatpara municipality, had long expressed before the party his desire to enter the Lok Sabha. He wanted a ticket from Barrackpore. Mamata Banerjee did not support the idea. Barrackpore was being represented by Dinesh Trivedi since 2009.

Trivedi, who succeeded Mamata Banerjee as Union railway minister after she took charge as West Bengal chief minister, had fallen out with Banerjee in 2012 over her opposition to the railway budget presented by him. However, they later patched up, and Mamata Banerjee was in no mood to deny him renomination merely to please Arjun Singh. TMC leaders gave Singh an alternative offer. He would be made a minister in the state cabinet after the elections were over. The day Mamata Banerjee announced her list of candidates, Mukul Roy reached out to Singh.

Roy and Singh's mutual dislike for each other was no secret – both when Roy was in the TMC and after Roy joined the BJP. Roy hailed from

Bhatpara's neighbouring town of Kanchrapara, and Roy's son, Subhranshu (who did not follow his father into the BJP), was a TMC MLA from Bhatpara's neighbouring Bijpur constituency. Arjun Singh wanted to control Bijpur too. But for Mukul Roy, his 'ego clash' with Singh was too minor an issue, considering the risk he had been running by taking on Mamata Banerjee. His was a one-point agenda of weakening the TMC.

Arjun Singh joined the BJP in New Delhi on 14 March, welcomed by his 'bete noire' Mukul Roy.

The Hunt for Candidates

Kailash Vijayvargiya had said to state unit leaders as early as on 20 December 2018 that if they were dreaming of getting Lok Sabha tickets, they had better stop doing so. This was at a meeting held at the National Library Auditorium. Four central leaders, Kailash Vijayvargiya, Shiv Prakash, Arvind Menon and Suresh Pujari, and state leaders Mukul Roy, Dilip Ghosh, Rahul Sinha and Subrato Chattopadhyay were present, along with the state unit general secretaries and the district unit presidents. Vijayvargiya said the office bearers will have to play the kingmakers. If they were keen on tickets, they had better work hard now and wait for their turn in 2021.

For becoming 'kings' – MPs in this case – the BJP looked for teachers, doctors, engineers and successful persons with a clean image from different walks of life, preferably also involved in social work. It was not an easy task. The TMC had almost pocketed Bengal's entertainment industry, while the public intellectuals – at least most of them – were either Left-leaning or pro-TMC, essentially opposed to the saffron camp. Mamata Banerjee had made it a practice to field celebrities wherever she was wary of infighting in the party.

Her party's MPs, MLAs and ministers included singer-songwriter-composer Kabir Suman, historian Sugato Bose, actor Mithun Chakraborty, painter Jogen Chowdhury, theatre personalities Bratya Basu and Arpita Ghosh, footballers Prasun Banerjee and Dipendu Biswas, cricketer Lakshmi Ratan Shukla, singers Indranil Sen and Anup Ghosal, and Tollywood stars Tapas Paul, Shatabdi Roy, Sandhya Roy, Moon Moon Sen, Debashree Roy,

Dipak 'Chiranjit' Chakraborty and Deepak 'Dev' Adhikari. Many other poets, singers and actors were frequently seen with her. She fielded former India football captain Bhaichung Bhutiya twice, though without any luck.

The BJP had limited success in its hunt for celebrity candidates. Their biggest catch since 2014 was Babul Supriyo, the Bollywood singer who hailed from Hooghly district. He was fielded from Asansol, the Lok Sabha seat that represents much of the Burdwan industrial belt. When Modi came to campaign for him in 2014, he indicated that he had Supriyo in mind for his bigger plan for India. Supriyo won, marking the first instance of the state BJP managing to win an assembly or Lok Sabha seat entirely on its own. The other seat that the BJP won in 2014 was Darjeeling, where the party veteran Surinder Singh Ahluwalia's fight was easier due to support from the Gorkha Janmukti Morcha that called all the shots in the hills. The party had also fielded singer Bappi Lahiri from Serampore, magician P.C. Sorcar Jr from Barasat, actors Nimu Bhowmik, George Baker and Joy Banerjee from Raiganj, Howrah and Uluberia, respectively. Later, actors Roopa Ganguly and Locket Chatterjee joined the party.

Among them, only five became closely associated with the party – Supriyo found a ministerial berth in Modi's cabinet, Roopa Ganguly was initially made the state unit chief of the women's wing and was later nominated to the Rajya Sabha, Joy Banerjee was made a member of BJP's national executive, George Baker was nominated to the Rajya Sabha, and Locket Chatterjee replaced Roopa Ganguly as president of the state BJP's women's wing.

In 2019, the BJP failed to attract big names from the celebrity world. Its list of candidates, in a way, reflected how the party had grown, and planned to grow, in Bengal. Of the forty-two candidates, fifteen were members of civil society, most of whom had close links with the RSS; seventeen were state- and district-level BJP leaders, eight had switched over from other parties, one was a priest of the Arya Samaj tradition, and the other was a leader of the Matua religious sect.

The civil society members included six doctors, two university assistant professors, one engineer, a journalist, a rights activist, a former India team footballer, an entrepreneur, and two former civil servants. Among them, journalist Rantidev Sengupta, the Howrah Lok Sabha candidate, had been editing the RSS's Bengali organ *Swastika* for more than a year after a long career as a Bengali print journalist. Jalpaiguri candidate Jayanta Roy, a doctor, was associated with Saksham, the RSS wing for the differently abled. Balurghat candidate Sukanta Majumdar, an assistant professor at Gour Banga University, had long been closely associated with the RSS. Krishnanagar candidate Kalyan Chaubey, former India football team goalkeeper, had grown close to the RSS over the past couple of years and had attended as a special guest the RSS's third-year OTC training in Nagpur in June 2018, as also its training camp in Howrah district in West Bengal. Burdwan East candidate Paresh Chandra Das, a retired IAS officer, had joined the BJP a couple of years ago but mostly remained associated with the RSS in the district. Barasat candidate Mrinal Kanti Debnath, also a doctor, had been campaigning for a long time highlighting the plight of the Hindu refugees from Bangladesh.

Party leaders who got tickets were the state unit president Dilip Ghosh, Union ministers Babul Supriyo and S.S. Ahluwalia, national secretary Rahul Sinha, national executive member Joy Banerjee, two state unit general secretaries, two vice-presidents, the state youth wing chief, the women's wing chief, a state unit spokesperson, a district unit president and five other district-level leaders. Of these seventeen, nine had an RSS background and three came from the entertainment world.

Carpet Bombing

During the seven weeks between end-March and mid-May 2019, Bengal witnessed one of the most bitterly fought electoral campaigns in recent decades, as the TMC was coming up with newer ways to disrupt BJP's planned events, and the BJP, determined not to give in, launching an all-out counter-attack.

On 27 March, the BJP submitted an application for use of the Kawakhali ground for Modi's rally on 3 April. The ground was owned by Siliguri Jalpaiguri Development Authority, headed by TMC MLA Sourav Chakraborty. Its officials informed the BJP on 31 March, though only verbally, that permission would not be given. The BJP had to shift the venue to a smaller field belonging to the railways.

The same uncertainty prevailed during Modi's 7 April rally in Cooch Behar. Mamata Banerjee had a meeting at the same venue, Rash Mela Math, on 8 April. The TMC had the venue booked from 4 April. The dais for Mamata Banerjee's meeting had been raised, and the TMC would not agree to stop work on the dais. This would not have allowed the BJP to construct the dais for Modi's rally, even though the ground was large enough to have stages on both sides. This ground, however, was under the administrative control of the district magistrate, who was already under the scanner of the Election Commission for a series of complaints against him lodged by the BJP. Finally, in the morning of 6 April, the TMC agreed to stop work until the time Modi's rally was over.

On 4 May, hours within the news breaking that Modi would be addressing a rally in Bankura district on 9 May, the TMC submitted an application to book the largest ground, Tamlibandh stadium, in Bankura town. The BJP then identified a large field four kilometres away from the town. Here, trouble started with getting no-objection letters from the owners. The plot of land had more than 100 owners. While the BJP obtained permission from some of them, some of the others, allegedly at the instigation of the TMC, raised objections.

The tug of war continued till 8 May, when the BJP's Bhupendra Yadav met the poll panel officers at Nirvachan Sadan in New Delhi and complained against the Bankura district magistrate. The same day, Amit Shah, while addressing a rally in another part of Bankura district for Bishnupur Lok Sabha, slammed the TMC and the administration for creating one hurdle after another to disrupt BJP's campaign schedule. The news in the state election office was that Delhi 'put immense pressure' on Kolkata to ensure the issue was resolved. Finally, permission came late in the evening on 8 May for Modi's rally, which was scheduled for 10.30 a.m. on 9 May.

The elections in West Bengal extended over seven phases, which gave Modi and Shah ample scope to find time for Bengal amid their nationwide travel schedule. They made full use of it. Modi and Shah addressed seventeen public meetings each. Rajnath Singh, Smriti Irani, Yogi Adityanath, Shivraj Singh Chauhan, Nirmala Sitaraman, Prakash Javadekar and Tripura chief minister Biplab Deb were among other star speakers who addressed multiple rallies.

The conflict between the two contenders was to reach its crescendo in the last phase. Shah was scheduled to address three rallies on 13 May – at Baruipur (Jadavpur Lok Sabha constituency), Canning (Jaynagar Lok Sabha constituency) and Rajarhat (Barasat Lok Sabha constituency). On the night of 12 May, the owner of the land where Shah's Baruipur rally was to be held went to the administration and withdrew the permission he had given to the BJP. It was not possible for the party to arrange for a different venue overnight. The meeting had to be cancelled.

However, what Kolkata witnessed the next day, 14 May, made the biggest news. Amit Shah was leading a road show on College Street for the Kolkata North Lok Sabha seat. Trouble broke out when the rally passed by Vidyasagar College, where some TMC student wing activists were still present even though it was already evening. It is difficult to positively ascertain whose was the first provocation, but clashes erupted, ultimately leading to vandalization of the college campus and destruction of a bust of Ishwar Chandra Vidyasagar.

News of the destruction of Vidyasagar's bust overshadowed everything else. This man, a polymath, was one of the central figures of the nineteenth century Bengal Renaissance, on whose character had been laid no blemish. He was a person undisputedly revered by the Bengalis, irrespective of their caste, religion, gender and political affiliation. Naxalites had beheaded a statue of Vidyasagar in College Square during the height of Maoist iconoclasm in the early 1970s. Kolkata never forgave the Naxals for this. The next-generation Naxalites admitted this act was a mistake.

Mamata Banerjee, who was addressing a public meeting in south Kolkata, wasted no time when the news broke. She asked Education Minister Partha Chatterjee to rush to the college. She too cut short her programmes for the day and followed Chatterjee. It was already 9 p.m. when she reached the college, inspected the damages and the broken bust and announced installation of a new and bigger bust once the elections were over. 'Those who can demolish Vidyasagar's bust must know nothing about Bengal and are essentially anti-Bengali in nature,' she declared. In view of the tension that prevailed since the incident, the Election Commission reduced the campaign schedule for the final phase, a move that Mamata Banerjee alleged was aimed at helping the BJP.

Modi and Shah had made no mistake in assessing the gravity of the situation. Shah kept blaming the TMC for the incident. On 15 May, he addressed the media at the party's central office in New Delhi. He presented a set of photographs which, he claimed,[4] conclusively proved that TMC supporters were behind the destruction of Vidyasagar's bust. He argued that since the gates of the college were closed, it was impossible for the participants of the BJP rally to enter the campus and carry out the vandalism. Modi, at a rally in Uttar Pradesh on 16 May, blamed 'TMC goondas' for the vandalism and then promised that the Centre would install a grand statue made of panchdhatu – an alloy of the five metals of copper, brass, aluminium, iron and zinc – used to make idols of gods.

Amid this blame game, some video clippings[5] of the vandalism at the college emerged, showing members of the BJP's rally scaling the iron grills, breaking open the lock of the iron gate of the college, then breaking open the wooden door in the first room where the plaster of paris bust of Vidyasagar was kept in a glass box.

The video clips went viral on social media.

Adding a new angle to the narrative, supporters of Bangla Pokkho launched a social media campaign stating that those involved in the vandalism were Hindi-speaking youths. Similar views were aired on social media. In fact, the *Telegraph*'s report on the incident in the next day's edition was titled, 'Clash of cultures: Shocked Bengal witnesses vandalism of Vidyasagar bust'.[6] It said:

> One of the greatest names of the Bengal Renaissance has been pitchforked into the final lap of an election so far yoked to muscular nationalism, calumny and preposterous claims. Smashed to pieces by suspected BJP supporters, a bust of the polymath appears to have brought to the fore a culture clash that has marked the BJP's foray

into Bengal. The vandalism, which carries the whiff of a targeted attack as the bust was accessed by smashing a glass case, has offered chief minister Mamata Banerjee a chance to underscore how Bengal's pride has been trampled upon.

A Battle of Two Narratives

In the midst of this high-voltage political battle and exchange of acerbic barbs, the TMC's basic electoral call was losing steam. They had pegged the Lok Sabha election as one that would create history by giving India its first Bengali prime minister. This narrative found not many takers with every passing week, as the state of disarray of the so-called 'federal front' was becoming clearer. In their rallies, Modi and Shah asked one simple question: do you want a *mazboot* (strong) or *majboor* (full of compulsions) government? This question became louder after the Pulwama terror attack and India's air strikes on Balakot in Pakistan. Opposition parties failed to show any signs of their ability to form a stable government after the election.

It was on their first and most successful grand gathering – the 19 January meeting in Kolkata – that the senior-most leader among them, Janata Dal (Secular)'s H.D. Deve Gowda, suggested that a common minimum programme be drawn first to earn the trust of the people. This author remembers speaking to the political analyst, Sabyasachi Basu Ray Chaudhury, a professor of political science at Rabindra Bharati University, that very evening. He said, 'Without a common minimum programme, this so-called front has no hope. They need to clearly spell out their policy against Modi's to gain people's confidence and remove apprehensions about stability of their government.'

Nothing of the sort happened. In the Lok Sabha elections, the Congress targeted the CPM hold of Kerala. In Uttar Pradesh, the Samajwadi Party and the Bahujan Samaj Party kept the Congress at bay. In Delhi and Haryana, the Aam Aadmi Party and the Congress failed to patch up. In Bihar, RJD and CPI locked horns over the Begusarai seat. The BJP lost no opportunity to mock the Opposition by saying that voting for the so-called grand alliance meant six different prime ministers for six days of the week.

The biggest electoral advantage for the BJP in Bengal, however, came in the form of the Left and Congress's failure to arrive at a seat-sharing deal, even though it was clear to both camps that fighting independently would fetch them little. The general perception was that in many seats voters would be confused about who, between the BJP contestant and the Left-Congress joint nominee, might be the stronger candidate against the TMC. In south Bengal, this could benefit the TMC as a result of a split in anti-TMC votes, but in north Bengal, the Congress and the Left may manage to retain their seats, upsetting both the TMC and BJP. But if the Left and Congress contested separately, people would have no difficulty in identifying the BJP as the TMC's principal opponent. Under such circumstances, the Left and the Congress were certain to face a rout; the TMC too could face losses, but the BJP was sure to make gains.

In spite of several rounds of talks, and despite there being agreement between the parties on most of the seats, the Left and the Congress failed to strike a deal. The equations got simpler and straight. Vote for Didi if you wanted to end the Modi regime. Vote for Modi if you wanted a strong government at the Centre and end Didi's rule in Bengal.

It was a no-holds-barred battle on the part of both contestants.

Mamata Banerjee targeted Modi for demonetization, GST and the Rafale deal. Modi and Shah targeted the TMC over Saradha, Narada and corruption and extortion at the grassroots level. Mamata accused the Centre of destroying the country's economy, federal structure and secular fabric. In an apparently veiled attack on Modi, she expressed her doubts as to whether a man who could not look after his wife could look after the country.[7]

Modi alleged that the people of the state were forced to pay 'Trinamool *tolabaji* (extortion) tax', and Shah alleged that the people were forced to pay '*Bhatija* (nephew) tax', targeting Abhishek Banerjee without naming him. They both accused the TMC of politicizing the administration and denying people justice. As Mamata Banerjee kept reminding the people that this election was to decide on the government at the Centre – 'It's Delhi's vote, our vote is due in 2021' – Modi and Shah kept urging the people to use this opportunity, when they had the protection of central security forces, to vent their anger on the TMC for their loot of votes during the panchayat elections.

A Multi-layered Campaign

The Trinamool Congress was busy countering the BJP's mega rallies that were to be addressed by its national leaders and the party's campaign on social media. But there were many layers to the saffron camp's campaign.

The BJP leadership started preparing its volunteer force of non-resident Bengalis to campaign in Bengal six months ahead of the elections. The Save Bengal campaign was launched in November 2018 in New Delhi, in the presence of Shiv Prakash and Dilip Ghosh. The focus was on Bengalis living in New Delhi, Noida, Ghaziabad, Lucknow, Meerut, Pilbhit, Chandigarh, Etawah and Bhopal.

With Shiv Prakash as the guiding force, Anirban Ganguly as the main organizer and Animesh Biswas as the key coordinator, a 'core team' was formed comprising Ranjana Mukhopadhyaya (associate professor of Japanese Studies in Delhi University), Susanta Kar (BJP's IT cell convenor of western Uttar Pradesh), Shoumendu Mukherji (advocate), Shantanu Mukherjee (advocate), Debapriyo Chowdhury (entrepreneur) and Malayendu Mukherjee (retired air force officer). The campaign also included some organizers who were not Bengali – Noida-based IT professional Vineet Chauhan, Ghaziabad-based IT professionals Anurag Tyagi, Nitin Garg and Naimish Kunwar, New Delhi-based entrepreneur Lakshmikanta Shaw and Lucknow resident Amresh Yadav.

Volunteers were enrolled over the next three or four months. Dilip Ghosh addressed Bengalis in Delhi and Pilbhit. Teams of volunteers started arriving in West Bengal from the end of March. Animesh Biswas and Sushanta Kar stayed in West Bengal, while Anirban Ganguly and Swapan Dasgupta kept travelling between Delhi, Kolkata and the farthest corners of Bengal. Twenty-nine seminars were organized across sixteen districts as part of what they called the 'New India Outreach Programme,' on topics such as 'National Security and West Bengal', 'Ensuring India's National Security and Perspective on West Bengal and Northeast', 'West Bengal's Resurgence – Challenges and Opportunities', 'In Search of New India: Bankim Chandra to Syama Prasad.'

The Save Bengal volunteers conducted indoor discussions, street-corner meetings and door-to-door campaigns, distributing leaflets and booklets.

Amresh Yadav and Rahul Chowdhury stayed in the state for nearly the entire duration of the election campaign. Shoma Mukherji, a faculty at Delhi School of Business who had been based in New Delhi for the past thirty-five years, came back to her home city for a week to hold informal discussions with friends, well-wishers and acquaintances on restoring Bengal's cultural and industrial heritage. She participated in the election rallies of BJP candidates from Kolkata South and Dumdum. Kishor Kumar Tarafdar, a Delhi-based Bengali businessman who was born and brought up in Pilibhit, came down to West Bengal in early May and took part in more than a dozen events – some of which he himself organized – in the Barasat Lok Sabha constituency.

The Save Bengal campaign in Bongaon was carried out by, among others, Bijoy Mondal, a BJP leader from Uttarakhand, and Achintya Mondal, who served as a West Bengal state executive member of the ABVP until his relocation to Delhi in 2018 to study in Delhi University, where he became an ABVP leader. From Etawah came Sharad Tewari, the BJP's IT cell head for Etawah district, and Anil Pandey, a swayamsevak. Noida-based Padmanava Lahiri came to campaign in Jadavpur, addressed street-corner meetings and accompanied BJP's Jadavpur candidate Anupam Hazra at his rallies. Prithviraj Patra, a doctor at the Post Graduate Institute of Medical Education & Research, Chandigarh, visited his native homes in East and West Midnapore districts, where he met local doctors, teachers and lawyers. He campaigned for BJP's Kanthi candidate Debashish Samanta, who too was a doctor. Shyamal Sil, who worked at the Delhi office of a German company, visited his native place in Hooghly district in April to engage in conversations with local members of the civil society.

The 'Team Meerut', comprising Sachin Chauhan (ABVP leader), Humanshu Goel (IT professional) and Shroya Garg (businessman), among others, campaigned in North Kolkata constituency for more than a week. Noida-resident Mihir Mallick and Delhi-resident Siddharth Ghosh came down to Dumdum, while Gajendra Dutt, who hails from Meerut, went to Asansol.

Overall, more than 200 volunteers came to campaign under the banner of Save Bengal. They, and the volunteers who did not come to Bengal but worked for the campaign, were trained in the use of social media to effectively spread the desired messages for the BJP. To further influence the discourse on social media, Swapan Dasgupta, Anirban Ganguly and Shishir Bajoria conducted a webinar with overseas residents who had their roots in West Bengal. Bajoria, an industrialist, was a member of the BJP's state executive and a core team member of party's central cell for NRIs, formally called Overseas Friends of BJP or OFBJP. The webinar was held on 14 April. As many as 135 Bengali NRIs from seven countries joined the discussion on 'The Role of West Bengal in New India'. It was expected that the opinions the participants would later express on social media would influence the opinions of their friends and relatives living in West Bengal.

One of the Save Bengal volunteers, however, had an unsavoury experience. The volunteer was Delhi resident Laxmikanta Shaw, who was part of the Save Bengal campaign right from the beginning and even addressed a gathering of the local Bengalis at Pilbhit in Uttar Pradesh in March, sharing the dais with Dilip Ghosh. Shaw came to West Bengal early in April, leading a team of Save Bengal campaigners to work in Midnapore Lok Sabha constituency, where Ghosh was contesting.

On 13 May 2019, Shaw, along with Gautam Chatterjee, who had been Dilip Ghosh's personal assistant until a few months ago, were standing on the platform at Asansol railways station, carrying a bag, when some railway police (GRP) personnel apprehended them for suspected possession of illegal goods. When taken to the GRP station, Rs 1 crore was found in the bag. Following their arrest, Ghosh did not deny his links with Chatterjee but said he did not remember knowing Shaw.

At Asansol, immediately after his arrest, Shaw told Bengali news channels that the money belonged to the BJP and was meant for use in the elections.[8] Shaw and Chatterjee could not get out of jail before the elections were over.

That was not all, though. The BJP's Tripura in-charge Sunil Deodhar camped in West Bengal after the third phase of elections, and travelled across the state. He was specially entrusted with the seats going to the polls in the final phase – the seats in and around Kolkata. After the elections were over in Gujarat, BJP's Yuva Morcha president Rutvij Patel came with a team of select organizers to camp in Barasat, which was to go to the polls in the seventh phase. Suresh Pujari, Bengal co-in-charge, who was a candidate in Odisha, came after the elections in Odisha were over.

Besides, various Sangh Parivar outfits were given charge of specific constituencies. The news within the Bengal BJP was that the VHP's Sachindranath Singha was the Sangh Parivar's in-charge for Midnapore and Bongaon seats, while Kreeda Bharati's all-India assistant secretary Madhumoy Nath, a pracharak, was in charge of Krishnanagar, and Hindu Jagaran Manch's state executive members Tapas Barik and Ranjan Bandyopadhyay in charge of Ranaghat. The Raiganj seat, where polarization had begun over the death of two ABVP organizers in the Darivit school firing in 2018, was the responsibility of the VHP and ABVP. Purulia was the responsibility of the Bajrang Dal.

In addition to all these volunteers and party officials, there were the swayamsevaks associated with RSS's social projects in education, health and self-employment who carried out 'jagran' work. Though their campaigns were pegged as apolitical, simply ensuring that voters exercised their franchise and did not press the NOTA button, the swayamsevaks also urged them to vote for a strong nationalist government that would make no comprise in matters of national security. At many places, these jagran campaigners distributed copies of *Shankhanaad*, an RSS-backed Bengali magazine edited by Subrato Chattopadhyay, Bengal BJP's general secretary (organization). The magazine's issues in March, April and May were packed with articles criticizing the Mamata Banerjee regime for turning Bengal into a hub of 'jihadi' activities.

And then there was Facebook, and Twitter; but above all, there was WhatsApp.

The BJP focused strongly on WhatsApp. A network of WhatsApp groups was opened simultaneous to the formation of social media cells. At least one person was entrusted with social media communications at nearly all levels of committees. For each of the forty-two parliamentary constituencies and 294 assembly constituencies, the BJP had a vistarak a palok (state-level leader in-charge of the seat) and a social media in-charge. The issues and contents for social media campaigns were often supplied from Delhi, from the team of Amit Malviya, but the contents in Bengali were created in Kolkata as well.

Messages from the state unit's social media cell cascaded down through the constituency in-charge, through the social media pointsmen at about 1,200 mandal committees, to nearly 10,000 of the roughly 13,000 shakti kendras that the BJP had created in the state. In some cases, the shakti kendra in-charges ran booth-level WhatsApp groups. Besides, those who gave missed calls to BJP's toll-free number to become members of the party were added on WhatsApp groups.

Many of these social media workers ran multiple WhatsApp groups. One IT warrior, Dipak Das from Cooch Behar district, told the *Indian Express* that he was 'admin' of 1,114 WhatsApp groups, with a team of forty reporting to him.[9] Overall, about 50,000 WhatsApp groups were created in Bengal.[10] In districts like Cooch Behar and Birbhum, the party did not have committees for many booths. But they had WhatsApp groups where some voters from some of those booths were members.

Anger

Touring many districts – Malda, Murshidabad, Cooch Behar and Nadia – during this period, this author witnessed first-hand the seething anger of the people wherever the TMC had turned the rural polls into a mockery. The people were waiting for a chance to vote. They had made up their minds. No campaign mattered. All they worried about was the strength of the Central paramilitary forces.

Insightful anecdotes came from some district-level TMC leaders about their campaign experience. At one house, a woman told a TMC worker, brother of a panchayat member, 'You all don't need to campaign at all, we know whom to vote for.' The tone of her voice created more discomfort than assurance for the TMC member. At the next house another woman told him, 'I don't remember any of you coming to us during the panchayat elections. We thought you didn't need votes anymore.'

'We did not spend much time there,' the TMC worker told this author, sitting on a bench in front of a tea stall along a state highway at Beldanga, sipping tea from a clay cup. This area fell in the Baharampore Lok Sabha constituency that Bengal Congress heavyweight Adhir Chowdhury has represented since 1999. Over the past five years, the TMC's Murshidabad district in-charge Suvendu Adhikary had destroyed much of Chowdhury's organizational strength by getting a large number of his close associates to defect to the TMC. The Congress was trounced in the district in the rural polls, having failed to field candidates in a majority of the seats.

In the erstwhile Bangladeshi enclave of Moshaldanga in Cooch Behar district, very few people were willing to talk politics. 'Could you just give us a hint of the strength of the Central forces who would be manning the booths? The only question that we are concerned about is whether we will be able to cast our votes,' said one of the couple of men who were willing to speak.

Shoaib Daniyal's report in Scroll.in reflected similar experiences faced by him. 'The episode (panchayat election) has sharpened support for the BJP in the ongoing Lok Sabha elections, which, conducted by Central paramilitary forces, will not allow the state government to effect any widespread malpractice,' Daniyal wrote in his piece dated 26 April 2019. The report also mentioned how the TMC's 'strong arm tactics' was prompting traditional Left voters to shift their votes to the BJP, which they found as the only party able to take on the TMC.

Taherpur, in Nadia district, offered an intriguing experience for this author. Taherpur was the only second town in West Bengal where the civic body was being run by the CPM. The local MLA, Rama Biswas, belonged to the CPM too. The other civic body run by the CPM was at Siliguri, where former urban development minister Asok Bhattacharya served as the mayor and MLA. The BJP had chosen Taherpur as the venue of Modi's rally for the Ranaghat Lok Sabha seat. Public enthusiasm was high near the venue. Charged up supporters had taken over the roads. At a tea stall about half a kilometre from the venue, a group of five or six youths were talking cricket. This author asked them about politics.

'It's BJP this time,' said one of them, 'Didn't you see the crowd? Didn't you hear them roar?'

'I did, but isn't it a stronghold of the Left? Won't the Left candidate split the anti-TMC vote?'

'Who are the Left?' another chipped in, 'We are the Left. We are all CPM. My whole family is CPM. But this time our votes will go to the BJP, the votes of all of my family and all these people sitting here.'

As the others nodded in agreement, a third spoke: 'We won't be able to retain the municipality if the TMC wins. Come the civic polls, we will vote for the CPM again. But the TMC has to be put on the backfoot first.'

A Saffron Tsunami

The evening of 23 May 2019.

> '*Har ghar Bhagwa Chhayega! Ramraaj bhi Ayega!*'
> (Every house will turn saffron! The rule of Ram is coming!)
> Saffron *abeer* (scented powder) was raining everywhere.
> '*Ek hi nara ek hi naam, Jai Shree Ram! Jai Shree Ram!*'
> (There is only one slogan: Jai Shree Ram!)

Nothing was audible, except for the song being played aloud. A strong female voice was singing, backed up by digitally mixed soundtrack, popularly known as 'DJ music' in Bengal. A group of youths was dancing in mad celebration on a small dais beside the statue of Syama Prasad Mookerjee on the narrow Muralidhar Sen Lane, bang opposite the Bengal BJP headquarters. There were two sound boxes on the dais that dozens of youths surrounded. They were all dancing – those on the dais and those around it.

'*Rajtilak ki karo taiari, aa rahe hain bhagwadhari!*' the song continued.

(Prepare for the coronation, the saffron-robed is coming)

It was a moment of celebration indeed. Not only had the people of the country returned Modi to power with a bigger mandate, half of Bengal had been painted saffron. It became evident from the afternoon onwards that the BJP was going to make huge gains in the state. By the time this author reached the state BJP office, at around 5.30 p.m., the BJP looked set to win anything between seventeen and twenty-one seats in the state. That was nearly half of the state's seats. That was very close to Amit Shah's ambitious target of twenty-three seats. The backward regions of north Bengal and southwest Bengal were virtually swept by the party.

The joy on the street in front of the BJP's office seemed boundless.

'Bharat mein rehna hoga to Vande Mataram kehna hoga!'

(If you want to live in India, you have to chant Bande Mataram)

The song and dance continued, celebrating the historic win.

Among the party's top leaders, only Mukul Roy was present in the office. He was coordinating with all counting centres and overseeing the work in the 'war room'. His room on the second floor was very crowded. State BJP IT cell members were taking his bytes. He looked deeply pleased and relieved, even as his assistant kept handing over his phone to him again within minutes of his ending one conversation. Bharati Ghosh, the IPS-turned-BJP leader, called Roy. She was probably upset that she was going to lose by a good margin in the TMC stronghold of Ghatal Lok Sabha seat, but Roy kept assuring her that the party was very satisfied with the efforts she had put in.

This author requested Roy for an interview. He did not agree to it. 'No interview today,' he said, looking calm and pleased. The others present in the room indicated that he would not speak a word to the media until Narendra Modi and Amit Shah had addressed the nation from the central office. Prodding elicited a few one-liners but he stopped answering altogether the moment this author asked if the Lok Sabha election results indicated an early assembly election in Bengal.

He came down to the press conference room on the ground floor after the Modi-Shah event at BJP's central office in New Delhi ended. He spoke for about five minutes. 'The Bengal elections were held on a single-point question – whether or not democracy should exist in Bengal. People have now given their mandate decisively – yes, democracy needs to be restored in Bengal.'

Now that their primary task had been achieved, he said, the newly elected MPs would work on using the floor of parliament to restore Bengal's industrial and cultural heritage.

As soon as he finished, this author asked: 'What's the future of the state assembly?'

'It's too early to comment, but as per the latest information available with me, the TMC is trailing in about 150 seats. Now, it's up to the people to decide the fate of the assembly.'

'What's the secret to your party's success?' asked another journalist.

'There is no secret. People fought out TMC,' prompt came the reply.

'When will TMC MLAs start joining your party?' asked another journalist. There was no answer.

'How many TMC MLAs are in touch with you?' asked another journalist. There was no answer.

One journalist asked for his comments on the trend of Muslim polarization in favour of the TMC in Bengal. Roy said, 'You must have missed the prime minister's speech. He said that our motto is '*Sabka Saath, Sabka Vikash aur Sabka Vishwas*'. I think you have got your answer.'

He ducked most of the questions that followed and stuck to his point that the press briefing was meant only to thank the people of Bengal for their courage and determination against an autocratic regime and to reassure them that the BJP would continue to support them in their quest for democracy.

Mamata Banerjee did not meet the press that day. From thirty-four seats in 2014, her party's Lok Sabha tally had come down to twenty-two. What's worse, three TMC defectors were among the BJP's eighteen winners.

TEN

Mission 2021

Mukul Roy: Unleashed, Leashed

RUBBING SALT ON MAMATA Banerjee's wounds, Mukul Roy, on 28 May 2019, got three MLAs to defect to the BJP. His son Subhranshu (who was still with the TMC), Congress-turned-TMC MLA Tushar Kanti Bhattacharya and CPM MLA Debendranath Roy, along with five dozen elected public representatives of local bodies, joined the BJP at the party's central office in New Delhi.

Roy junior's switching of camps was only a matter of days. He had already been suspended by the TMC immediately after the Lok Sabha elections for praising his father. 'I'm proud of my father. Some people said a hundred thousand of Mukul Roys could be created. I will say only one thing, the man who built the party with his own hands has now single-handedly ravaged it,' he had said[1], a day after the results were announced. However, the defection of the Left and the Congress MLAs came as a surprise. No one had a clue about them.

This was the first case of mass joining of the BJP by elected public representatives – three MLAs, fifty-six municipal councillors and three rural body representatives. The defection of the councillors – seventeen each from Halishahar and Kanchrapara municipalities, including the chairman and vice-chairman, and twenty-two from Naihati municipality – brought the civic bodies under the BJP's control. The ruling party lost three municipalities in West Bengal in a single day – all in the Barrackpore Lok Sabha area. Mukul Roy and Arjun Singh had for years bitterly fought each other – within the TMC and later outside – allegedly for political control of the Barrackpore industrial belt. Now, Roy and Singh had joined hands to uproot the TMC from the area. Capturing Bhatpara municipality in the same area was just a matter of formality for the BJP.

Mukul Roy's smile was getting wider. Sitting next to him at the joining ceremony – which most Bengali TV channels aired live – Kailash Vijayvargiya too looked pleased and confident as he addressed the media: 'When Modiji said during his election campaign in Bengal that forty MLAs are in touch with us, TMC leader Derek [O'Brien] said not a single corporator would desert the TMC for the BJP. Today there are more than fifty corporators. There are three MLAs. Just like we had a seven-phase election, there will be a seven-phase defection from the TMC in the coming months.'[2]

Asked about the possibility of the BJP coming to power in Bengal before the scheduled assembly elections – Amit Shah had said at a rally in Bengal that the Mamata Banerjee government would fall in no time if Bengal gave the BJP twenty-three seats – Vijayvargiya said, sporting a mischievous smile: 'We want to win Bengal through elections. We have our best wishes for Mamata Banerjee till then. But if her MLAs start deserting the party in such numbers, we should not be blamed [for an early fall of the government].'

The very next day, the TMC's Labhpur MLA Manirul Islam, former MLA Gadadhar Hazra and a few other district-level leaders joined the BJP in New Delhi. Mukul Roy and Vijayvargiya welcomed them into the party. Bhatpara municipality was captured on 4 June. Noapara MLA-cum-Garulia civic body chief Sunil Singh joined the BJP with a majority of the councillors on 18 June, and on the next day the TMC's Bongaon MLA, along with the majority of councillors from Bongaon municipality, joined the BJP. On 24 June, TMC MLA Wilson Champramari and the TMC's Dakshin Dinajpur district unit president Biplab Mitra joined the BJP in New Delhi. The majority of the members of Dakshin Dinajpur zilla parishad, including its sabhadhipati, followed Mitra to the BJP. Loss of a zilla parishad, or the highest administrative body in the district, was considered the rudest shock for the TMC.

Mukul Roy was bulldozing the TMC organizations. Sometimes he claimed as many as 107 TMC MLAs were in touch with him; at other times he said even newly elected TMC MPs were in touch with him. Even if he was exaggerating, an air of suspicion gripped the TMC's rank and file. Who would be next?

The beginning of Roy's political innings in the BJP was not smooth. His equations with the state BJP leaders were not clear. A number of state-level BJP leaders privately expressed to journalists their apprehensions that New Delhi could impose Roy on them. One thing was clear, though . . . he would not be taking orders from the state leaders. His first attempt at poaching for the BJP not only failed but also put the party in an embarrassing spot. Bye-elections for two assembly seats had been scheduled in January 2018. The national leadership, especially Kailash Vijayvargiya, entrusted Roy with getting influential TMC leaders to defect and contest as BJP candidates.

In Noapara in North 24 Parganas – Mukul Roy's home district – TMC announced Sunil Singh, a brother-in-law of Bhatpara MLA Arjun Singh, as its candidate. Mukul Roy lost no time in getting in touch with Manju Basu, former two-time MLA from this constituency, and sealed the deal with her. The BJP's central office, on 7 January, named Basu as its Noapara candidate. Basu remained incommunicado throughout the day. The next day, she said she was still with the TMC and that Mamata Banerjee continued to be her leader. The BJP lost no more time in announcing its Barrackpore district unit president as its Noapara candidate and the Howrah (rural) district unit president as its Uluberia candidate.

The BJP's central leadership, however, kept their trust in Roy. They knew only too well that getting members to defect from the TMC was difficult. On 24 February, the party appointed Roy the convenor of Bengal's panchayat election management committee. After the BJP emerged as the TMC's principal rival in the panchayat elections, Roy was inducted into the BJP's national executive in August 2018, eight months after his joining the party. In October, the party named him the convenor of Bengal's Lok

Sabha election management committee, which made him the second-most important leader of Bengal BJP after state president Dilip Ghosh. By that time, Roy had emerged as the BJP's Bengal in-charge Kailash Vijayvargiya's closest comrade.

When the BJP had finished finalizing its candidates for all forty-two seats, Mukul Roy's influence was evident. The candidates were: Arjun Singh in Bhatpara, Nishith Adhikari in Cooch Behar, Saumitra Khan in Bishnupur, Anupam Hazra in Jadavpur, Khagen Murmu in Malda North, Bharati Ghosh in Ghatal and Nilanjan Roy in Diamond Harbour. They all joined the BJP, courtesy Mukul Roy. Four of them – Singh, Adhikari, Khan and Murmu – had emerged victorious. Mukul Roy had all reasons to be pleased. He had shaken the Trinamool Congress.

Following the post-poll defection drive, TMC leaders had started looking nervous. But Mukul Roy's steamroller hit a hurdle from within. The influx of TMC leaders and functionaries en masse did not go down well with a section of the Bengal RSS leadership and BJP old-timers. Protests erupted within the party and a message of disapproval came from the Sangh, particularly after the induction of Manirul Islam. A Forward Bloc MLA-turned-TMC legislator, Islam had earned notoriety and disrepute for a series of speeches full of threats to his opponents, including one in which he proudly claimed to have killed three youths. Two consecutive issues of the RSS's Bengali organ, *Swastika,* expressed concern over induction of TMC toughs into Bengal BJP.

One article in the 10 June issue, a post-editorial, was written by Jisnu Basu, secretary of the RSS's south Bengal chapter. Titled '*Kandari Hushiyar*' (Beware, Captain!), Basu strongly advocated that the BJP needed to depend on its devoted and time-tested workers and swayamsevaks. Referring to the dedicated workers of the BJP and RSS, several of whom had laid down their lives during the Left and the TMC regimes, Basu wrote, 'These people laid the foundation of the BJP's victory. If the BJP's present-day leadership fails to read this writing on the wall, they are in for a bleak future.'[3]

'The argument that criminals are required to fight criminals is lame and dangerous ... hundreds of the likes of Prashanta Mondal, Abhijit Sardar, Anadi Naskar, Patit Paban Sardar and Srijit Sadar (RSS martyrs in Bengal) are waiting to offer their blood. Give them a call and see for yourself! But all our efforts of years would be in vain if you induct mercenaries, jihadi elements and branded criminals,' Basu wrote.

The following issue of *Swastika* was themed, 'Would the BJP be able to check the entry of bad elements?' It had on its cover a photograph of a joining ceremony in the BJP's New Delhi office during which Monirul Islam was given party membership.

These articles were shared in BJP circles fast, with a section of the party's old-timers sharing photos of the cover image and paragraphs from the articles on social media. Pressure started building. Kailash Vijayvargiya had to keep Mukul Roy under control. None of these joining events took place after consultation with the state unit leaders. The BJP's Bengal leadership remained in the dark as Mukul Roy dealt directly with Vijayvargiya. From the end of June, however, the BJP's Bengal leadership started telling the central leadership that for important inductions the state leaders should be kept in the loop. A section of the BJP state leadership had never been comfortable with Roy's increasing clout. He was becoming a separate power centre. He often operated from his own office at his Elgin Road residence. Now, Roy's choice of new inductees was getting central approval, almost as a norm.

The voice of these state unit leaders became louder after Mukul Roy suffered a major setback when the TMC reclaimed Halishahar municipality on 9 July and Kanchrapara on 13 July. Most of the councillors who defected to the BJP returned to the TMC. Kanchrapara was Mukul Roy's home town. His son, Subhranshu, the local MLA, was also a councillor of Kanchrapara municipality. Halishahar was made a part of Roy Junior's Bijpur assembly constituency. In short, it was a personal blow to Mukul Roy.

Finally managing to give Mukul Roy a suitable reply, Mamata Banerjee's nephew Abhishek said, after reclaiming Kanchrapara, 'He (Mukul) might be a Chanakya, but one made in China!'[4]

Over the next one month, the TMC regained its majority in Bongaon and Naihati municipalities, and in Dakshin Dinajpur zilla parishad. Subsequently, Mukul Roy was leashed. A committee was formed to scrutinize joining proposals from leaders of other parties. If Roy had to bring someone to the BJP, he could no longer do it bypassing the state's BJP leadership. The party had decided that all entries of state-level leaders would have to take place at the state headquarters, and after consultation with the state leadership, announced Dilip Ghosh, on 16 July 2019.

Didi Unnerved

Mamata Banerjee looked jittery in the immediate aftermath of the Lok Sabha elections. In the first press conference she addressed, two days after the results were announced, she vented her anger more on the people than on her party. Instead of going into an introspection mode, which most of her supporters wanted her to do, she said she had possibly done more work than she was supposed to and that from now on she would focus more on her party.

'Everyone is getting rice for Rs 2 a kilogram; there are no expenses on treatment (in government facilities). There is no power cut. Availability of irrigation water has been made easier. I have done too much of government work. I will give more time to the party henceforth,' she said[5].

She was so upset that at one point she even said, 'I don't need the chair, the chair needs me!' She lost her temper when a journalist asked if she was going to attend an Iftar that night. She said, 'Yes, I'll be going to the Iftar. I'll go a hundred times. One should swallow the kicks of a milch cow.'

These remarks did not go down well with the masses. Even hard-core TMC supporters asked the likes of us, journalists, 'What's happened to her?'

In a few days, her reaction to the shouting of 'Jai Shree Ram' by a group of young BJP supporters made news again.

During the election campaign in early May, she had lost her cool when a group of youth shouted, 'Jai Shree Ram', as her car was passing through Chandrakona in West Midnapore. She got down and dared them to face her. Post the polls, a group of youths shouting Jai Shree Ram in front of her car, near Bhatpara in North 24 Parganas, elicited a cruder response. Seven days after the results, on 30 May, Mamata Banerjee was on her way to Naihati when, a few kilometres before her destination, she stopped her car, got down, and literally chased a group of youths who were standing by the road and shouting 'Jai Shree Ram' to welcome her convoy with. She took it as an abuse.

'I am not yet a thing of the past. I will close down everything. I will close down all industries. What audacity! You all get your bread and clothes from us! You survive because of us! Tomorrow, you will be gone in a second. I will see which *dada,* which *mastan* comes to your rescue,' she said,[6] pacing restlessly from one side of the road to the other. '*Merey chamra gutiye debo,*' she said, literally meaning that she would skin them alive.

The spot was in front of a jute mill. By distinguishing between 'you' and 'us', she meant the north-Indian, or Hindi-speaking people from Bihar and Uttar Pradesh, hundreds of whom have made Bengal's Hooghly industrial region, of which the Barrackpore Lok Sabha constituency is a prominent part, their home for decades. Most of the jute mills' industrial workers are Hindi-speaking people. Threatening to close down industries, of course, were not comments expected from a chief minister. But she was too angry to stop herself at this. Visuals aired live on TV channels showed her asking the policemen accompanying her to find out who all had shouted 'Jai Shree Ram'. 'Everyone,' she said, 'search every single home'.[7]

Those accompanying her included Virendra, the director general of state police. She was not ordering him, though. After a few minutes she boarded her car, and the moment the vehicle was started, some people from the crowd shouted, 'Jai Shree Ram'.

She got down again.

'Hey, you, come here and say it if you have the guts! Hey, you, criminal, come here!' a furious Mamata Banerjee was heard saying. She even called them '*saala* criminals'.[8] A few dozen of journalists, including TV channel crews, were following her. She kept muttering, 'We have taken care of them. They are all outsiders. They are not Bengal's local people!' Referring to the shouting of 'Jai Shree Ram' by the youths, she told the journalists, 'What audacity! They are hurling abuses.'

Video footage of this dominated TV channels through the rest of the day. Mamata Banerjee had still more anger to vent. At the party's meeting in Naihati, where the TMC had lost its majority in the civic body barely two days back after the mass defection of councillors to the BJP, she nearly uttered actor Mithun Chakraborty's super-hit dialogue from a Bengali film based on the life of a near-legendary Bengali strongman. The dialogue from the film, *MLA Fatakeshto*, was: '*Saala marbo ekhane, lash porbe shmoshane*' (I'll hit you here and your body will land in the crematorium).

'I hope you know Mithun Chakraborty's dialogue,' she said, '*Marle ekhane* . . .' and paused, while the audience completed it for her: '*lash porbe shmoshane*'. She raised her hands in objection. 'No, there will be no killings, I won't talk of killing, and I can't say that. *Marle ekhane, bichar hobe onyokhane* (If you beat us up here, justice will be meted out elsewhere). Is it alright? Take the message you want.'

Continuing with her newly adopted stance of seeing the Hindi-speaking people as oppressors of the Bengalis, she alleged that '400 Bengalis' had been driven homeless.

Was the TMC falling back on Bengali identity politics? Mamata Banerjee had raised the issue in April 2017, in the immediate aftermath of the Sangh Parivar's mega Ram Navami celebration. She, as also other leaders of her party, had started saying that the BJP was bringing in north Indian culture and imposing it on Bengal's own.

Later, though, she had her party competing with the BJP in celebrating Ram Navami and Hanuman Jayanti. She also left no stone unturned to address the Hindi-speaking people and sometimes even appeased them, in her trademark appease-all politics. She attended Hindi conferences and announced the founding of a Hindi university. Her administration allowed, despite strong criticism from the Bengali media and environmentalists, the Bihari people to use the ecologically sensitive Rabindra Sarobar lake in south Kolkata for Chhat Puja rituals. The results of the Lok Sabha election, however, made it clear that areas dominated by Hindi-speaking people had voted overwhelmingly in favour of the BJP. So, was she now going to dump them altogether and reorient her party?

There was another aspect of the elections that the politically aware were talking about. The TMC had trounced the BJP in the final phase – the one held after the destruction of the Vaidyasagar bust. The one question that people in general and politicians in particular were asking was: 'Did Vidyasagar save the TMC in the final phase?'

Perhaps a more important question was: is Mamata Banerjee drawing any such conclusion?

She came up with two slogans to counter 'Jai Shree Ram': 'Joy Bangla' and 'Joy Maa Kali'. 'Joy Bangla' was being popularized by Bangla Pokkho, since mid-2017. 'Joy Maa Kali' was being popularized by both Hindu Samhati and Bangla Pokkho to highlight the distinctiveness of the Bengali Hindus from the Hindus of north and west India.

'We already had "Jai Hind". From now on, "Joy Bangla" and "Joy Maa Kali" are also our slogans. Will the BJP say, "Joy Bangla"? Will they say "Joy Maa Kali"?' she asked.

Dilip Ghosh, who initially said the BJP found nothing wrong with 'Joy Bangla', since it was Bangladesh's independence war cry against Pakistan, later alleged that Mamata Banerjee was adopting a foreign slogan. He pointed out that it had, over the recent years, become the slogan of Bangladesh's ruling party, Awami League. The controversy over 'Joy Bangla' even reached parliament, with Dilip Ghosh criticizing Mamata Banerjee for the slogan in his speech in the Lok Sabha. Kailash Vijayvargiya paid a visit to a Kali temple and told journalists that they had no problem in hailing Maa Kali. He said 'Joy Maa Kali' a few times.

In effect, though, only 'Jai Shree Ram' and 'Bharat Mata Ki Jai' rent the air at BJP programmes in the following days.

Results: The Analyses

The one-line story of the Lok Sabha results was this: despite increasing its vote share, the TMC lost one-third of its 2014 Lok Sabha tally as a result of consolidation of anti-TMC votes, especially the traditional Left votes, in favour of the BJP.

The mathematics looked simple. The Left's vote share dipped by 22.3 percentage points – from 29.7 per cent in 2014 to 7.4 per cent in 2019, while the BJP's gained by 23.2 percentage points – from 16.8 per cent in 2014 to 40.25 per cent in 2019. The TMC gained 4.25 percentage points, taking its share of votes to 43.3 per cent, and the Congress lost 4 percentage points. It looked like the bulk of the Left votes went to the BJP and the TMC further ate into the Congress's vote share. The assembly bye-election held simultaneously revealed a similar trend. Of the eight seats that went to polls, BJP candidates backed by different Gorkha parties won Darjeeling, where the voting pattern is traditionally different from that of the rest of West Bengal. In rest of the seven seats in the plains, the TMC received 41.58 per cent of the votes and won three seats, all in Muslim-dominated areas. The BJP too won three seats, all in Hindu-dominated areas, receiving 37.88 per cent of the votes. Apart from the one seat that went to the Congress, that party had no influence in the seven other assembly seats, and the Left were left behind in all eight.

The BJP's spectacular performance was attributed to a number of factors – from the people's pent-up anger against the workings of the grassroots-level TMC leaders to the Modi-created wave of hyper-nationalism and the lack of a credible alternative to Modi. Veteran journalist Anirban Choudhury, editor of Zee 24 Ghanta, one of the leading Bengali news channels, cited four reasons to this author: 'First, it was the people's warning to Mamata Banerjee against the highhandedness, corruption and nepotism of her party's local leaders. Second, Modi-Shah's high-pitched campaign against TMC's Muslim appeasement somewhere struck a chord among voters. Third, the TMC fought the elections on an agenda set by the BJP. Instead of portraying the good work done by their government, the TMC spent all its energies in countering the BJP. And fourth, a section of the administration and the TMC secretly helped the BJP.'

Political scientist Amal Kumar Mukhopadhyay cited the reasons as: backlash after the panchayat elections, corruption at the grassroots level, and the gradually fading prospects of Mamata Banerjee's 'federal front'. 'Questioning the government's versions of the Pulwama attack and the Balakot airstrike was counter-productive,' Mukhopadhyay told this author.

The BJP's gains triggered a blame game between the Left and the TMC. Mamata Banerjee alleged that the Left had transferred their votes to the BJP in a planned manner. 'I lost because of the CPM, not the people. The CPM sold all their votes to the BJP. Monetary transactions can never be proved but statistics nail the truth,' Subrata Mukherjee, the panchayat minister and Bankura candidate, told journalists. A political veteran, he was the only minister from the controversial Congress stalwart Siddhartha Shankar Ray's 1972–77 cabinet to again grab a ministerial berth after the fall of the Left regime in 2011. 'Just think of it, Amiya Patra is such a big leader of the CPM, a central committee member. He got 75,000 votes from Taldangra assembly seat in 2016. His votes can never be only 100,282 in a Lok Sabha poll comprising seven assembly segments.'

In the 2019 Lok Sabha elections, Amiya Patra got only 20,569 votes from the Taldangra assembly segment of Bankura Lok Sabha. The BJP's candidate Subhas Sarkar pulled in 6.75 lakh votes in Bankura, defeating Subrata Mukherjee by 1.75 lakh votes.

Patra refuted Mukherjee's charges and blamed the TMC for the rise of the BJP. 'People have voted for the BJP to get freedom from TMC's atrocities. Mukherjee knows it very well that my house came under attack from the TMC during the panchayat elections. Many of our comrades were physically assaulted. Some are staying away from home. People thought that, to survive, they had to go with the BJP for this election at least. This is simply because the BJP is ruling at the Centre.'

Micro analyses of the assembly-wise and booth-wise results of the Lok Sabha elections revealed that the Left got virtually no share of the Muslim vote and the Congress too received little support in Muslim-dominated pockets, except in parts of Malda and Murshidabad districts. Muslims overwhelmingly voted for the TMC. In Kolkata South Lok Sabha, in the Hindu-dominated Behala Paschim and Behala Purba assembly segments, the Left candidate Nandini Mukherjee received 39,836 votes and 33,794 votes, respectively. But she was favoured by only 3,976 voters in Kolkata Port and 8,518 voters in Ballygunge – the two assembly segments with a large proportion of Muslims.

Booth-level analysis of a portion of the Muslim-dominated Beniapukur area in the Ballygunge assembly segment showed that in twelve booths, numbered 7 to 18, the BJP polled only 375 votes altogether, against 6,145 votes in favour of the TMC. Congress got slightly more votes than the BJP, and the Left scored less. In the Kolkata Port segment, in booth numbers 1 to 32, the BJP received only 667 votes, against 14,791 polled in favour of the TMC. In the thirteen polling booths in ward IV of Kharagpur municipal town, in the Kharagpur Sadar assembly segment in Midnapore Lok Sabha, the TMC secured between 393 and 840 votes, while the BJP managed to get between eleven and forty votes. In booth number 79, for example, the TMC got 820 votes against the BJP's twenty. In booth number 85, the TMC bagged 840 votes against the BJP's twenty-four. In the neighbouring ward, numbered V, represented by municipal vice-chairman Md. Hanif, more than 9,000 of the roughly 11,400 voters favoured the TMC.

The booth-level picture broke the myth that Left votes went only to the BJP. In Muslim-dominated areas, the traditional Left votes evidently went to the TMC.

There was another takeaway. The BJP made deep inroads among the SC and ST communities. In a state where SCs constitute 23.5 per cent of the population – West Bengal is home to India's second largest SC population, after Uttar Pradesh – and the STs another 6 per cent, this could have crucial political implications. The BJP won both the Lok Sabha seats reserved for STs and five of the ten Lok Sabha seats reserved for SCs. Of the state's 294 assembly seats, eighty-four are reserved for SCs and STs. In the Lok Sabha elections, the BJP took the lead in forty-six of these reserved assembly segments, while the TMC led in thirty-seven and the Congress in one.

A deeper look at the reserved seats revealed that the TMC led over the BJP mostly in those seats reserved for SCs and STs where Muslims made more than 25 per cent of the population. Among the reserved SC seats in which the TMC led, Hingalganj had a Muslim population of more than 50 per cent, while Swarupnagar, Horoa, Nabagram and Kharagram had Muslim populations of more than 40 per cent. Sitai and Nanoor had Muslim populations of more than 30 per cent.

The results inevitably brought back memories of the 2009 Lok Sabha elections, which marked the beginning of the Left's fall in the state. The *Telegraph* even headlined the front-page lead story in their 24 May 2019 issue, 'BJP in 2019 looks like TMC in 2009'. To some extent, it was correct. The TMC won nineteen seats in 2009, fighting in alliance with the Congress that bagged another five, and a Socialist Unity Centre of India (SUCI) candidate won with the TMC's backing.

The BJP won eighteen seats in 2019, fighting the elections all alone.

TMC leaders, however, argued that Mamata Banerjee in 2019 had a better chance of a comeback than the Left did in 2009. The Congress-TMC alliance had reduced the Left's Lok Sabha tally to less than half – from thirty-five in 2004 to fifteen in 2009. Analysing the elections assembly-segment-wise, the TMC-Congress alliance was leading in 190 of the 294 segments in 2009, well above the required mark of 147 seats. In 2019, the BJP was leading in only 128 seats. In 2009, the TMC-Congress alliance's vote share stood two percentage points above the Left's. In 2019, BJP's vote share stood 3 per cententage points below the TMC's.

In a sense, in 2009, more than half of the 2011 assembly battle was won. But for the BJP in 2019, more than half the assembly battle for 2021 remained to be won.

Mamata's Makeover

One day, Mamata Banerjee's nephew Abhishek entered the state secretariat of Nabanna, bringing along political strategist Prashant Kishor. This marked the beginning of a new chapter in West Bengal politics. The date was 6 June 2019. For the first time, a political party in the politically vibrant state had appointed a political strategist to plan recovery of its public image.

The three had a meeting for about an hour and a half, following which news spread in TMC circles that Mamata Banerjee and Prashant Kishor were close to an agreement to work together. Four days after their meeting, Mamata Banerjee, after convening an administrative review meeting at the state secretariat, announced a telephone helpline number for the public to register their grievances about delays in implementation of projects and corruption. It was not known whether this idea was originally hers, her nephew's or Kishor's. The complaints could be lodged on the phone, through text messages and email. She also announced a new cell in the chief minister's office, named 'Programme Implementation and Grievance Monitoring Cell', which would scrutinize the complaints.

Briefing the press about the decision, she said, in an apparent warning to her own party leaders, 'I remind people that no one needs to pay a paisa to get the benefits of government-provided projects such as Khadya Sathi, Sobuj Sathi and Kanyashree.'

About a week later, on 18 June, she hurled a virtual bomb at her own party in an apparent crusade against corruption.

At Nazrul Mancha auditorium in Kolkata, she was addressing TMC councillors from all parts of the state – about 2,500 of them, when she suddenly raised the issue of 'cut-money'. The term refers to illegal cuts or commissions that elected representatives take from government grants for various social welfare schemes. 'I hear people are taking Rs 25,000 from the urban housing scheme. Some of you are even taking Rs 200 from the Rs 2,000 grant under the Somobyathi project!' she said, with a shell-shocked expression on her face. Somobyathi, the Bengali word for sympathizer, is a project meant for providing funeral assistance to people below the poverty level.

And then she dropped the bombshell: 'Those of you [who] have taken cut-money, return it!' This remark would be quoted again and again by the people of her state.

Over the following weeks, starting from the very next day, Bengal stood witness to a series of unique scenes. People gathered at the residences of TMC leaders – panchayat members, municipal councillors and office-bearers at various unit levels of the TMC – seeking return of the commissions they had paid them. In most cases, the villagers told the TMC leaders that since Didi herself had ordered return of illegal commissions, they had better oblige. Some leaders had their residences gheraoed; some were manhandled and the houses of a few vandalized. Some of these leaders denied that they had taken commissions. Some said the money had already been distributed among many. Some of the leaders actually returned the amounts. Police in two districts arrested a panchayat pradhan and a panchayat member, after locals lodged complaints. The BJP, too, started organizing people to gherao TMC leaders' homes.

This decree by Mamata Banerjee created myriad controversies. The BJP's Kailash Vijayvargiya said she was sacrificing foot soldiers to protect lieutenants. Mukul Roy said Mamata Banerjee's home itself was the prime hub of cut-money. The CPM's Sujan Chakraborty and Mohammad Salim asked whether those who were seen accepting cash in the Narada tapes would return the money too. TMC MP Shatabdi Roy publicly said she was wondering how the grassroots-level corrupt would get back the share they had passed on to their political bosses. Is it ever possible that refunds would come down to the lowest ranks from the top, she asked, speaking to journalists at her constituency of Birbhum. A few TMC councillors from distant districts publicly said Didi had landed them in trouble, that she had stolen their sleep. At some places, clashes broke out between those claiming refunds and those refuting the charges against them, branding the agitation as a BJP-hatched conspiracy.

There were other noticeable changes in Mamata Banerjee. Her attendance in the assembly increased. The monsoon session started on 21 June and ended on 10 July. She attended six of the fourteen functioning days – her highest session attendance during her two regimes, opposition leaders claimed. She convened, for the first time, a meeting with all MLAs representing seats reserved for SCs and STs to discuss issues requiring immediate attention. This was her first meeting to which MLAs from opposition parties were invited, according to Abdul Mannan, leader of the Opposition.

'Of course, she is now keen on knowing the issues that ruined her fortune,' Mannan remarked, in a conversation with this author.

Enter 'PK'

The cut-money row was continuing for over a month, when Mamata Banerjee launched the 'Didike Bolo' or 'Tell Didi' campaign, designed by Prashant Kishor's organization Indian Political Action Committee (I-PAC), on 29 July. Kishor had already met the TMC's state unit leaders and district unit presidents to know about their opinion of the electoral debacle.

Didike Bolo was a multi-layered, public outreach campaign. In addition to the existing toll-free number at the CMO, this was another phone number, to be manned by an I-PAC team. There would also be a website, on which people could complain about anything. A dedicated team would coordinate between the administration and TMC ranks to solve them. The most significant part of the programme was perhaps the 'gramey chalo' (go to the villages), under which 1,000 elected public representatives, from panchayat members to MPs and ministers, would have to visit 10,000 villages in the next 100 days, engage with local residents and civil society personalities, dine and spend the night at the residence of a booth-level party worker, and hoist the party flag the next day before moving out.

On these tours, the leaders would distribute cards with the contact details of the Didike Bolo helpline printed on them. However, no leader could tour the village of his or her own choice. Team PK would provide every detail – the name of the village and the name of the village influentials who must be met. The leader, however, was at liberty to choose the party worker at whose residence one night was mandated to be spent.

Pushing her leaders to face the public amidst the raging cut-money row was like throwing them into a snake pit. But the leaders had no alternative. They could face agitations, they were told, but they were not to lose their cool. They would have to be patient listeners. They would have to report their tours to the top leadership, with photographs and videos as evidence.

The helpline became a hit. In one month, one million citizens used the phone and website facilities to flag their concerns, the TMC claimed. There were many success stories – of people having their problems solved at striking speed – and the TMC's newly-revamped IT cell focused all its energies on broadcasting these stories. People sought help for hospitalization, people telephoned seeking ambulances, people complained about panchayat-level corruption, administrative red-tape, about crime and criminals and malpractices, and even personal difficulties.

The village outreach programme too resulted in a flood of stories in the mainstream media, as people vented their grievances about a range of issues when they saw the netas coming to them, now mandated by their leader to adopt a soft approach.

Soon, Mamata Banerjee herself started paying unscheduled visits to different villages and slum areas during her tours of the districts. She walked into people's homes, sat in front of their slums and at roadside tea stalls, inquiring from the residents about their key problems.

Saffron Renaissance

14 August 2019. 'Bengal does not need guidance from outside. Bengal is showing the path to the whole country,' said Surendra Jain, international joint general secretary of Vishwa Hindu Parishad.

'Jai Shree Ram!' the audience of about 200 roared in approval.

He was in the Jamini Roy auditorium of the International Centre for Cultural Relations (ICCR) in Kolkata to launch the VHP's Hindi mouthpiece, *Hindu Vishwa*'s special issue on West Bengal, titled *'Bangal ek aur Navjagran ke Rah par'* (Bengal on the Verge of another Renaissance).

Jain elaborated on this notion: 'Take the case of Howrah. The whole country was concerned about the practice of offering namaz blocking roads. They jam train compartments and rail stations; create traffic jams on roads, block ambulances, and people die. And yet they are so shameless about it! This is not at all about showing your devotion to Allah. It's all about displaying power. But Howrah showed the way. Howrah said that we are not going to be scared of your power. They read Hanuman Chalisa on road. And the namaz on the roads stopped. Yes, if they block roads for namaz, we will block roads for reading Hanuman Chalisa and offering maha aarti. The governments are bowing and laws are being made. Uttar Pradesh has brought a regulation already and others will follow too!'

On 25 June, about 100 members of the BJP's youth wing sat on the Grand Trunk Road (NH2) in Howrah, blocking traffic, to read the Hanuman Chalisa. Such events were repeated at different places in Howrah on NH2 on two more Tuesdays – 2 July and 9 July. This programme then spread to Uttar Pradesh, first on 14 July in Sambhal district, and then in the districts of Hathras, Aligarh, Baghpat and Bulandshahr. The maha aarti was added to the reading of the Chalisa. Other organizations, including the BJP's Kisan Morcha and the VHP's Bajrang Dal, joined the 'protest' bandwagon, following which the administration (first in Aligarh district) announced prohibition on the offering of namaz and the performing of Hindu rituals on the roads. The saffron camp took it as a victory.

Back in Howrah, the practice stopped after trouble broke out between the police and BJP supporters, leading to a terrible traffic jam on 16 July.

It triggered a debate within Howrah district BJP, as a section of the party thought such events could antagonize the general public that had to suffer the traffic jams.

In the Jamini Roy auditorium, Jain was visibly upbeat. 'This year, the auspicious fourth Monday or the month of Shravan and the Eid collided. In twenty places in the country, Muslims attacked Hindu processions. There was not a single case in Bengal. This is a direct impact of the new Renaissance in Bengal.'

On the dais sat the RSS's south Bengal secretary Jisnu Basu, *Swastika* editor Rantidev Sengupta, the BJP's refugee cell convenor Mohit Ray and the national head of the chain of Hindu Milan Mandirs of the Bharat Sevashram Sangh, Swami Gurupadananda. Almost all the speakers stressed on the need to have the Mamata Banerjee government overthrown to save the Hindus of Bengal.

Jisnu Basu said that the series of episodes of political violence that the state had witnessed along the areas bordering Bangladesh 'is in reality part of a project for ethnic cleansing of the Hindus so that the areas could turn into hubs of infiltrator-run rackets of fake currency and terror networks.'

He lauded the VHP for helping the slogan of 'Jai Shree Ram' reach every nook and corner of the state and said that popularization of the slogan would continue to top Sangh Parivar's agenda in Bengal. 'Without 'Jai Shree Ram', the people of Bengal will no longer remain Hindus,' he said.

The audience cheered him with 'Jai Shree Ram'! Once, twice, thrice. 'Jai Jai Shree Ram!'

Mohit Ray's speech was brief and to the point. He suggested that a movement was needed in Bengal seeking removal of mosques that had been built on the ruins of Hindu temples. 'There is a good example to start with,' Ray said, 'The Zafar Khan Ghazi dargah and masjid at Tribeni in Hooghly district was built on the compound of a Hindu temple that was destroyed by a Muslim raiding party during the thirteenth century. It's history. The pre-existing Hindu temple is still visible. There are signboards put up by the Archaeological Survey of India. And the place is also a Tribeni, or confluence. In Uttar Pradesh, Ganga, Yamuna and Saraswati meet. In Hooghly's Tribeni, Ganga (Bhagirathi), Jamuna (not the same as north India's Yamuna) and Saraswati (not the same as north India's elusive Saraswati) separate. I think there is a need to initiate a prayag yatra in Tribeni and to build a movement around the dargah and the mosque of Zafar Khan Ghazi.'

The Zafar Khan Ghazi mosque is considered Bengal's oldest. The Archaeological Survey of India's website describes it thus: 'The mosque is the first available example of the brick and stone style and is far advanced than the Qutbud Islam Mosque in Delhi. At the front part of the complex are located two roofless square chambers, one at the east contains graves of Zafar Khan Gazi, his sons and a daughter-in-law, while the other one contains graves of another son and grandsons. In the construction of both the Mosque and Dargah profuse use of carved stone members of various religious affiliations are noticed.'

NRC vs CAB

The BJP took its post-Lok Sabha-election organizational expansion drive in two stages – a membership drive over June-July-August, and organizational elections between September and December. The ideological battle was renewed with the Centre's moves on Kashmir – abrogation of Articles 370 and 35A and bifurcation of the state.

The TMC was not yet sure what had caused its electoral debacle but the party leadership had started wondering if 'taking Modi's hyper-nationalism head on' was a blunder. So, when the parliament debated the Centre's moves, the TMC took no stand and walked out before the voting, protesting 'procedural hara-kiri' on the part of the Centre. They were cautious about not getting branded as 'anti-national' and maintained absolute silence, even as voices of protest started emerging from a section of Bengal's Muslim community leaders. Sensing Mamata Banerjee's dilemma, the Left parties in the state started talking about 'gross injustice to the people of Kashmir' in their bid to woo the Muslims.

The BJP launched a state-wide micro- and macro-level campaign, describing 'the integration of Kashmir with the rest of India' as the fulfilment of Syama Prasad Mookerjee's dream that ultimately caused

Bengal's great son his untimely death. Modi had pegged the decision as a tribute to Mookerjee, and Bengal BJP organized celebrations across the state, thanking Modi for helping realize Mookerjee's dream. '*Jahan huye balidan Mookerjee woh Kashmir hamara hai*' was a slogan concerning Mookerjee that never found popularity in his homeland of Bengal. It now started rending the air, as the BJP leaders addressed street-corner meetings, indoor conventions and public gatherings in all districts and assembly segments. '*Woh Kashmir hamara hai, jo saarey ka saara hai!*'

The TMC was trying to address its organizational deficiencies by revamping its different wings, reviving the near-defunct farmers' wing and the SC-ST-OBC cell. However, it was yet to find an answer to the BJP's ideological challenge on issues concerning nationalism, patriotism and terror. The exclusion of 1.9 million names from the final list of the Assam NRC, published on 31 August 2019, gave Mamata Banerjee an issue on the ideological front once again.

For decades, action against infiltration and infiltrators had been one of the BJP's top concerns in West Bengal, the state with India's third highest population density. The issue of infiltration from Bangladesh into West Bengal and Assam has been one of the top items in the Sangh's agenda for years. In Assam, an exercise to detect and expel foreigners was agreed upon by the Rajiv Gandhi government through the Assam Accord signed in 1985 to end a six-year-old militant-movement in the state seeking expulsion of illegal immigrants who entered the state after 25 March 1971.[9] However, the process of citizenship screening did not start and, in 2009, the matter reached the Supreme Court, which in December 2013 ordered the Centre to complete the process of identifying bona fide Indian citizens as per rules set by the Assam Accord.

The work actually started in February 2015. There was no concept of religious discrimination in the Assam Accord. So, both Hindus and Muslims, mostly Bengalis, faced the trouble after the publication of the draft list in July 2018. When the final list was published in August 2019, media reports indicated Hindu Bengalis made the majority of those excluded from the citizenship list. This had put the BJP in a spot of bother in West Bengal, as for Bengal they had a proper plan of differentiating between Hindu and

Muslim migrants, welcoming the first group as persecuted refugees and seeking expulsion of the second group as infiltrators.

In September 2019, panic gripped the people of West Bengal, Hindus and Muslims alike. The list of documents required for the Assam NRC came into circulation in West Bengal through Facebook and WhatsApp. Many realized that they did not have the kind of papers sought for the Assam NRC. Mamata Banerjee made no delay in making good use of the situation. She was for 'inclusionary politics', she said in the first week of September, 'as against their exclusionary politics.' To suit her position, she also dumped her Bengali-first approach adopted in May-June 2019 and started addressing the Hindi-speaking population once again, saying that Bengal belonged to all, to people from all castes, creeds, religions and sects.

From mid-September, panic spread, especially in the districts bordering Bangladesh and those around Kolkata, over the routine exercise of updating digital ration cards and correcting voter ID cards. People turned up at those correction centres in their hundreds and stood in serpentine queues from dawn to dusk. The death of two persons on the morning of 20 September were attributed to panic over NRC by their relatives. By evening, Mamata Banerjee had grabbed the issue. She announced Rs 2 lakh in compensation to each of the families and assured the people of Bengal, saying, 'They will have to throw me out first before touching a single one of you.'

Dilip Ghosh retorted soon: 'Mamata Banerjee has no power. She can do nothing. She could not impede the removal of Article 370. She could not stop the triple talaq bill. She won't be able to save a single infiltrator from NRC.'

Over the following week, as more such deaths and suicides started to get attributed to panic over NRC, the TMC intensified its campaign, blaming the BJP's threat of implementing NRC in Bengal for the mess. The state government ran a series of campaigns on TV channels and in daily newspapers, urging people not to panic and assuring them that the state government would never allow any citizenship screening exercise in Bengal.

The BJP's Bengal unit leaders were visibly under pressure. It had been decided early in September that the party's focus in Bengal should be the highlighting of BJP's move on Kashmir as a tribute to the neglected

Bengal luminary S.P. Mookerjee, and the cornering of the TMC over the Citizenship Amendment Bill. The CAB was the BJP's trump card for Bengal. It would protect the Hindus from facing what the Hindu Bengalis in Assam had to undergo. The state's BJP leaders were advised to avoid talking about NRC unless it became necessary.

It was about five months ago, on 12 April 2019, that Amit Shah had made his controversially famous '*aap chronology samjhiye*' (please understand the chronology) remark when addressing the media at a hotel in Rajarhat area in Kolkata's eastern fringes early in the morning.[10] To appeal to the Hindu migrant vote bank, Shah had said, 'First, the Citizenship Amendment Bill (CAB) will be brought and all refugees will be given citizenship. Then the NRC will be implemented. So the refugees need not worry but the infiltrators must worry.'

After the Lok Sabha election, the party realized that even this was not sufficiently reassuring, and there were pockets where the party missed out on prospective votes because a section of Hindu migrants continued to be in a panic over the prospect of the NRC. The VHP's Sachindra Nath Singha and BJP's Dilip Ghosh had told this author in July 2019 that the party should avoid talking about the NRC until the CAB had been passed. However, as Mamata Banerjee centred her campaign on the NRC, all guns blazing, BJP leaders failed to find a suitable response without raising the subject. The tone of Dilip Ghosh's comments on the NRC was fluctuating. Finally, Amit Shah decided to address a gathering in Kolkata to clear all confusion about the NRC. That would be on 1 October. It would be his first visit to Bengal after taking charge as the Union home minister.

In another change of tactics on the part of the state administration, the police did not allow the Left workers to show black flags to Shah. When a group of CPM leaders and workers gathered near Kolkata airport, the police swiftly picked them up, took them to a police station and kept them detained until Shah had taken the return flight. The TMC called protecting Shah a 'constitutional duty'.

At Netaji Indoor Stadium, Shah lashed out at Mamata Banerjee. 'We introduced CAB in the Rajya Sabha to grant citizenship to the Hindus, Sikhs, Buddhists, Jains, Christians and Zoroastrians who were forced to migrate from the neighbouring Islamic countries in the face of religious persecution. But TMC MPs did not allow the Rajya Sabha to function. CAB could not be introduced in the Rajya Sabha. If the refugees have not been able to get Indian citizenship till date, it is because of the TMC. However, the situation has changed. However much the TMC may oppose it, CAB is set to be introduced in the Rajya Sabha.'

'After ensuring the rights of Hindus and other minorities (from the neighbouring Islamic countries), each and every infiltrator will be thrown out,' Shah said.

On the ground, Shah's assurance had little effect. A Facebook group named 'No-NRC Movement' was created on 5 September. By 15 October 2019, it had 57,000 members and recorded more than 58,000 posts between 17 September and 15 October. It seemed like the majority of its members, or at least the more active ones, were Hindus. They hailed from various backgrounds – supporters of the Left and the TMC, members of organizations for Dalits, Muslims and refugees, human rights groups and Bengali ethnic rights associations. Their BJP bashing had so far centred on their opposition to the NRC. But from October, after Shah's speech, the so-called 'no-NRC' movement started showing signs of adopting a 'no-CAB' stance too. The protestors pointed out, citing examples from Assam, how CAB posed a great danger to Bengali Hindus. Another similar group, called 'Joint Forum against NRC', also began an anti-CAB campaign as part of its agenda.

Kolkata is often called *michhil nogori,* or the city of rallies. About this time, almost whole of Bengal turned into a land of rallies; some opposing the NRC and CAB and others supporting them.

Governor Dhankhar

Governor Keshari Nath Tripathi left Bengal on 28 July 2019, with a parting shot at Mamata Banerjee – he said that 'her policy of appeasement has the effect of adversely affecting societal harmony'. He said that discrimination in Bengal was 'apparent' and that the CM's statements themselves reflected the discrimination.[11] His successor, Jagdeep Dhankhar, a sixty-eight-year-old lawyer practising in the Supreme Court of India, was sworn in on 30 July. He started from where Tripathi left off, only to take the criticism of the CM and the confrontation with the government to an unprecedented level.

Like Tripathi, Dhankhar too had a background in the BJP. He served as a Janata Dal MP (1989-91) from Jhunjhunu in Rajasthan and a minister of state in V.P. Singh's government. In 1991, he switched over to the Congress, contested from Ajmer Lok Sabha, but lost. In 1993, he became a member of the Rajasthan assembly from Kishangarh, but in 1998, contesting from Jhunjhunu Lok Sabha, he came third. He joined the BJP in 2003. A 2008 report in the *Indian Express* described him as 'a prominent Jat leader' who was part of the BJP's 2008 assembly election campaign committee.[12] In 2016, he was the national convener of the BJP's law and legal affairs department. After taking charge as Bengal's constitutional head, he took less than two months to get involved in a confrontation with the state government.

It was on 19 September. Union minister Babul Supriyo had visited the campus of Jadavpur University to attend an event organized by the ABVP and found himself amidst a gherao by activists of various leftwing student groups, who were demanding an apology from Supriyo for 'BJP's divisive plots named CAB and NRC'. After about an hour of chaos, Supriyo managed to move into the auditorium where the event was being held. However, a section of the leftwing students kept waiting outside the auditorium and the siege resumed as soon as Supriyo tried to move out.

With Supriyo failing to move out of the campus for hours, Dhankhar first asked the JU vice-chancellor Suranjan Das to call in the police – which Das flatly refused to do – and then telephoned the chief secretary Malay De and also Mamata Banerjee, asking for the immediate rescue of Supriyo. Then he himself left for the campus to rescue the minister. He too fell in the middle of the gherao, did not get down from his car, but ultimately left the campus taking Supriyo along. That was about five hours since Supriyo tried to move out of the auditorium. While the gherao was continuing near Gate No 3, the office of the arts faculty students' union, at that time run by the CPM's student wing Students' Federation of India (SFI), was vandalized, and Che Guevara's images defaced, and 'ABVP' written all over the walls, allegedly by ABVP activists.

Mamata Banerjee was furious. The TMC government, after initially trying to increase its influence on the JU campus and falling utterly short, failing to bring any significant number of teachers or students under its influence, had adopted a no-confrontation policy. The teachers and students were still mostly under the influence of various Left organizations. Now, according to some senior TMC leaders, Banerjee not only had requested Dhankhar to remain patient but also told him that the government was in favour of dealing with students' issues 'softly'; but Dhankhar, apart from doing exactly the opposite, also issued media statements criticizing the state government. 'The incident of gherao of Union Minister Babul Supriyo and others by a section of the students in Jadavpur University is a very serious matter. It is an adverse reflection on the law enforcement agency in the state,' news agency PTI quoted him as saying.

The TMC spokesperson and state education minister Partha Chatterjee issued a statement the next day, stating that the party 'strongly opposed' Dhankhar's 'political views'. 'Hon'ble Governor went there without taking the State Government into confidence. On his way, he rang up the CM. CM requested him several times that the Governor being the constitutional head need not go at this moment. The CM requested him to give the government some time to peacefully solve the issue. But instead of taking the government into confidence, the Governor went there to help the BJP. Before going there, he released two press statements that I quote: "This is a very serious reflection on the law and order in the State." He, of course, did not offer any comment on the vandalism perpetrated by the BJP and ABVP goons in the Jadavpur University campus today,' read Chatterjee's statement.[13]

While Dhankhar kept defending his move, and indeed did not offer any comment on the vandalism of the union room, Dilip Ghosh said that the right thing had been done. 'It is appropriate that the union office was vandalized. Just as we demolished the camps in Pakistan in surgical strike, the rooms that are cradles of anti-nationals should be demolished. We know how to break the arms that attacked Babul,' he told the media[14].

If that was the beginning of the governor's acrimonious relationship with the government, the intensity kept increasing and the confrontation soon appeared to be the new normal. The next confrontation started over Dhankhar's announcement that he would start holding administrative meetings with top officials in different districts. This was something Mamata Banerjee used to do on a regular basis and these meetings in the districts, in which top state officials used to accompany Banerjee, used to be broadcast live on social media, and often TV channels.

But the government was not happy with Dhankhar's announcement, arguing that there was no precedence of any governor holding such meetings and interfering with the daily affairs of an elected government. When Dhankhar reached Siliguri for an administrative meeting on September 24, he found no senior official present at the venue. Dhankhar slammed the government and said that he would call and attend similar meetings in other districts too to inquire into the state of affairs as regards to the people's well-being.

His 23 October visit to Dhamakhali in Sunderbans, where he called a meeting of all top administrative officers and public representatives from North 24 Parganas and South 24 Parganas, elicited similar response. No official turned up. Dhankhar questioned if the government had enforced a censorship on officers. When Dhankhar turned his focus on the state-run universities of which he was the chancellor, deciding to start attending their 'court' meetings – which his predecessors hardly ever did – and started issuing directives to different vice-chancellors, the government in December 2019 framed rules for an Act related to governing of universities, and curbed the chancellor's role in the functioning of the varsities. All communications between the governor and the VCs/ varsities will have to be channeled through the state education department, the rules said.

Dhankhar gradually emerged as one of the most vocal critics of the state government, prompting the TMC to say that Dhankhar was trying to play the leader of the opposition. The party accused him of abusing his chair to serve the BJP's purpose. Dhankhar repeatedly justified his role, saying, 'I am not a proactive governor, I am an active governor.' He said that his role was not merely of a rubber stamp, he was 'not a tourist', not there for holidaying. The state of the people of the state was his concern and that he had to perform the duties for which he was sworn in.

Finally, on 5 December, Mamata Banerjee herself targeted the Centre and the governor, referring to the dramatic developments in Maharashtra over the formation of the new government, and accused the Centre of running parallel governments. 'We'll fight it out,' she said, while referring to how the Bengal governor's delay in according permission for introducing a Bill in the assembly had led to the untimely adjournment of the assembly session. Dhankhar retorted, saying the blame could not be put on him since it was the government which had not supplied him with adequate information he had sought.

The battle continued ceaselessly, as Dhankhar emerged as one of Mamata Banerjee's sharpest critics, while being full of praises for the Modi-led Centre.

A Blow in the Bye-elections

Despite all the chaos and panic over the NRC, the BJP looked the clear favourite in two of the three assembly seats going for bye-elections on 25 November 2019. Kharagpur Sadar and Karimpur seats fell vacant after the BJP's Dilip Ghosh and TMC's Mahua Moitra got elected to the Lok Sabha. In Kaliaganj, Congress MLA Pramatha Nath Roy's death had necessitated the bye-election.

Going by the 2019 Lok Sabha election trends, the BJP had a lead of 56,762 votes over the TMC in Kaliaganj in North Dinajpur district and of 45,123 votes over the TMC in Kharagpur Sadar, Dilip Ghosh's own assembly constituency in West Midnapore district. In the Kaliaganj segment, the BJP had secured 52.15 per cent of the polled votes and in Kharagpur 57.23 per cent. The leads were considered unsurpassable in a matter of just six months. In Nadia district's Karimpur, the TMC had a lead of about 14,340 votes over the BJP and was expected to retain the seat.

Adding a slight twist to the Lok Sabha equation, the Left and the Congress patched up this time. Congress decided to support the Left candidate at Karimpur and the Left would support the Congress candidates in the two other constituencies.

The three constituencies represented three different segments of the society. Kaliaganj was dominated by the Rajbanshi, Bengal's largest scheduled caste community and the area's original inhabitants. Karimpur was about 30 per cent Muslim, and a significant number of its Hindus were migrants from Bangladesh. Kharagpur Sadar's population was dominated by people speaking Hindi and Telugu. Therefore, the results of the three elections could indicate a general trend, political parties and analysts thought.

A high-voltage campaign in the constituencies, involving MPs, MLAs, senior state-level leaders and celebrities belonging to both parties, started in the beginning of November. Behind the limelight were two other groups of players – the swayamsevaks associated with different Sangh Parivar organizations aiding the BJP, and 'Team PK' handling electoral micro-management for the TMC. How the swayamsevaks worked to build public opinion in favour of the BJP without holding up the BJP flag has already been discussed earlier.

Team PK, as they were known in TMC circles, started working in Kharagpur and Kaliaganj from mid-October, even before the parties had decided on their candidates. Each of these teams comprised about forty I-PAC employees, who drew a volunteer force from the TMC's booth-level workers to prepare the booth-management mechanism. I-PAC members did discrete surveys in different localities to get hints of the public image of local TMC leaders and identified netas with a bad reputation. These netas were kept out of the campaign. Team PK met for one hour every day, prepared the daily campaign schedule for all sorts of leaders – a very tight schedule, as the leaders described it – and advised them on the specific issues needed to be addressed in each locality. Also, for the first time, the TMC released constituency-specific election manifestos.

'Their team monitored the activities of all leaders – to see whether their full efforts were behind the campaign or not. This kept all of us under the scanner and under pressure,' a TMC leader from Kaliaganj told this author. This was a step taken to deal with the issue of infighting within the TMC, he said. In Kharagpur Sadar, where the TMC was fraught with factionalism, team PK ensured that everyone backed the party's nominee, the young and energetic civic chairman, Pradip Sarkar.

The BJP's initial plan was to target the TMC for misgovernance and corruption, but most of their top leaders in the state ended up devoting the lion's share of their campaign time speaking on the NRC and CAB, trying to assure the Hindus of no harm when a citizenship screening exercise takes place, as the TMC, the Left and the Congress were repeatedly citing the Assam example to warn Hindus in West Bengal against falling into the BJP's trap.

The results came as a shock to the BJP in general and to Dilip Ghosh in particular. It was a green sweep, with the TMC winning all three seats. The election result in Kharagpur Sadar was construed as a personal defeat for Dilip Ghosh, as the TMC trounced the BJP by 20,853 votes. Its vote share, which was 29.58 per cent in the May 2019 Lok Sabha election from this assembly area, was 47.66 per cent in this election. The BJP, which had a vote share of 57.23 per cent in the Lok Sabha election, had a vote share of 34.02 per cent now.

The Kaliaganj results were no less disastrous for the BJP. The TMC won by 2,414 votes. Its vote share in this assembly segment had been 27.25 per cent in the Lok Sabha election. It was 44.65 per cent this time. The BJP's share had been 52.15 per cent in the Lok Sabha elections. The assembly elections gave it only 43.54 per cent. In May, the parliamentary candidates of the Left and the Congress had together secured 37,801 votes in Kaliaganj. In the bye-election, the Left-backed Congress candidate got only 18,857 votes. The TMC evidently gained from both the BJP and the Left-Congress camps.

Overall, in the three seats, the TMC secured 47.53 per cent of the polled votes, and the BJP 39.29 per cent.

The TMC had reasons to celebrate. Its vote share had not only increased, compared with its Lok Sabha electoral performance, but the party had also won Kharagpur Sadar and Kaliaganj seats for the first time since the birth of the TMC twenty-one years ago.

A section of the BJP leaders, including Dilip Ghosh, tried to downplay the defeat by arguing that bye-election results tended to favour the state's ruling party everywhere across India. However, in a similar tumultuous political situation in Bengal in 2009, the TMC-Congress combine, after dealing the ruling Left a deadly blow by winning twenty-five of the forty-two Lok Sabha seats, had continued their victory run in the assembly bye-elections held six months later, winning eight of ten seats. The Left managed to win only one. The Left's fall had become almost certain.

But the BJP's dream run had hit a speed breaker.

The Blame Game

Two reasons, in general, were attributed to such a swing of the vote – mass panic over the NRC, and the TMC's image makeover drive, managed by Team PK. The TMC's winning candidate in Kaliaganj, Tapan Deb Singha, cited NRC, Team PK and the concerted efforts of the state leadership behind the party's success. Karimpur winner Bimalendu Singha Roy, a retired teacher, echoed him. Dilip Ghosh, however, blamed 'overconfidence' among a section of the BJP workers.

'The NRC is the main factor. It came as a terrible blow. People got scared and we failed to counter the TMC's campaign,' the BJP's Kaliaganj candidate Kamal Chandra Sarkar told this author in a telephonic conversation a day after the results. 'There was extreme Muslim polarization against us and in favour of the TMC. Muslim votes didn't split at all,' he said, citing the results from three booths to support his analysis. At booth number 185, the BJP got one vote against 734 in favour of the TMC and ninety-one for the Congress; in booth number 157, the BJP got eleven votes against 777 in favour of the TMC and 117 in favour of the Congress; and in booth number 175, the BJP got twelve votes against 1,052 in favour of the TMC and twenty-five for the Congress.

Dilip Ghosh had no hesitation in admitting that the party had failed to address properly 'the confusion spread by the TMC over the NRC'. 'But their gain is only for a short time, as their weapon will be blunted the moment we bring CAB in parliament. It's going to be soon. Let the TMC oppose it,' Ghosh said, while interacting with the media at the state unit office, looking unfazed as always, even as the BJP's opponents kept labelling the party's loss in Kharagpur as the defeat of Ghosh's brand of politics.

Rubbing salt on Ghosh's wounds, two articles in the RSS's *Swastika*, in its 9 December issue, sharply criticized the BJP's state unit for letting Mamata Banerjee regain lost ground. One article, titled, 'Dependence on Modi-Shah's magic must be reduced for winning Bengal Assembly elections', was written by Swapan Dasgupta, whose involvement in affairs related to Bengal had been steadily increasing over the recent months. 'The swing observed in the elections has proved it beyond doubt that people believed Mamata Banerjee's devastating campaign on NRC. In contrast, the BJP failed to launch a counter-attack citing the positives of NRC and CAB. The local leaders' relentless campaign insisting that NRC will surely be carried out in the future only led the BJP into Mamata's trap,' Dasgupta wrote.

He went on to say, 'In the absence of a competent local leader, there is excessive dependence on the brains of major national leaders. As a result of this, the old branding of the BJP – that the party does not fit into the psyche, characteristics and culture of the Bengali people – has revived.'

The other article, titled 'No room for complacency', was written by *Swastika* editor Rantidev Sengupta. It said that the by-polls were 'extremely important' from the perspective of the 2021 assembly elections and that the defeats brought the BJP 'not only discomfort but also utmost disgrace'. He opined that in creating a public perception for the battle of 2021, 'the TMC has marched way ahead [of the BJP]' and that the results reflected 'ominous portents' for the BJP.

These criticisms in the public forum did not go down well with the party's state leadership. 'One of the writers is a Rajya Sabha member and the other was the party's Lok Sabha candidate. They would have done better by placing their views within the party,' state unit general secretary Sayantan Basu told this author.

The state BJP's internal assessment, carried out by three general secretaries Sayantan Basu, Raju Banerjee and Sanjay Singh, blamed overconfidence, complacency and infighting among party workers and functionaries, a member of the party's state committee told this author.

Citizenship Amendment Act

The CAB was tabled and passed in the Lok Sabha on 9 December 2019 and in the Rajya Sabha two days later – thus turning it into the Citizenship Amendment Act (CAA). The TMC took a leading role in opposing the CAB, alleging that its provisions violated the basic tenets of the Indian Constitution. 'What citizenship are you (Modi) giving? Don't these people already have their documents? Why should anyone enjoying all benefits here suddenly declare himself as a foreigner?' Mamata Banerjee had said in Kolkata. 'No NRC, no CAB,' she made her stance clear.

But barely two days after the passage of the bill in the Rajya Sabha, lawlessness broke out in the Muslim-dominated pockets in the districts of Howrah, Malda and Murshidabad, with protests by hundreds of people against the passage of the CAA turning violent and targeting Central government properties such as railway stations and highway toll plazas. Banerjee was trying to contain the protests – the vandalism went on for three days – with a soft policing approach (under no circumstances could the police open fire) supplemented by her own aggressive political moves, consisting of a series of peaceful agitations against the CAA, while repeatedly assuring the people that she would never let the legislation be implemented in the state.

When rights activists and left the parties demanded that she also scrap the process of updating the National Population register (NPR), on the ground that NPR was the first step towards the nationwide NRC, she even halted all process related to updating NPR, which the Centre had described as a mandatory exercise to be carried out along with the house-listing phase of Census between April and September 2020. 'Census will happen,' she said, 'but not NPR.'[15]

The BJP was not sitting silent either. Initially, celebrations took place in the areas dominated by Bangladeshi Hindu migrants over Amit Shah's announcement in parliament that no one needed to submit any proof of their entry to India or of religious persecution in Bangladesh (self-declaration would do), and that everyone seeking citizenship under the new Act will continue to enjoy all the rights and facilities they had been enjoying on the day of the application. 'These two declarations have killed all apprehensions created in the minds of the refugees by the TMC's misinformation campaign,' Matua-leader-turned-BJP Bongaon MP Shantanu Thakur told journalists, a day after the Bill was passed in the Rajya Sabha. The BJP lined up an abhinandan jatra (congratulatory march) across the state, to be led by state-level leaders, to congratulate Modi and Shah. Rallies would be held in every assembly segment, and street corner meetings in every panchayat area.

Leading from the front, Dilip Ghosh unleashed a stream of headline-grabbers at his rallies in different parts of the state. Here are some of them:

- 'Lungi-clad terrorists are holding Bengal hostage'.[16] (16 December, Kolkata)
- 'A conspiracy is being hatched to turn West Bengal into West Bangladesh. Those opposing CAA are all infiltrators who have got their names enlisted as voters here and are voting for a particular party.' (17 December, Kolkata)
- 'We are seeing Didi-inspired lungi dance all over Bengal over the past three days. Wearing lungi, they uprooted railway tracks, set buses and trains on fire and vandalized railway stations. It's these people for whom Bengal needs NRC. These people need to be identified and sent back.' (18 December, Hanskhali, Nadia)
- 'Those who drove Hindus out of Bangladesh have crossed over to our land, creating disturbances and terror and destroying national assets, as the chief minister is taking their side. Didi is afraid that these people will have to go back once NRC happens.' (21 December, Bankura)

Ghosh took a break from insisting on NRC for only a few days after Modi, on 22 December, said that there had been no plan at any level of the government to implement the NRC at the national level.

Amit Shah subsequently supported Modi's statement, in effect countering his own remarks that he had repeated over and over. Top BJP ministers repeatedly said that the CAA had nothing to do with the NRC. But Ghosh's silence on NRC was short-lived. On 26 December, at the BJP state unit headquarters, he told journalists, 'NRC is required in India and first in West Bengal. When and how, whether through the government or the court, remains to be decided. But NRC is a must for Bengal. I want NRC in Bengal.'

The publication of the BJP's booklet on the CAA in the first week of January 2020 indicated that the NRC could be the BJP's Bengal-specific agenda. The booklet was published centrally, from New Delhi, in Hindi and English, and was translated into regional languages by the state units. The Hindi and English booklets made no mention of NRC. There was no report in the media of any regional language edition of the publication mentioning the NRC. But the Bengali version of the booklet was a slightly altered version. On the last of its twenty-three pages, a question read, 'Is NRC coming next? How necessary is this? Won't Hindus, too, land in jail in case of an NRC, just like in Assam?' The answer says, 'Yes, NRC comes next. At least that's the intention of the Union government.'

The booklet claimed that two crore Bangladeshi infiltrators were living in West Bengal and Assam and it was necessary that they were turned into D-voters (doubtful voters) and driven away. The final sentence of the booklet read, 'After the passage of the CAB, no Hindu, Sikh, Jain, Buddhist, Christian or Parsi will find their name in the D-voters' [doubtful voters] list. The Hindus and the Sikhs [in Punjab] have their homeland secured.'

Owing to such a heated war of words, panic continued to spread over the NRC. Anyone travelling to the villages to carry out any kind of survey carried the risk of being gheraoed by villagers as a suspected 'enemy'. On 4 January 2020, several hundred people gheraoed the residences of Jesmina Khatun and Rakiba Khatun at Dharampur village within Hariharpara police station jurisdiction in Murshidabad district. The two worked with the New Delhi-based Digital Empowerment Foundation (DEF) for implementation of Internet Saathi, the Google and Tata Trust joint venture for bringing digital literacy to women. The two had trained some women in December and had collected the names and addresses of those trained. Later, news spread that they were collecting data for the NRC. It took a huge contingent of police to rescue the women.

On the same day, under the jurisdiction of the same police station, Pratima Mandal, an auxiliary nursing midwife working with the state health department, was gheraoed at Mamudpur village. Mandal had visited the place for a survey on the Centre's immunization programme, Mission Indradhanush. The residence of Khodabax Mandal, a ration dealer, was under siege by the locals after people accused him of sharing with the Centre the details of their ration cards.

Over the next few days, health workers, ration dealers and Internet Saathi trainers came under attack in areas in the Domkal, Lalbag and Sagardighi police station jurisdictions, all in Murshidabad district. All the thirty-five women associated with the Internet Saathi programme in Sagardighi block were taken to safe shelters by the police, according to Prasenjit Banerjee, sub-divisional police officer of Jangipur. The panic then spread to neighbouring Birbhum district.

Sensing the gravity of the situation, the state government now halted all works related to the census. The situation was simply not conducive for carrying out the census, with or without the NPR. The leaders of almost all political parties were agreed on this. The enumerators could face a risk to their lives. The Internet Saathi programme was also halted in the state.

But incidents of belligerence towards strangers, or anyone whose activity entailed collection of any kind of information, continued to happen. On 4 February, two employees of a private bank were gheraoed in Kolkata after the Aadhaar updation form they distributed was found to be carrying a column for 'NPR number'. On 8 February, eight beggars from Solapur in Maharashtra were gheraoed at Ilambazar in Birbhum district. On 10 February, a group of students from a college at Gobra area in North 24 Parganas district was gheraoed while conducting a survey for a project related to their study. The students were released only after the teachers gave it in writing to the local people that the students were not collecting data for the NRC or the NPR.

If one reason for this panic was Dilip Ghosh's consistent remarks that the NRC would be implemented in West Bengal and that all the infiltrators agitating against the CAA would be driven out, the other was, quite obviously, Mamata Banerjee's persistent warning to the people not to share any personal information with anyone who might come knocking at their door. She said the BJP was using NGOs to collect data for the NPR and the NRC, and later alleged that the Centre was using banks and the postal department to collect data for the NRC and NPR. She even asked people to be watchful of anyone coming to their home identifying themselves as state government employees, as they could be carrying fake ID cards of the state government.

At a rally in Bongaon on 4 February 2020 she had said, 'I warn you against the NPR. If someone knocks on your door and asks for your parents' names and other details, do not share your papers. If someone asks for the number of family members at your home, don't tell a thing ... share personal information only when I tell you. Don't trust anyone even if they are carrying my photos. Don't trust my photos. Listen to only what you hear me say. You know me, you can recognize my voice.'[17]

'Big Brother Is Watching'

The Trinamool Congress was changing and Prashant Kishor was the change agent. If the BJP was gaining from the work of the RSS, the TMC was gaining from PK's I-PAC. Mamata's trust in PK's ways of working increased manifold, and PK started emerging as one of Didi's top confidantes after the party's assembly bye-election success.

So, what did PK advise Didi? According to a senior minister, who wished to remain anonymous, PK told the TMC top brass that four things were essential – administrative delivery, a vibrant party organization, ideological consistency and a clear perspective on what went wrong and how.

The first two aspects were covered under the elaborate, three-tier grievance redressal system, involving the grievances monitoring cell at the chief minister's office, the Didike Bolo helpline, and the survey teams of I-PAC that travelled the state's length and breadth, inquiring from the common people, grassroots-level TMC workers, panchayat members and municipal corporators their perception about administrative delivery and the reputation of local TMC leaders. There was synergy between the three tiers.

Didike Bolo helpline was used by the people to complain about anything and everything – from administrative affairs to the TMC's internal matters. The complaints were verified and acted upon. It is not that all problems were solved, but as the reach of the programme expanded with time, newspapers, TV channels and news portals were reporting an increasing number of success stories. A youth who lost a leg in an accident got a job in the education department; poor parents got their children enrolled in schools; distant villages got roads and footbridges; slums got improved sewerage and drainage systems, ambulances were booked for critical patients and pregnant women, and so on. It became the general helpline for the people.

Besides, four major policy decisions were taken based on large-scale demands: institution of a monthly pension scheme of Rs 1,000 for senior citizens from the SC and ST communities, a housing scheme for tea garden employees, relaxation of norms for obtaining caste certificates, and limiting transfer of school teachers to within their home districts.

There was another significant change – the TMC had a special focus on the backward classes, who made more than one-third of Bengal's population of 9.03 crore, according to the census of 2011. Hindus formed 70.54 per cent of the population, with the share of the SCs being 23.5 per cent of the whole population and the STs being 5.8 per cent. Even though the OBC population did not feature in census data, the state had a 7 per cent reservation for OBCs in jobs and education before Muslims too were brought under the OBC category in 2013. From a demographic perspective, Bengal was an ideal state for winning elections based on Dalit-Muslim political unity, with the two communities making up 50.5 per cent of the state's population.

'PK told us that we needed to solve the mystery of why the backward classes, especially the SCs, were in general voting against the BJP all over India but in favour for them in West Bengal,' said the TMC minister. 'PK's explanation was that corruption and highhandedness on the part of TMC leaders had hit the backward classes most, as they made the lowest strata of society and were easy prey.'

This author, however, had a feeling that Dalit votes turned towards the BJP not only because of the TMC's malpractices and highhandedness but also because of the RSS' social work. The RSS in Bengal had the state's backward regions dominated by the backward classes as their focus areas for myriad social work, penetrating the society deeper than what the TMC perceived.

From November 2019, the TMC revived its virtually defunct SC-ST-OBC cell, whose new state unit chief Paresh Chandra Das started travelling the state's nooks and corners. The party also launched a refugee cell, led by refugee leader Mukul Chandra Bairagya soon after he joined the TMC. On 14 April, B.R. Ambedkar's birth anniversary, the TMC planned programmes for SC communities across 277 assembly constituencies to felicitate well-known Dalits. In all, 2.5 lakh SC members would attend these functions. Similar programmes for the ST community would be held in ninety-seven assembly constituencies on 19 April, targeting a total audience of 50,000.[18]

On the ideological front, Kishor told the party that there should be no inconsistency in the ideology of the party so that no doubt is ever created among its core support base. The TMC, in reality, had frequently displayed ideological inconsistency. Born out of the Congress, it had joined hands with the BJP and was a partner in Vajpayee's government. Later, it took a left turn, hijacked the Left's traditional issue of land rights and brought prominent leftist intellectuals into its fold, borrowed the Left's slogans and even appropriated the Left's cultural heritage to topple the Left regime. But when the BJP and RSS targeted Mamata's rule with their right-wing questions and countered her Muslim appeasement with the slogans of Hindutva, her party struggled to come up with an appropriate strategy, and even competed with the BJP in celebrating the saffron camp's flagship religious festivals.

The party also swung between a pro-Bengali and all-inclusive stance. To make things worse for Mamata, Asaduddin Owaisi's All India Majlis Ittehad e Muslimeen (AIMIM) was trying to launch the party in the state, and was doing ground work, especially in the districts where the population is dominated by Muslims, while Mamata still had to win over a section of Muslims who voted for the Congress in the districts of Malda and Murshidabad.

'It's a very critical act of balancing. The BJP was growing banking largely on their campaigns against the TMC's Muslim appeasement and the Left; the Congress and the AIMIM were trying to tell Muslims that Didi could not be trusted, that Didi had struck a secret deal with the BJP. We had only one way open – that was to preach inclusiveness. From that perspective, we should also refrain from taking any kind of Bengali regionalist stance. We may, at the most, accuse the BJP of having no knowledge of and connect with Bengal,' a senior TMC MP told this author about the party's new approach.

By early March 2020, PK was at the forefront of the TMC. At the party's 2 March meeting at Netaji Indoor Stadium, where Mamata Banerjee addressed about 25,000 leaders from various levels in the party, Kishor sat among the top-ranking leaders. The next day, during a meeting at the TMC state unit office in Topsia, Abhishek Banerjee and Kishor addressed the attendees. Both told the gathering, in no uncertain terms, that the party was bent on seeing a free and fair election in the civic polls. The 2020 polls in about 100 civic bodies were being seen as a dress rehearsal for the 2021 assembly elections, but the TMC was in no mood to lose the state by earning a bad name if it attempted to win a few municipal wards and civic bodies that it did not deserve to win.

Among the TMC leaders in the districts, Team PK, and PK himself, became a feared name. Leaders felt they were being shadowed and were under surveillance. I-PAC's surveying teams were travelling everywhere. All the reports they gathered would be scanned and the extracts would reach Abhishek Banerjee and Mamata Banerjee, via PK. Fear spread among them the leaders after *Anandabazar Patrika* reported how Kishor, during a meeting with the party's district leaders in Kolkata, showed a photograph on his mobile phone to Bachchu Hansda, the junior minister for north Bengal who represented Tapan assembly seat in South Dinajpur district. The photo was of Hansda's own house. PK reportedly told him that his palatial house in the midst of the tiny homes of his poor neighbours had created a bad impression among the public. *Anandabazar* also published a photo of

Hansda's house. Hansda reportedly said he had built his house with his own hard-earned money and that it was large because he needed space for accommodating travelling relatives, friends and colleagues.

'We are all under surveillance. Big Brother is watching,' a TMC Lok Sabha MP told this author.

Politics in the Time of the Pandemic

The battle against Covid-19 took a political turn in Bengal. Mamata Banerjee initially did not take the threat from the novel coronavirus seriously. Early in March she was busy targeting the BJP for the Delhi riots, calling them 'a planned genocide'. She even alleged that Delhi was creating a hullabaloo around Covid-19 to divert the country's attention from the Delhi riots.[19] However, by the second week of March she had taken the threat seriously, and started to close down schools, gradually moving towards a total lockdown even before Modi announced the country-wide lockdown.

The first case of Covid-19 positive was recorded in the state on March 17 and the very next day four TMC MPs entered the Rajya Sabha wearing face masks, the first instance of any member of parliament doing so. They sought curtailment of the parliament session due to the pandemic. On 22 March, the TMC asked its MPs to withdraw from parliament.

Since then, she was seen leading the battle from the front, holding one meeting after another, frequently addressing the people using video messages and media advertisements, visiting hospitals and markets, convening all-party meetings, personally supervising relief work, in short, putting in every effort expected of a chief minister. She wrote to chief ministers of eighteen states, providing them with details of migrant workers from West Bengal stranded there and requested help for them. By the end of the month, she had started earning a lot of praise on social media from a wide cross-section of people for her proactive role in the fight.[20]

The BJP, after remaining silent during the initial days, started targeting her from the end of March, when Dilip Ghosh, Babul Supriyo and Swapan Dasgupta began to criticize her. First, they accused her of politicizing the relief work – they alleged that BJP leaders, including MPs, were not being allowed to carry out relief work – and then her administration for mismanagement.

Indeed, Bengal was seamlessly sharing data on Covid-19 till 31 March, when the state put the death toll at three and the cumulative number of persons testing positive at twenty-seven. Till then, the state gave data for past twenty-four hours and also cumulative data for deaths, persons testing positive and recovery. The first change happened on 1 April, when three persons died and ten tested positive, but the health department's daily bulletin kept the cumulative death figure still at three and said that the declaration of the three other deaths were 'subject to confirmation'.

The state did not issue any bulletin for the next two days and, from 4 April, the format of the bulletin changed. It now shared data only for active Covid-19 cases instead of the cumulative numbers and mentioned only those deaths that had been attributed to Covid-19 by the expert committee of doctors. The committee was formed by the CM on 4 April to find out which patient died of coronavirus infection and who died of co-morbid conditions. The number of deaths attributed to co-morbidity was not being revealed, while journalists were receiving reports of deaths of Covid-19 patients from different hospitals. It led to utter confusion. There also was allegations that Bengal's Covid-19 testing rate was abysmally low.

The BJP tried to flog these matters into a massive issue, projecting them as proof of the administration's incompetence. Supriyo wrote in one of his tweets: 'WB Govt is into serious hara-kiri'. In another he said: 'WB under #TMchhi is lying thru their teeth!!' Another post had a video attached. Contents of the video claimed: 'Mamata Banerjee is doing what China did to the world.'

The BJP was also trying to mount pressure on Mamata Banerjee over the controversial 15 March event of the Tablighi Jamaat at Nizamuddin Markaz in New Delhi, which allegedly led to a spike in the number of Covid-19 patients across India. Unlike the governments in Delhi and some other states, the Mamata Banerjee administration did not divulge much information about the number of Markaz returnees to Bengal, their whereabouts and number of people infected. When journalists asked her for the details at a press briefing at the state secretariat, she even said, 'Don't ask communal questions.' Dilip Ghosh, while accusing Mamata Banerjee of playing with the lives of hundreds to please a particular community, himself released a list of mosques in Kolkata where Markaz returnees, including foreign nationals, had been lodged.

'Jamaat cases have exploded across the country, but there is no clarity on the latest numbers in Bengal. How many of them traced and tested? Results? No update at all. Has she made it about vote bank?' The BJP IT cell chief Amit Malviya tweeted on 8 April 2020.

Though she was trying to avoid talking politics as much as possible, Mamata Banerjee did target the Centre for not providing the state with adequate support and its financial dues. 'Delhi is not giving us any support, not even paying our dues. We are doing everything on our own, from our limited resources,' she said in the beginning of April. On 8 April 2020, she targeted Delhi over the Nizamuddin Markaz event.

'They allowed it to happen. The event was on 15 March. Two days ago, on March 13, the Union health secretary Preeti Sudan wrote in an official letter that Covid-19 was not an epidemic in India. You can't blame the organizers when the government itself woke up late,' she said, addressing the media from the state secretariat, with chief secretary Rajiva Sinha sitting next to her. She added, 'Those who are saying these things (blaming the Tablighi Jamaat and the state government) are responsible for this. External affairs and home affairs do not come under state jurisdiction. Several people, including foreigners, had gathered at Nizamuddin. They were allowed to gather. Had steps been taken from the beginning, it would not have happened. I don't want to play politics in these times.' Before ending the press briefing on 11 April, she also said, 'It is not a communal virus.'[21]

Step by step, tension between the Centre and the state escalated. The Ministry of Home Affairs shot off a letter to the West Bengal state chief secretary on 10 April, accusing the state of 'gradual dilution of the lockdown'. The letter turned into ammunition in the hands of the BJP leaders – Babul Supriyo and Swapan Dasgupta shared it on Twitter, and so did Governor Dhankhar, who had virtually made it a norm to toe the Centre's line on any issue. There already was utter confusion over the government's Covid-19 data. Even the general public suspected that the government was hiding certain information. This author received phone calls from politically non-oriented persons, asking if the government was really hiding information.

On 15 April, when the state's official death toll stood at seven, the CPM's Bengali mouthpiece, the daily *Ganashakti*, put the figure at thirty in its lead story on the front page. Even the BJP leaders shared photos of the report in their archrival's publication. Reacting to these, Mamata Banerjee threatened legal action, though without naming *Ganashakti*, for 'spreading misinformation.' Unperturbed, leaders of opposition parties launched a thorough campaign accusing the government of data fudging. Amid this trade of barbs, the Centre's decision to send two Central inter-ministerial teams to have a first-hand experience of the ground reality in West Bengal triggered a fresh bout of political blame-game.

The two Central inter-ministerial teams landed in Bengal on 20 April. Under the Disaster Management Act, the Centre has the right to send such teams. But the state cried foul, alleging that the Centre was trying to ruin the country's federal structure. The chief secretary told the media that the state government was informed about the teams' arrival after they had already landed in the airport. The political blame-game intensified when the Central teams asked the state questions that would make them uncomfortable, and the TMC began branding the Central team members as the BJP's political agents. TMC spokesperson Derek O'Brien cited how the letters from the Centre critical of the state government were reaching the media even before they reached the government. However, as it happened, the first time the state came up with data on the deaths attributed to co-morbidity was on 24 April, two days after an inter-ministerial Central team sought Bengal's explanation on its way of Covid-19 death declaration. Chief secretary Rajiva Sinha, on 24 April, announced fifty-seven deaths, attributing eighteen to coronavirus infection and thirty-nine to co-morbidity. Now, the state's death toll, in the eyes of the public, jumped from eighteen to fifty-seven overnight.

Amidst this raging battle between Bengal and the Centre, public agitation against the public distribution system was spreading to different parts of the state. While the government said there were some gaps in distribution due to a mismatch between demand and supply – the demand had suddenly increased with people who usually purchased from open markets also queuing up in front of ration shops – Governor Dhankhar alleged, in tune with other opposition parties, that there was a massive ration scam involving ruling party leaders and ration dealers.

An irate Mamata Banerjee took sharp digs at the governor in a letter to him, dated 23 April, 'You appear to have forgotten that I am an elected chief minister of a proud Indian state. You also seem to have forgotten that you are a nominated governor.'[22] She then quoted from B.R. Ambedkar's speech, and from the report of the Sarkaria Commission, to elaborate how nominal a governor's role is intended to be.

Dhankhar reciprocated with two more letters to Banerjee – both shared with journalists – accusing the CM of 'abject failure in combating and containing coronavirus in West Bengal', 'appeasement of the minority community' and 'cover-up mechanism'.

On the administrative front, the Mamata Banerjee government continued to face embarrassments. State health secretary Vivek Kumar's 28 April letter to Union health secretary Preeti Sudan landed the state in a spot of bother, as the figures given by Kumar exceeded what the government had told the media. Finally, as the controversy raged, the government decided, on 30 April, to shelve the report of the death audit committee. That day, chief secretary Sinha said that the committee had attributed thirty-three deaths to Covid-19 and seventy-two to 'co-morbidity.'

After the state came clean with detailed data on 4 May, following another letter from the inter-ministerial Central team, it also became clear that the state had reported 214 fewer cases of persons testing positive till April 30. Sinha admitted that there were gaps in the state's Covid-19 reporting system. In a damage control mode, the state then changed the daily bulletin's format yet again, this time coming up with detailed data, not only for the state but also district-level, on the number of daily increase and the cumulative tally on the infected and the deceased, as well as testing and other details. The BJP proudly proclaimed victory, saying that the Centre's intervention saved Bengal from the TMC government's attempts to hide the real picture.

The political tug of war was not to end though, as the Centre now targeted the state government for being reluctant to bring back migrant workers stranded in other states. Mamata Banerjee had already made her mind clear – that she preferred to go slow on bringing the migrant workers back so that the state could take proper precaution for each of them and ensure the infection did not spread through them. The BJP, the Congress and the Left, however, accused Banerjee of being apathetic towards the migrant workers. The Congress's Adhir Ranjan Chowdhury, who was now the party's leader in the Lok Sabha, carried out a particularly high-pitched campaign, mounting pressure on the chief minister.

The intensity of the political battle increased following Amit Shah's letter to the chief minister. While the whole letter never got leaked in the media, its contents did, early in the morning of 9 May. The letter reportedly said, 'Migrants from West Bengal are also eager to reach home. Central government is facilitating but we are not getting expected support from W.B. State Government, which is not allowing the trains to reach W.B. This is injustice with W.B. migrant labourers. This will create further hardship for them.'[23]

In the evening, the TMC hit back, with O'Brien holding an online press conference, presenting some documents showing eight trains had been finalized for Bengal. 'Amit Shah's letter is full of outright lies', he alleged. Justifying the state government's stance on the issue, he said, 'We have a seven-stage plan to bring back the migrants. We are doing it in a staggered manner. The PM announced the lockdown without an iota of planning. We don't want to bring the migrant workers without a proper plan, as we are considering all possible implications to find the best way to do it.'

Even before this issue could die down, the BJP found another. Communal clashes in Malda and Hooghly district – triggered by people's panic about Covid-19. On the night of 9 May, a clash broke out between the residents of two villages, Manikbari and Chandipur, within Rashidabad gram panchayat jurisdictions in Harishchandrapur administrative block of Malda district. Several residents of Manikbari had recently returned from Ajmer Sharif and some of them tested positive for Covid-19. According to a report in the *Indian Express*, and what this author gathered through interaction with local politicians, residents of Hindu-dominated Chandipur raised fencings around their village, blocking anyone's entry from Muslim-dominated Manikbari. However, since the residents of Manikbari were dependent on the market at Chandipur, tension between the two villages escalated and altercations led to vandalism, in Chandipur, by some residents of Manikbari.

On 10 May night, a similar clash took place at Telenipara, within Bhadreshwar area in Hooghly district. Some persons from a Muslim neighbourhood were tested positive and the neighbouring Hindu-dominated area fenced off their neighbourhood. People from both neighbourhoods used to use a common public toilet. This triggered tension, which was diffused by the police later, but ultimately, resulted in arson and clashes with sharp and blunt weapons.

On 11 May, all senior BJP leaders started highlighting the cases of Chandipur and Telenipara. Vijayvargiya wrote on Twitter, in Hindi, that people from a special community (in Telenipara) were bent on not abiding by the Covid-19 norms and turned violent. Shiv Prakash alleged in a tweet that first the police were assaulted when they went to the place at Telenipara to fetch those tested positive for the disease and then there was violence 'on the society'. Vijayvargiya shared a short video clip showing a Hindu idol broken inside a temple and claimed that the scene was from Malda. He wrote, 'People from a special community today attacked a Hindu temple and broke the idol.'

In another tweet on the same day, sharing a video of a few people pulling down a fence, he wrote in Hindi, 'Some people from a special community who returned from Ajmer Sharif tested positive for Covid-19. And yet they opened their shops, opposing which the Hindus cordoned off their area. Pulling the fencing down, people from the special community vandalized the temple and Hindu households.' Sharing the same video, Amit Malviya wrote on Twitter, 'After Telinipara, reports of violence from Malda too. Those who returned from Ajmer, tested +ve for Covid, but refused to follow lockdown. When the locals protested, a local temple and homes were vandalized. But Mamata Banerjee, home minister of WB, is missing!' Swapan Dasgupta too alleged on Twitter, 'Rioters determined to drive out local Hindus from area.'[24]

Telenipara's local BJP MP and the state BJP's women's wing chief, Locket Chatterjee, who represented the Hooghly Lok Sabha constituency, alleged before the local media and on video messages posted on social media that there was a planned attack on Hindus. 'Why is one community getting so much encouragement that they would not get tested, they would not get quarantined and they would only keep spreading corona and the police would keep quiet? When the police are saying something, they are taking the revenge on Hindus,'[25] she said, and added, 'If we cannot control this community, they would hold West Bengal for ransom.'

The TMC MLA-turned-BJP MP Arjun Singh, who represented Barrackpore on the other side of the river Hooghly, shared on Twitter, on 11 May, a video of a man profusely bleeding and asked Mamata Banerjee when would the spilling of the blood of the Hindus stop. He would not stand a mute spectator if the administration turned a blind eye when the Hindus were being targeted and attacked, Singh threatened.

The state police from its social media accounts called several posts made by BJP leaders as fake. These included Malviya's and Vijayvargiya's 11 May tweets sharing the video of the pulling down of the fences that we already referred to.[26] In another tweet on 12 May, Malda district police wrote, 'Harischandrapur PS has taken strong action in Chandipur incident triggered by an objectionable communal remark by one person of Krishnapur vill on 10/05 and stone pelting by a group of persons of nearby vill Manikbari enraged by the remark. Complete peace is maintained in area.'

When this author inquired from a senior officer of Malda district police what was the 'objectionable communal remark' mentioned in the tweet, he said, 'Muslims were called Covid-spreaders.'

Besides, Altnews later established that the bleeding man seen in a photo shared by Arjun Singh was actually a Muslim, named Manzur Alam.[27] The Wire[28] and Altnews[29] also called a viral photo claiming to be of attack on Hindus in Telenipara as fake – it was a photo from Pakistan. The Wire's ground report[30] pointed at planned attack on Muslim-owned houses and business, referring to the cases of Hindu-owned shops remaining intact amidst charred remains of Muslim-owned businesses.

Mamata Banerjee, who had remained silent for the first two days, warned on May 12 that no rioter will be spared. 'I am clear about it. Whoever it may be, none will be spared. They will be booked under Disaster Management Act. And what the BJP is doing is pitting one community against the other. This is dirty politics and shameful, even more so at the hour of a pandemic,' she said. The next day, she asked the district magistrates to appoint district-wise nodal officers for social media.[31]

The situation at Chandipur and Telenipara calmed down by 13 May but the political tension between the state and the Centre did not. On 14 May, when Banerjee announced that the government has arranged for 105 trains over the next one month to bring back migrant workers, railway minister Piyush Goyal replied to Banerjee's tweet, saying Bengal needed 105 trains daily. 'I feel sad that while there is a need for 105 trains/day to bring back migrants to WB, the State is accepting only 105 trains over thirty days. I once again hope for the state of Bengal brothers and sisters in different parts of the country, that WB will accept them back with open arms,' Goyal wrote[32].

The TMC countered him by alleging that the Centre was trying to upset the state's Covid-19 management plan. The party also alleged that the Centre created the crisis over stranded migrant workers by announcing the lockdown without a plan. Over the next one month, the treatment of the migrant workers dominated the state's political discourse. And with the return of the migrant workers, Covid-19 indeed spread to Bengal's rural belt, with migrant returnees in their dozens testing positive for the virus infection.

One significant political development in the post-Covid period was that, according to psephologist Biswanath Chakraborty, the BJP which was on the backfoot till March 2020 due to the intense opposition it was facing over the CAA and NRC, recovered its front-foot stance on account of the Mamata Banerjee government's manipulation of Covid-19 data. 'Mamata Banerjee's credibility had come under question, and that's quite significant,' Chakraborty said.

Even Nobel laureate economist Abhijit Vinayak Banerjee, whom CM Banerjee had appointed as the chairperson of the state's global advisory committee for Covid-19 management, said during an interview with *ABP Ananda* on 11 May that it would have been better had the controversy been avoided altogether. 'Transparency is very crucial at this hour to assure people,' he said, 'The lack of it could lead to the spread of rumours.'

While the state government managed to douse the controversy with detailed data in its Covid-19 daily bulletins, and also normalized ration distribution, cyclone Amphan of 20 May simply doubled the state's challenges. Dubbed as the worst cyclone to hit West Bengal in three centuries, the cyclone wreaked havoc, literally devastating the districts of South 24 Parganas and North 24 Parganas, besides paralyzing Kolkata with about 15,000 trees uprooted, and causing heavy damage in the districts of Hooghly, Howrah and East Midnapore. Mamata Banerjee invited Modi to pay a visit and see for himself the extent of damage – she estimated the losses at about Rs 1 lakh crore – and Modi responded promptly by accepting her invitation. Modi, Mamata and Dhankhar took a helicopter ride, following which Modi announced instant assistance of Rs 1,000 crore for West Bengal and Rs 500 crore for Odisha. The extent of damage in West Bengal was in any case far greater than that of Odisha. Mamata Banerjee herself announced a slew of relief measures, including immediate cash assistance of Rs 20,000 to every house entirely damaged. This mostly meant the mud-houses.

Her announcement of direct cash transfer won her accolades but a major scam at the panchayat level soon emerged over the distribution of the relief. Bengali media outlets reported dozens of cases of TMC leaders, panchayat members and their kith and kin getting the relief despite owning two-storied brick houses that were hardly damaged by the cyclone. In contrast, many genuine victims of the cyclone did not receive the grant.

The chief minister did not lose time in nipping the controversy in the bud. She said that she herself had received 2,100 complaints about irregularities in relief distribution, had asked the district administration to examine all lists and publicly display the lists of beneficiaries at the block development offices so that utmost transparency is maintained.

She also asked the administration to recover money from the false beneficiaries. The administration launched a massive drive to recover money and started freezing bank accounts of such false beneficiaries. Simultaneously, the TMC launched a purification drive, issuing show-cause notices to and expelling several hundred panchayat-level leaders involved in such malpractices.

Nevertheless, new cases of such false beneficiaries were reported by the local media almost every day. It emerged that there were gram panchayats where 80 to 90 per cent of the beneficiaries did not meet the criteria. Dealing with corruption at the grassroots level had evidently emerges as one of Mamata Benerjee's major challenges ahead of the 2021 elections. People had started talking that her so-called jihad against 'cut-money' in 2019 had no real impact on her party.

It Is Didi vs Didi

The battle for 2021 had started with about one year to go, with the BJP swinging to the election mode by the end of May 2020. From the morning of 27 May, when the Mamata Banerjee government completed four years in its second term, a social media campaign was launched, branded as 'Aar Noi Mamata', literally meaning no more Mamata, with the top BJP leaders of the state and at the national level taking to Twitter and blasting the state government, using the hashtag #aarnoimamata.

In the evening, Dilip Ghosh released a nine-point charge sheet against her. He said, while addressing the media at the state unit office, that the nine points where she failed the state in the past nine years were – the Covid-19 mismanagement, malpractices in the public distribution system, collapsed law and order situation and lack of democratic space, collapsed economy, collapsed education system, rampant corruption and taking an anti-Hindu and anti-refugee attitude. 'The government must be toppled in 2021,' Ghosh said. The party also announced a series of five 'virtual rallies', the first of which will be addressed by Amit Shah.

During his speech on 9 June, Shah tore into the Mamata Banerjee government and reiterated the party's promise of building 'Shonar Bangla'.

'We are on the streets not only to increase organizational strength but to build Bengal according to its original culture and heritage', he said.

The TMC hit back at the BJP and the Centre in the evening, accusing the ruling party at the Centre of focusing on politics and an election still one year away when the priorities should have been on battling Covid-19, dealing with the border stand-off with China and, for Bengal in particular, dealing with the post-cyclone relief and reconstruction.

But perhaps the most striking element in Shah's speech was the revival of the CAA issue. He targeted Banerjee for opposing the CAA and said that the Hindu refugees from Bangladesh would turn her into a 'political refugee'. By calling for an end to infiltration, Shah also raised the issue of the NRC, though without referring to the controversial word.

The TMC said they could see through the BJP's plan. 'The rules for the CAA were to be notified in six months, which ends this week. So, the Centre will now seek another six months' extension, which will drag the time till December, which will be just three or four months ahead of the elections,' Derek O'Brien alleged. In a few days, apolitical social organizations opposed to the NRC and CAA, such as No NRC Movement, had started reviving social media activities.

In July, Mamata Banerjee responded. 'We have not forgotten the NRC or NPR fight. Preoccupation with the Covid situation does not mean we have forgotten the CAA or NRC', she said while addressing party workers through social media on 21 July.

Besides, by June-July 2020, both parties revamped the state leadership. The BJP announced its new state leadership early in June, bringing into prominence deserters from other parties. It appointed the TMC-turned-BJP MP, Saumitra Khan, as the youth wing chief; the TMC MLA-turned BJP MP, Arjun Singh, as vice-president; Sabyasachi Datta, a TMC MLA who had defected to the BJP as secretary; another defector TMC MLA Dulal Bar as SC Morcha chief; the CPM MLA-turned-BJP MP, Khagen Murmu, was made the chief of ST Morcha; and another former Left MLA, Mahfuza Khatun, was appointed as a vice-president.

The TMC made its changes over the fourth week of July. The thirty-nine-member state committee, the twenty-one-member state coordination committee and seven-member steering committee were reconstituted. Among the significant new appointments were those of Chhatradhar Mahato, who headed the Maoist-backed Lalgarh movement during the Left Front regime and was released in January 2020 after serving more than ten years in jail, expelled CPM leader Ritabrata Banerjee, and the Saradha-scam-accused Kunal Ghosh, who had repeatedly tried to drag Mamata Banerjee's name in the Saradha scam during 2013–16. Explaining Ghosh's reinstatement in the party – he was a sitting Rajya Sabha MP in 2013 when the TMC first suspended him and then the state police arrested him – a TMC Rajya Sabha MP told this author, 'Ghosh and Mukul Roy are the two leaders who have tried to harm the party the most. By reinstating Ghosh, she gave a clear message that anyone who wanted to come back would be forgiven.'

There were also hints that the BJP would go for another round of poaching drive. Even though Mukul Roy was working mostly behind the scenes, the party's central leadership did not forget to recognize his contribution in public. During his March 2020 rally in Kolkata, Amit Shah had introduced Roy as 'the one under whose chairmanship of the Lok Sabha election management committee we won eighteen seats in Bengal.' And during Shah's 'virtual rally' (speeches from daises inside BJP offices in New Delhi and Kolkata) for Bengal on 9 June, only two persons got a chance to speak before him – Dilip Ghosh and Mukul Roy. It was mostly on Roy that the BJP central leadership depended for weakening the TMC organizationally.

And who was going to be the BJP's chief ministerial face for Mission 2021? The buzz in Bengal BJP circles was: no one. Indeed, Amit Shah has twice given indications that the party will go to the elections with Modi as its face. He said this first in his 1 October 2019 speech in Kolkata: 'You have expressed your wish for a change in the government (in Bengal) by giving us eighteen Lok Sabha seats. The wish will now be realized under Modi-ji's leadership.'

During the 1 March 2020 rally in Kolkata's Brigade Parade Ground, he said: 'Mamata Banerjee is obstructing PM Modi from developing Bengal. Give Modi five years and we will change it. We will turn Bengal into Shonar

Bangla (golden Bengal).' And during his 9 June address to the people of Bengal, Shah again sought a chance for Modi: 'People who changed the communist rule expecting development are now saying that even the communists were better than the TMC. They are so upset. You gave the communists thirty-four years and ten years to Didi. Now, give a chance to Modi-ji and you will see,' Shah said and cited Bihar as an example of walking the path of development from being treated as a 'bimaru state' once the BJP-led National Democratic Alliance (NDA) government took charge.

'Only the BJP can change Bengal. I appeal to the crores of people to give Modi-ji a chance for a corruption- and violence-free Bengal,' said Shah, 'You will see an end to violence, corruption, scam, extortion, terror, infiltration, and dynasty politics. If you want these, give Modi-ji the rights to take the steps.'

Shortly after Shah's 9 June address, Derek O'Brien presented data to prove Bengal was doing better than BJP-ruled states both in terms of employment and communal harmony. According to a top TMC strategist, the party was preparing to face Modi in the 2021 elections. 'It would be easy for us if the BJP names a chief ministerial candidate,' he said, 'The battle would be between that person and Mamata Banerjee, and there is no person in Bengal who can match her. But if they keep their options open, if they keep people guessing, the battle will turn into one of Modi vs Mamata. And that would be a close one. There is no room for complacency.'

Quite significantly, the TMC was mostly banking on (apart from Muslim votes in bulk) the beneficiary base created by the government's social welfare schemes – which opposition parties criticized as 'politics of dole' – and Mamata's MSME-oriented industrial policy that helped reduce rural unemployment. By the end of June 2020, she had already announced free ration to all till June 2021. However, it appeared that corruption had hampered that beneficiary base, too. 'The high-handedness and rampant corruption in TMC's rank and file have forced people to look for an alternative,' Anil Mahato, a resident of Kalsibhanga village in Salboni block of West Midnapore district, told this author. Salboni is part of the former Maoist stronghold of Jangalmahal region, where the TMC fared poorly in the 2019 Lok Sabha elections despite carrying out development work with unprecedented speed and infusion of funds since 2012.

Several political observers told this author during May-June 2020 that they were expecting a close contest in 2021. The TMC's prospects were 'rather precarious,' said Amal Kumar Mukhopadhyay, a former principal of Presidency College, 'because there is a strong wind of anti-incumbency and that's due to her own failures in initiating industrial development and checking corruption'.

'Unless she can start a mass expulsion of corrupt leaders in the coming months, there is every possibility of the BJP routing the TMC in 2021,' Mukhopadhyay said. He, however, did not rule out the BJP committing political blunders in the days to come. Mukhopadhyay was convinced that communal polarization was a minor issue compared to people's disgruntlement over corruption.

Veteran psephologist Biswanath Chakraborty said that no prediction of the assembly elections was possible as of August 2020. According to him, Covid-19 made future 'extremely unpredictable' and if the situation in Bengal, and in the country, kept worsening, both the Mamata Banerjee government and the Narendra Modi government could face the people's ire. In that case, a slight revival of the Left-Congress camp could complicate all equations. In case the assembly elections got delayed due to Covid-19 and Bengal witnessed President's Rule, equations could be complicated further.

For the record, the Left and the Congress had almost finalized contesting the 2021 elections in alliance, offering the voters a third alternative. The left parties had also managed to reopen several hundreds of their closed offices after the TMC's electoral setback in 2019. They did not face much of an obstruction, except in the Muslim-dominated areas where the TMC did not want them to grow.

Chakraborty mentioned among the TMC's disadvantages the 'public resentment against corruption, highhandedness, the politicization of the administration, the lack of democratic space and failure in employment generation'. He felt that the BJP leaders, on the other hand, had 'antagonized all sensible and liberal-minded people with their senseless, unscientific and rubbish talks', failed to strengthen the party's organization in the districts, and gave Bengal no importance in the Union cabinet.

He reminded that after the 2009 Lok Sabha elections, the TMC with nineteen MPs had Mamata Banerjee as the railway minister in the UPA II government and six others as ministers of state. Besides, she kept announcing projects for Bengal. The BJP gave Bengal only two ministers of state even when the party had two MPs in 2014, and when they had eighteen, after 2019 elections.

'As of July-August 2020, I can tell multiple points in favour of the TMC rule and against it. But there is nothing to say in favour of the BJP. The battle is more likely to be between Mamata Banerjee's successes and the undercurrent against her failures,' Chakraborty said.

This author feels that one of the BJP's principal contributions to Bengal politics during 2013–20 is the removal of fear from the people's mind emboldening them to question and counter the TMC's misdeeds. This could very well prove to be their chief claim to succeed the TMC as the ruling party, aided by the saffron camp's success in giving a certain religious bent to the Bengali Hindu psyche.

Mamata Banerjee had *Bodla Noy, Bodol Chai* (no revenge, only change) as one of her central slogans for the 2011 campaign. Quite intriguingly, the BJP's call for change had a striking slogan. Dilip Ghosh started saying from the end of July 2020: '*Bodol o hobey, Bodlao hobey*' (there will be change and revenge).[33]

Notes

ONE: Rise of the Sangh

1. Officially, the name of the party is All India Trinamool Congress or AITC.
2. On 2 March 2016, in Birbhum district, Ghosh said that anyone saying 'Pakistan Zindabad' would be 'chopped by six inches from the top'; on 6 August 2017, at Haldia, he threatened he would have TMC workers 'buried six feet under the soil'; on 22 April 2018, in Bongaon, he said: 'I have said, we can send you six feet under the soil and can also shorten you by six inches from the top. You are free to tell me your preference.'
3. Even at the height of the frenzy over the Ram Temple movement, BJP's vote share in West Bengal in the 1991 general elections stood at 11.7%, only to dip to 6.9% in the 1996 Lok Sabha and to 6.45% in the 1996 state assembly elections.
4. Bhattacharjee's comment created a huge uproar, after which he took an about-turn two weeks later, telling the media that he had earlier been wrongly quoted.
5. The position in the BJP is general secretary (organization).
6. C. P. Bhishikar, *Shri Guruji: Pioneer of a New Era*, translated into English by Sudhakar Raje, Bangalore: Sahitya Sindhu Prakashana1999.

7. Author's telephonic interview with Sukumar Bandyopadhyay, one of the RSS' early pracharaks in Bengal, conducted in 2014. He was ninety but still had his memory sharp. He died in July 2019.
8. 'RSS' work is expanding consistently across the nation – Dr. Manmohan Vaidya', 16 October 2019. Source: rss.org.
9. Founded in February 1966 and led by the just-removed state Congress president Ajay Mukherjee.
10. Those who deserted the CPM in support of armed agrarian revolt initially gathered under the platform of All India Coordination Committee of Communist Revolutionaries in 1967, out of which two underground and armed organizations – CPI (Marxist-Leninist) and Maoist Communist Centre (MCC) were born in 1969. Both these Maoist parties were founded in West Bengal and spread to other parts of the country.
11. 'WEST BENGAL- A Made to Order Election', *Economic and Political Weekly*, Vol. 7, issue No. 13, 25 March 1972.
12. The record was later broken by Sikkim's Pawan Kumar Chamling.
13. A group of Bangladeshi refugees who had settled on an island in the Sunderbans defying the state government's orders and repeated warnings were allegedly attacked by armed policemen on boat from all sides, resulting in the death of a great many. https://tinyurl.com/ugrj33s.
14. Seventeen monks, including a woman, belonging to the religious group Ananda Marg, were beaten to death in the morning of 30 April 1982, allegedly in front of hundreds of people, before their bodies were set on fire. Ananda Marg had forayed into the political arena with its wing Aamra Bangali, and the ruling CPM was widely accused of orchestrating these killings. No inquiry took place until Mamata Banerjee ordered one in 2013.
15. http://www.mainstreamweekly.net/article2874.html
16. 'Mamata Banerjee's antics put the Marxists on the defensive in the past. This time it bombed', *India Today*, 9 November 1998.
17. Ibid.
18. Dwaipayan Bhattacharyya, 'Making and Unmaking of Trinamul Congress', *Economic and Political Weekly*, Vol. 39, No. 14/15, 3–16 April 2004.
19. 'After defeating the censure motion on Gujarat, the Vajpayee government looks confident', *India Today*, 13 May 2002.

20. The TMC won 184 seats and the Congress won only forty-two.
21. The author was present during the BJP delegation's visit.
22. 'Pratinidhi Dol Pashey, Gramey Firlen Kormira', *Anandabazar Patrika*, 16 June 2014.
23. 'BJP steps up heat for NIA probe in Bengal blast', IANS, 7 October 2014, Kolkata.
24. https://www.anandabazar.com/national/hasina-s-statement-to-those-people-who-supports-terrorists-1.82553
25. Copies of the letter were shared with journalists.

Two: Bengal, Islam, Hindutva

1. The population density of West Bengal was 1,028 per sq. km in 2011 and Bangladesh's was 976 per sq. km in 2011, according to Census of India, 2011 and Population Monograph of Bangladesh, 2015. India's population density was 382 people per sq. km in 2011 and Pakistan's was 275 per sq. km in 2018, according to the World Bank.
2. 'Archaeological evidence confirms that already in the second millennium B.C., rice-cultivating communities inhabited West Bengal's Burdwan District. By the eleventh century B.C., peoples in this area were living in systematically aligned houses, using elaborate human cemeteries, and making copper ornaments and fine black-and-red pottery.' Richard Maxwell Eaton, *The Rise of Islam and the Bengal Frontier (1204–1760)*, Berkeley: University of California Press, 1993.
3. *Bangala Sahityer Itihas*, Vol. I., Calcutta: Modern Book Agency, 1940, p. 5
4. *Bangaleer Itihas - Adiporbo*, first published 1949, Kolkatta: Dey's Publishing, 8th edition, 2013, pp. 495–97.
5. Charles Stewart, *The History of Bengal: From the First Mohammedan Invasion until the Virtual Conquest of that Country by the English, A.D. 1757*, London: Black, Parry, and Company, 1813. This book was republished by the Council of Education, East India Company in 1847 for government schools and colleges in Bengal, and in 1903 by the Bangabasi Office.
6. Abdul Karim, *Social History of the Muslims in Bengal (Down to A.D. 1538)*, Dacca: Asiatic Society of Pakistan, 1959.

7. Sukumar Sen, *History of Bengali Literature*, New Delhi: The Sahitya Akademi, 1960, p. 37.
8. H Baverley, Inspector-General of Registration, Bengal, 'Report on the Census of Bengal', Calcutta, 1872
9. *Haqiqat-i-Musalman-i Bangale*, the English translation of which was published as *Origin of the Musalmans*, Bengal, 1895.
10. Dhirendra Nath Majumdar and C. Radhakrishna Rao, 'Race Elements in Bengal: A Quantitative Study', *Indian Statistical Series*, No.3, Calcutta, Statistical Publishing Society, 1960.
11. *Bangladesh: Tradition and Transformation*, Dhaka: University Press, 1987.
12. *The Rise of Islam and the Bengal Frontier (1204–1760)*, Berkley: University of California Press, 1993.
13. 'Islam and Its Early Introduction in Bengal,' a paper read at the 56th session of the Indian History Congress, 1995.
14. Calcutta: G. Bharadwaj & Co., 1973, pp. 196–97.
15. Two of Bengal's most illustrious families – the Tagore family, with innumerable luminaries, and the Ray family (Upendra Kishor, Sukumar and Satyajit, among others) were Brahmos.
16. Printed by Kashinath Bhattacharya, Hooghly: Baishakh 1276 [April/May 1869].
17. *Bangashree* (a Bengali periodical), (Shravan 1341). Translated from the Bengali by the author.
18. Author's translation.
19. *The Swadeshi Movement in Bengal, (1903-1908)*, New Delhi: People's Publishing House, 1973, chapter titled 'Hindu-Muslim relations'.
20. *Shoto Borsher Ferari Bankim Chandra Chattopadhyay*, Dhaka: Prachyabidya Prakashani, 1997.
21. Bhupendranath Dutta, *Bharater Dwitiyo Swadhinata Sangram*, first published in 1949, Kolkata: Radical Impression, 2017, p. 17.
22. Hem Chandra Kanungo, *Banglay Biplob Proceshta*, first published by in 1928, Calcutta: Kamala Book Depot, present edition, Kolkata: Chirayata Publication, 2012.
23. The Shimla delegation on 1 October 1906 had demanded separate electorates and quotas in civil service; the All India Muslim League was founded in Dhaka on 30 December 1906.

24. Lt Col. U.N. Mukherji, *A Dying Race,* Calcutta: Bhaskar Mukherje [publisher], 1929. First published in 1909 by Mukherjee & Bose, Calcutta.
25. Pradip Kumar Datta, 'Dying Hindus': Production of Hindu Communal Common Sense in Early 20th Century Bengal', *Economic and Political Weekly,* Vol. 28, No. 25, 19 June 1993.
26. Muslims neither accepted the educational nor the employment opportunities that came along with the British rule.
27. Nitish Sengupta, *Land of Two Rivers: A History of Bengal from the Mahabharata to Mujib,* New Delhi: Penguin Books, 2011, pp. 278–79
28. *The Indian Mussalmans,* London: Trubner and Company, 1871.
29. *Roots of Separatism in Nineteenth Century Bengal,* Calcutta: Ratna Prakashan, 1974, p. 19.
30. Both movements gradually included economic and political issues and attained complex characters.
31. J.A. Vas, 'Indian Civil Service officer', in Eastern Bengal and Assam District Gazetteer's publication on Rangpur, pp. 44, 48.
32. Sumit Sarkar has cited a list of Calcutta university graduates from 1858 to 1881 where only 38 names out of a total of 1,720 'appeared indisputably Muslim'.
33. Lawrence John Lumley Dundas, Marquess of Zetland, 1876–1961.
34. Joya Chatterjee, *Bengal Divided: Hindu Communalism and Partition 1932-1947,* Cambridge: Cambridge University Press, 1994.
35. 'Communal Violence in Twentieth Century Colonial Bengal: An Analytical Framework,' *Social Scientist,* Vol. 18, Nos. 6-7, June-July 1990.
36. In the 1937 general elections to the 250-seat Bengal assembly, Congress emerged as the largest party with fifty-four seats, and Muslim League the second largest, with forty seats. Hindu Mahasabha, which had only just entered politics, won two seats.
37. Author's translation from the Bengali of the quotation in *Anandabazar Patrika.*
38. Seats were reserved for such institutions as universities, railways and chambers of commerce.
39. He was still living as a pracharak in Bankura district in 2017.
40. Narayan Chandra Dutta, 'Problems and prospects of the BJP in West Bengal, 2010', Department of Political Science, University of Burdwan. (http://hdl.handle.net/10603/66844)

41. 'With sympathy, PM goes to tea at Mamata's', Calcutta, *The Telegraph*, 6 July 2000.
42. https://channelhindustan.com/syama-prasad-mukherjee/

Three: From Laddu to Fish Fry

1. Full speech at https://youtu.be/3FV714UivkI
2. Ibid.
3. Ibid.
4. 'Congress-Baam-ke Top, Sur Norom Mamatar Proti', *Anandabazar Patrika*, 6 February 2014.
5. https://youtu.be/LmCLWSQ62_s
6. https://zeenews.india.com/bengali/zila/modi-criticised-on-mamata-in-silguri_21641.html
7. Full specch at https://youtu.be/GkSm6hsXBmQ
8. 'Saradha chief used fake mobike plant to dupe investors', Hindustan Times, 25 April 25, 2013. The scam drew people's investments into innovative and attractive schemes, promising astronomical returns. This author reported a case in which a closed motorbike factory was purchased and maintained neat and clean, with no operations taking place, and a group of staff kept ready-to-wear uniforms and pretend to work whenever visitors (prospective investors) would arrive. The group raised crores of rupees, showing this building as an operational factory.
9. Full speech at https://youtu.be/SEXTnrGMZvw
10. UCRC, an amalgamation of the CPI, Forward Bloc, Revolutionary Socialist Party and other left groups, was set up on 12 August 1950 to voice the grievances and demands of the East Bengal refugees. Ambica Chakrabarty, who was a comrade of Masterda Surya Sen in Chittagong, had joined CPI after being released from jail in 1946 and took charge as UCRC general secretary in 1950.
11. Mohit Ray, 'Illegal Migration and Undeclared Refugees - Idea of West Bengal at Stake', https://www.asthabharati.org/Dia_Oct%2009/Moh.htm
12. https://eisamay.indiatimes.com/election-news/mamata-demands-to-arrest-modi/articleshow/34669555.cms

13. Full speech at https://youtu.be/VWO0orp5RQs
14. https://www.ndtv.com/elections-news/congress-soft-on-narendra-modi-i-would-have-jailed-him-with-rope-around-waist-mamata-banerjee-560969
15. Constant Traffic, *Frontline*, 15 June 2007: https://frontline.thehindu.com/cover-story/article30191822.ece
16. Full speech: https://youtu.be/-jwUEsQFnK0
17. 'Is Modi a donkey asks Mamata', PTI, 8 May 2014
18. UNI report dated 14 June 2008; https://www.oneindia.com/2008/06/14/trinamool-to-organise-sit-in-demonstration-at-singur-from-aug-20-1213454154.html
19. She went back to NDA in 2002 but did not get the portfolio of her choice.
20. 'Appeased RSS calls Mamata Durga', *The Telegraph*, 16 September 2003, Calcutta.
21. 'Mamata's date with RSS', *The Times of India*, 16 September 2003, New Delhi.
22. On the Margins: Muslims in West Bengal, *Economic and Political Weekly*, Vol. 44, No. 16 (18 – 24 April 2009), pages 91-96
23. 'In Search of Development: Muslims and Electoral Politics in an Indian_ State', *Forum for Development Studies*, Vol. 38, No. 3, 2011.
24. This group had started to unearth 'Hindu nationalist' elements from the works of Bengal's cultural stalwarts and adopted '*Joi Maa Kali*' instead of '*Jai Shree Ram*' as their main religious slogan. The group split in 2018, apparently over political orientation.
25. https://eisamay.indiatimes.com/west-bengal-news/left-front-workers-furious-over-leaders-meeting-mamata/articleshow/36362917.cms
26. Telephonic conversation with this author the day after her joining.

Four: Grassroots Grow Greener

1. Justices T.S. Thakur and C. Nagappan, Supreme Court order, in Writ Petition (C) No. 401 of 2013, 9 May 2014. Source: https://main.sci.gov.in/jonew/bosir/orderpdfold/2019634.pdf
2. Ibid.
3. 'CPI(M), Congress, CBI face the wrath of Mamata', *The Hindu*, 28 August 2014.

4. https://youtu.be/Sdi_iwUgfZY.
5. '*Saradha-Kande ebar Mukul-ke CBI Tolob*', *Anandabazar Patrika,* 12 January 2015.
6. Ibid.
7. 'No Special Favour Shown to Saradha Arm: IRCTC'; IANS, 4 September 2014.
8. 'CBI Jerar Shesheo Rohosyo Jiyiye Rakhlen Mukul Roy', *Anandabazar Patrika,* 31 January 2015.
9. Mirza was arrested by CBI in 2019 and Mukul Roy was questioned.
10. Jean Drèze, Souparna Maji, 'Food matters in West Bengal', *The Indian Express,* 16 September 2016.
11. In June 2017, Kanyashree fetched Mamata Banerjee recognition in the shape of the United Nations Public Service Award, when the project was adjudged first in the category 'Reaching the Poorest and Most Vulnerable through Inclusive Services and Partnerships'.

Five: The Widening Fault Lines

1. https://www.facebook.com/bimochan.bhattacharya/posts/989492104425465.
2. Secularism in Bangladesh was removed with the Proclamations (Amendment) Order, 1977 (Proclamation Order no. I of 1977), dated April 23. It was legalized by the passage of the Constitution (Fifth Amendment) Act 1979 on 6 April 1979.
3. https://www.rediff.com/news/column/a-rally-for-war-criminals-why-are-tmc-left-silent/20130403.htm.
4. https://www.livemint.com/Opinion/x9ZrrLFPFaSJ6OFG4GSw9J/West-Bengal-a-zone-of-silence-in-India.html.
5. https://www.thehindu.com/opinion/lead/a-dangerous-connivance/article4585420.ece.
6. Justice Dipankar Datta, in Writ Petition 24471 (W) of 2016 (*Sandeep Bera Vs. Chief Secretary, Government of West Bengal & Ors*), 6 October 2016. http://164.100.79.153/judis/kolkata_app/index.php/casestatus/viewpdf/WP_24471W_2016_06102016_O_74.pdf
7. Md. Kamrul Hasan, 'No Hindus will be left after 30 years', *Dhaka Tribune,* 21 November 2016.

8. https://www.facebook.com/jubi.saha.73/posts/516344448573506, translation from the Bengali, author's.
9. Abhijit Saha, *'Hamlar Chinha Sarbatra, Tran Police Kormider'*, *Anandabazar Patrika*, 5 January 2016. https://tinyurl.com/r3f87hh
10. Bibhas Bhattacharyya, 'Opium, fake money racketeers blamed for mob attack on Bengal cops', *Hindustan Times*, 6 January 2016. Source: https://tinyurl.com/rhr22mt.
11. Aniruddha Ghosal, 'Birbhum clashes break out over Facebook post, I killed in police firing', *The Indian Express*, 3 March 2016. https://tinyurl.com/w7hyjjv
12. Aniruddha Ghosal, 'Homes ransacked in communal violence in Bengal, people flee', *The Indian Express*,17 October 17, 2016. Source: https://tinyurl.com/r3d4n5j
13. Suvojit Bagchi, 'Bengal stares at a new, divisive communal equation', *The Hindu*,23 October 2016. https://tinyurl.com/yx4v5yso
14. 'Dynt Inside: Dhulgarh Riots', YouTube, 28 April 2017. https://youtu.be/2axz_-gF38M
15. Reverse journey of the chariot carrying lords Jagannath, Balaram and Subhadra held a week after the Rath Jatra.
16. 'Bengal violence: Basirhat's Muslim leaders tried to pacify the rioting mob, but couldn't', *Hindustan Times*,16 July 2016. https://tinyurl.com/udcxmzv.
17. Two years later, the family would turn down an official invitation to attend Modi's 2019 swearing-in ceremony, arguing that they did not want to 'politicize the family and the death'.

SIX: The Bengal Plan

1. 'RSS ABPS-2017 Resolution: Grave concern on Jihadi Violence in West Bengal', Coimbatore, 21 March 2017. https://tinyurl.com/sxuwnkp.
2. *'Poschimbonge Pathyopustok-e "Ramdhonu" na "Rongdhonu" Bitorko'*, *BCC News Bangla*,16 January 2017. https://tinyurl.com/usjoou3.
3. https://tinyurl.com/vkja7dq.
4. The Vishwa Hindu Parishad's eastern regional organizing secretary Sachindra Nath Singha, a veterinary doctor, told this in a telephonic interview with the author in April 2017.

5. '*Banglar Katha*', compiled in *Deshbandhu Rachana Samagra*, Kolkata: Tuli-Kolom, 1958.
6. Anisuzzaman, 'Creativity, Reality and Identity', International Centre for Bengal Studies, Dhaka, 1991.
7. https://tinyurl.com/ss4wqqe, official website of Purulia district.
8. https://www.facebook.com/bsaikat/posts/10154992566987534.
9. A large male goat is called *Ram-chhagol* or *Ram-pantha* in Bengali.
10. Telephonic interview with author, April 2017.
11. Ibid.
12. '*Swami Vivekanander Bani O Rachana*', Vol. 6, *Prachya O Paschatyo*.
13. Of the two sects of Shaktism – Srikula (lineage of Lakshmi) and Kalikula (lineage of Kali), Bengali Hindus follow Kalikula.
14. Gunter Grass, *Show Your Tongue*, New York: Harcourt Brace Jovanovich, 1989.
15. Saptarshi Chakraborty, 'The non-believer's guide to Durga Pujo'. https://tinyurl.com/t5gfxvu
16. 'Anti-Hindi movement re-surfaces in Bengal, leader says BJP's rise a threat to regional languages', *Hindustan Times*, 6 July 2018. https://tinyurl.com/tfgsjxj.
17. 'Bankim Chandra to Swami Vivekananda: Icons are BJP's new weapon in Bengal', *Hindustan Times*, 6 August 2018. https://tinyurl.com/yb53x6ku.
18. https://youtu.be/YslTUrtJ8Zw.
19. 'Congress divided Vande Mataram in 1937, and it led to Partition', Amit Shah quoted in *Hindustan Times*, 27 June 2018. See for full speech: https://youtu.be/_i24eZ6Hu8U.

Seven: The Sangh Spreads Its Wings

1. For the whole speech see - https://youtu.be/jQ4ClrD-mBw
2. Interview with this author during first-year OTC camp at Tantiberia in Howrah district, May 2014.
3. Administratively, Barrackpore is a sub-division of North 24 Parganas district.
4. Author's translation from the Bengali.
5. Telephonic interview with Sukumar Banerjee in January 2015. He also served as the BJP's Bengal unit president twice.

6. Tathagata Roy, *The Life & Times of Dr. Syama Prasad Mookerjee: A Complete Biography*, New Delhi: Ocean Books Private Ltd, 2012.
7. This author was present at the programme at Sukanta Sadan.
8. https://www.ekal.org/pdf/ekal-annual-report-2016-17.pdf
9. According to the Census of 2011, 4.93 lakh people in Bengal registered as followers of Sari and 2.64 lakh as followers of Sarna.
10. Interview with author at the TMC office in Jalpaiguri town, 2 May 2018.
11. Ekal Abhiyan Annual Report 2018-19. https://www.ekal.org/pdf/ekal-abhiyan-annual-report-2018-19-v1.pdf.
12. 'Bengal govt launches crackdown on RSS-inspired schools', *Hindustan Times*, 20 February 2018. https://tinyurl.com/yd4ng2uv
13. Telephonic interview with this author in February 2018.
14. Most of them were for students up to class V, except in about half-a-dozen schools that had the sanction to hold the classes up to the class X.
15. Puffed rice and yellow pea curry
16. 'How coastal Karnataka was saffronised'; 'Part 7: Hindu groups rally behind love jihad'; 'Anti-Muslim sentiments seep into local consciousness', Firstpost, 8 April 2019.
17. Shravan Krishna Paksha Amavashya Sankhya (August 2018).
18. Block-level organization.
19. Directive sent to organizers via WhatsApp messages.
20. VHP south Bengal spokesperson Sourish Mukherjee said this to journalists.
21. 'Islampur firing Bengal's biggest issue, say RSS-BJP; line up prolonged agitation plans', *Hindustan Times*, 28 September 2018. https://tinyurl.com/y7eh4az5.
22. https://eisamay.indiatimes.com/west-bengal-news/rss-wants-to-new-step-for-teachers/articleshow/61625140.cms
23. Author's telephonic interview with the minister
24. Interview with author at state BJP office, January 2015.

EIGHT: Changing Equations

1. *Anandabazar Patrika*, 14 May 2016: https://www.anandabazar.com/state/bjp-leader-dilip-ghosh-s-insulting-comments-for-women-dgtl-1.386716

2. *Anandabazar Patrika,* 21 February 2016: https://www.anandabazar.com/state/bjp-targets-suranjan-das-as-shadow-of-jnu-engulfs-jadavpur-university-1.314530
3. *Anandabazar Patrika,* 12 February 2017: https://www.anandabazar.com/state/bjp-state-secretary-dilip-ghosh-indecently-criticised-amartya-sen-dgtl-1.563185
4. https://www.kolkata24x7.com/again-dilip-ghoshs-controversial-comment-in-purulia-here-is-the-details/
5. https://www.thewall.in/12-12-2018-distnews-dilip-ghosh-threats-police-at-keshiari/
6. https://www.sangbadpratidin.in/bengal/bjp-state-president-dilip-ghosh-makes-controversial-remarks-in-a-public-meeting-at-islampur/
7. https://bengali.news18.com/amp/news/dilip-ghosh-explosive-statement-to-cm-143124.html
8. For the speech delivered on 29 May 2016, see: https://youtu.be/XfbTJy80nyc
9. Mohammad Aklakh was lynched at Dadri in Uttar Pradesh in September 2015, allegedly by cow vigilantes.
10. 'BJP Rajyo Sabhapatir Kuruchikar Nishanay: Amartya Sen', *Anandabazar Patrika,* 12 February 2016.
11. https://peoplesreporter.wordpress.com/2017/07/09/dilip-ghosh-bjp/; he also told this to this author during a telephonic conversation in February 2017.
12. It was only once, in June 2019, when a Bengali news portal quoted him belittling Mukul Roy, that Ghosh issued a statement disowning his remarks.
13. A committee to look after affairs involving voters of one polling booth, often called 'part', in Election Commission jargon.
14. Anirban Ganguly and Shiwanand Dwivedi, *Amit Shah and the March of BJP,* New Delhi: Bloomsbury India, 2019.
15. Author's interview with Dilip Ghosh at the state unit office of the BJP, June 2017.
16. Author's telephonic interview with a BJP state executive member who did not want to be identified, 19 December 2016.
17. For the whole speech: https://youtu.be/rAevU0tUfHc
18. Ibid.

NINE: Battle for Bengal

1. Video message on 1 January 2019. https://youtu.be/GM5RmDL3mB8.
2. Speech at Chopra, Uttar Dinajpur district, 14 December 2018. https://youtu.be/WAmls6RFPR0,
3. According to one of the vistaraks who spoke to this author on condition of anonymity.
4. https://twitter.com/i/status/1128572174921375745; https://youtu.be/e_3A_kg2lsQ
5. https://tinyurl.com/rzvg6az; https://youtu.be/b_2zwJpjXtk; https://tinyurl.com/tgsnnsb; https://vimeo.com/336351259; https://vimeo.com/336351858
6. 'Clash of cultures: Shocked Bengal Witnesses Vandalism of Vidyasagar Bust', *The Telegraph*, Kolkata, 15 May 2019.
7. https://english.kolkata24x7.com/who-cannot-look-after-his-wife-how-will-he-look-after-country-mamata.html/
8. https://www.hindustantimes.com/lok-sabha-elections/bjp-bengal-unit-chief-s-aide-among-two-arrested-with-rs-1-crore-cash/story-akmN78kjjVwhIspCXfADIM.html
9. 'In Cooch Behar, BJP's social media boss is 36-year-old shop owner who juggles 1,114 WhatsApp groups', *The Indian Express*, 12 April 2019.
10. 'Ujjwal Pareek: The Calcutta boy who made Modi go viral'; *The Telegraph*,24 May 2019.

TEN: Mission 2021

1. https://youtu.be/IH2_Ep0P8Ro
2. https://www.hindustantimes.com/india-news/in-7-phases-bjp-sneers-at-mamata-after-exit-of-2-trinamool-lawmakers/story-7xzwT4TjZecdzNirabktdO.html
3. http://www.eswastika.com/20190610.pdf.
4. https://zeenews.india.com/india/mukul-roy-is-made-in-china-chanakya-says-tmc-leader-abhishek-banerjee-2219044.html
5. https://www.facebook.com/watch/?v=715863392163772
6. https://youtu.be/0JN6-Zt0CsE.

7. Ibid.
8. https://youtu.be/JevWiiQbd7Y.
9. Pakistan Army's onslaught on East Pakistan's liberation movement began on this day.
10. For the full speech, see: https://youtu.be/TABPaNXZqfE.
11. https://www.telegraphindia.com/states/west-bengal/keshari-nath-tripathi-s-parting-shot-at-mamata-banerjee/cid/1695348
12. http://archive.indianexpress.com/news/the-jat-myth-results-show-backing-for-cong/397484/
13. Full statement at: http://aitcofficial.org/aitc/trinamool-statement-on-governors-visit-to-jadavpur-university/?lang=bengali
14. 'Jadavpur University, a hub of anti-nationals, will be destroyed in a Balakot-like surgical strike': BJP's Dilip Ghosh; PTI, 20 September 2019.
15. https://www.hindustantimes.com/india-news/mamata-banerjee-retreats-on-npr-govt-stays-all-work-related-to-it/story-LAuGgVR6ER7P069BsqLC4I.html
16. In Bengal, the lungi has been more popular among Muslims, even though Hindus in West Bengal wear it too. Following Ghosh's identification of the lungi with Muslims, the *Anandabazar Patrika* published a report, titled *'Bangali Jiboney Lungi Kono Samprodayer Ekchetiya Noy'* (22 December 2019), mentioning some of the stalwart Bengali Hindus who used to wear the lungi – Abanindranath Tagore, Shambhu Mitra, Debabrata Biswas, Jyoti Basu, Nirode Majumdar, Soumitra Chatterjee and Shirshendu Mukhopadhyay.
17. Link to video of the speech: https://youtu.be/SfgAXAJh-2I
18. Both events got postponed due to the Covid-19 lockdown.
19. 'Centre creating hype around coronavirus to divert attention from Delhi riots, claims Mamata', *Hindustan Times*, 4 March 2020.
20. 'Trinamool Congress uses Covid-19 lockdown to reverse electoral fortunes', *Hindustan Times*, 29 March 2020.
21. 'Lockdown to continue with a human face, says Mamata', Shiv Sahay Singh, *The Hindu*, 12 April 12, 2020.
22. 'Bengal CM, guv trade barbs over inspections', *Hindustan Times*, 24 April 2020.

23. 'West Bengal not cooperating, Amit Shah tells Mamata Banerjee', *The Hindu*, 9 May 2020.
24. https://twitter.com/swapan55/status/1260166726441820162
25. https://youtu.be/JktIepagjLY
26. https://twitter.com/WBPolice/status/1260246555875061760/photo/1
27. https://www.altnews.in/bjp-mp-arjun-singh-shares-video-of-bleeding-muslim-men-as-hindus-attacked-in-west-bengal/
28. https://thewire.in/media/pakistan-hindus-attack-bengal-telinipara
29. https://www.altnews.in/images-of-hindus-attacked-in-pakistan-falsely-linked-to-communal-clashes-in-west-bengals-telinipara/
30. https://thewire.in/communalism/ground-report-what-really-happened-in-violence-hit-telinipara-west-bengal
31. Video of press conference: https://www.facebook.com/watch/?v=262270571587285
32. https://twitter.com/PiyushGoyal/status/1260936322174251008
33. https://twitter.com/DilipGhoshBJP/status/1291429031426977792

Acknowledgements

THIS BOOK WAS AN idea of author Sudeep Chakravarty. I was working on a different subject when he convinced me that this was the book I should be doing first. Thereafter, conversations with him, and a reading of his book, *The Bengali: Portrait of a Community,* helped me get a better understanding of the historical perspective.

This book is, to a large extent, a by-product of my activities as a *Hindustan Times* journalist. I am grateful to Avijit Ghosal, who was my 'boss' at the office, for giving me all the time and freedom to dig deeper into socio-political and cultural issues.

Intense political debates with journalist Bhaskar Narayan Gupta, who had been a friend and elder brother to me, led me to a thorough reading of Bengal's, and India's, political history. I lost him in January 2019 and am really missing him today. He would have been overjoyed to see this book.

I had to battle multiple health issues while working on the book and, at one point of time, even lost the hope of finishing it. My family stood by me in those difficult times.

I am thankful to Antony Thomas and Kripa Raman for their help with the edits.

And last but not the least, Swati Chopra, executive editor at HarperCollins India, took great care of the book. The time she invested and the value she added helped the work get its present shape.

About the Author

SNIGDHENDU BHATTACHARYA is a Kolkata-based journalist who has reported for different national media houses including the *Hindustan Times*, The Wire and *Outlook*. He has been writing on politics, security, history, socio-economic and cultural affairs since 2005. His book *Lalgarh and the Legend of Kishanji: Tales from India's Maoist Movement* was published in 2016.

ALSO BY SNIGDHENDU BHATTACHARYA

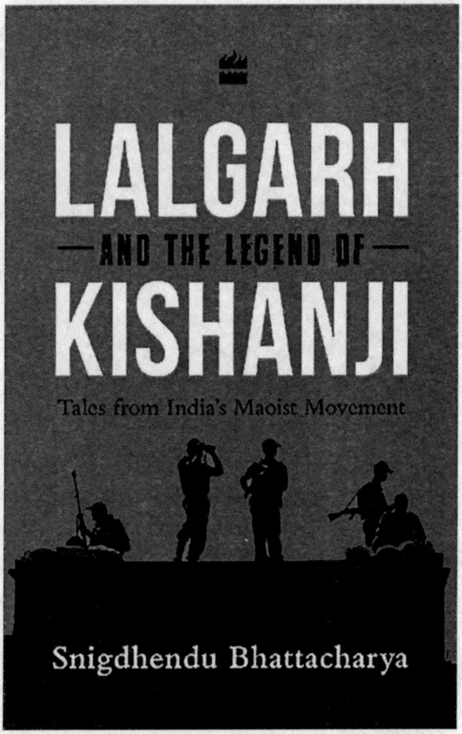

In 2009, unexpectedly, Lalgarh in West Bengal exploded on to the national consciousness. A tribal upsurge against police atrocities escalated into a fierce, full-fledged guerrilla warfare against the Indian state. Lalgarh and the *Legend of Kishanji: Tales from India's Maoist Movement* by Snigdhendu Bhattacharya is an epic tale of war between the state and the Maoists, and also between a callous state and its desperate citizens.

'It is a comprehensive book that places the Lalgarh movement in a historical perspective and provides a deep insight into and first-hand account of all that transpired in the Maoist belt.'

– *Frontline*